P9-CBM-442

HOT
POTATO

HOT POTATO

How WASHINGTON and NEW YORK Gave Birth to BLACK BASKETBALL and Changed AMERICA'S GAME Forever

BOB KUSKA

UNIVERSITY OF VIRGINIA PRESS

CHARLOTTESVILLE AND LONDON

University of Virginia Press
© 2004 by the Rector and Visitors of the University of Virginia
All rights reserved
Printed in the United States of America on acid-free paper

First published 2004

1 3 5 7 9 8 6 4 2

LIBRARY OF CONGRESS CATALOGING-IN-PUBLICATION DATA
Kuska, Bob.
Hot potato : how Washington and New York gave birth to Black
basketball and changed America's game forever / Bob Kuska.
p.   cm.
Includes bibliographical references and index.
ISBN 0-8139-2263-1
1. Basketball—Washington (D.C.) 2. Basketball—New York (State)—New
York. 3. African American basketball players—Washington (D.C.)
4. African American basketball players—New York (State)—New York.
5. African Americans—Recreation—Social aspects. I. Title.
GV885.73.W18 K87 2004
796.357′64′08996073—dc22
2003018322

The players today are much better than we were. . . .
But there is one thing that we could do better. We could pass
the ball better than they can now. Man, we used to pass that
basketball around like it was a hot potato.

SAM "BUCK" COVINGTON,
FORMER MEMBER OF THE WASHINGTON BRUINS

CONTENTS

Illustrations follow page 74

PREFACE

I grew up during the 1970s in a quiet, tree-lined neighborhood called Arden Park on the far northeast side of Sacramento. With the NBA Kings still a decade away from relocating to Sacramento, which would turn the city hoops crazy, Arden Park and the surrounding upper-middle-class neighborhoods didn't take basketball too seriously. Area courts stood empty most of the year, and our best suburban high school teams usually lost early in the postseason playoffs to the more talented, predominantly black city schools. As most kids from my all-white neighborhood believed—myself included—it was just a fact of life: Basketball is an inner-city playground game in which speed, quickness, and superior jumping ability win championships.

Supporting this idea was a stack of books and magazine articles that I had accumulated on the subject, most of which were written by noted national authorities who often served up their own theories. One of the better known names was the popular *Sports Illustrated* reporter Rick Telander. In his book *Heaven Is a Playground,* published in 1976, Telander wrote, "Obviously, black superiority in basketball rises from a combination of many factors. But one would not be far wrong in saying that in the cities, environment and black potential have merged to form unusually fertile ground." I translated Telander's words to mean that black basketball was one of those fuzzy, gene-and-environment things. It made intuitive sense, but you couldn't wrap your fingers around any hard scientific evidence to prove it. Like jazz or a good Chianti, black basketball just happened.

For years, I went with the flow of popular opinion. If someone asked me how black players had come to dominate basketball, I would speak authoritatively of playground heroes, much like a jazz aficionado rattles off the names of obscure saxophone players. There was Earl the Goat, Herman the Helicopter, Jumpin' Jackie, and so many others. I would even quote the late, great Pete Axthelm: "Other young athletes may learn basketball, but the city kids live it."

In late 1990, everything changed for me. That's when I decided to write a newspaper article on playground basketball in my adopted city of Washington, D.C. I began with a basic question that would come to dominate the next ten years of my life: When did the black game begin in Washington? My guess was the game started with Hall of Famers Elgin Baylor and Dave Bing in the 1950s. Or maybe with one of their predecessors from the 1940s, names I had learned such as Greeky Watson, Bernard Levi, or Earl Lloyd.

The answer was none of the above. While scrolling through microfilm one evening in a dark cubicle at the Library of Congress, I happened upon a short newspaper article from 1911 that bore the headline, "Colored Athletes Show Proficiency in Basket-Ball." A week and dozens of rolls of microfilm later, I had learned that black basketball bounced into Washington in 1907 and, far more significantly, it hadn't bounced there by accident.

The game had been introduced by a Harvard-educated African American physical education teacher who recognized an opportunity. His name was Edwin Bancroft Henderson, and this was the opportunity that obsessed him: "When competent physical directors and equal training are afforded the colored youth, the white athlete will find an equal or superior in nearly every line of athletic endeavor," he wrote a good thirty-five years before Jackie Robinson donned Dodger blue.

Henderson added in the Darwinistic language of the day that we now find racist: "The native muscular development and vitality of the Negro of the South, if directed in channels of athletic activities, would lower many records now standing, and our leaders should grasp the situation and develop agencies to conserve the vital forces of the race."

That's when it hit me. As interesting and important as the history of playground basketball was, there was another perspective from which to explain the social phenomenon of black basketball. Henderson and his contemporaries envisioned basketball—and sports in general—as providing a rare opportunity to combat Jim Crow.

These men realized that in sports, unlike politics and business, all races played by the same rules. Same balls, same bats, same objectives. They reasoned: The top black high school students from Washington often matriculated in white Northern colleges, so why not train them in grade school to excel in athletics? These students would join their college teams, outperform the competition, and become public role models who would force whites to accept African Americans as equals. "I doubt much whether the mere acquisition of hundreds of degrees or academic honors has influenced the mass mind of America as much as the soul appeal made by our top athletes," Henderson later wrote. "Fairness creeps out of the soul in the athletic world to a larger extent than anywhere else."

Black basketball was not born on playgrounds in the 1960s as the illegitimate child of a slow, flat-footed white game. It had been a planned birth a half century earlier in New York City and Washington, D.C. As such, black basketball is a continuum that stretches from Ed Henderson to Cumberland Posey, from Fat Jenkins to Pop Gates, from Wilt Chamberlain to Julius Erving, from Michael Jordan to Kobe Bryant. Each generation is linked not only by its athletic contributions and its love of the game, but by the social opportunities that its premier players have helped create for all African Americans.

As Ed Henderson wrote in his autumn years, still thirty years before Air Jordan sneakers and just a dozen years past school integration: "It is our opinion that when the final record is written as to contributing values in the battle for human and civil rights, our Negro athletes should be accorded high esteem."

Shortly after my discovery in the Library of Congress, which inspired me to turn my newspaper article into a book, I interviewed the late Sam Lacy, the Hall of Fame sportswriter and living legend who helped integrate major league baseball in the 1940s. As the interview wound down, Lacy reflected on his then nearly seventy-year career in journalism, casually offering tidbits about Jackie Robinson and other legends. He paused, then looked me in the eye and said, "The best journalists always have the same trait. They are the restless ones, the ones who always keep digging for more information. They are never satisfied."

With this conversation etched in my mind, I spent a decade "digging for more information." My restlessness allowed me to piece together from disparate primary sources the story that you are about to read. But in digging so deeply into the past, I discovered a segregated black world that was wonderfully vibrant and hardly fit the bleak images of Jim Crow America that now pass for fact in most history books. That's not to say the historians are wrong; rather, it shows that racial conditions in Washington and New York were far less oppressive than those portrayed in the Deep South. Though African Americans certainly felt the sting of racism on a daily basis in these cities, angry white mobs and lynchings were rare events. These themes, so dominant in other texts on the politics and social life of this era, did not directly influence the development of black basketball in New York and Washington.

More conspicuous was the fact that both cities were home to large, well-educated African American middle classes. These accomplished men and women elevated the cultural lives and institutions of their communities in the face of tremendous social obstacles, to an extent unrivaled in the Deep South. Though the pursuit of black unity, racial equality, and justice was a cherished philosophical ideal in their lives, most were motivated, day to day, by a more immediate and tangible objective. It was the concept of "makin' good," or bettering one's own lot in life to uplift those below and open new opportunities for future generations.

The idea of makin' good is expressed poignantly in a letter from Charles Drew, the father of modern blood banking, to his mentor Ed Henderson: "I owe you and a few other men like you for setting most of the standards that I have felt were worthwhile, the things I have lived by and for and wherever possible have attempted to pass on. Some few always have to set the pace and give the others courage to go into places which have not been explored."

Insofar as this book conveys the concept of makin' good, I will have succeeded in highlighting the origins of the black game. It is my sincere hope that this story becomes common knowledge among basketball players, fans, and historians alike. It is to those who played in the early 1900s—in recognition of their vision, sacrifice, and example—that I dedicate this book.

ACKNOWLEDGMENTS

This book grew out of a telephone call to a great basketball mind, Arnold George. Though we've fallen out of touch, thanks. Your words inspired me. I'd like to thank all the wonderful people whom I've met along this journey: the late Buck Covington, Wallace Conway, the late Sam Lacy, Shootmoore Brown, the late Pop Gates, Willie Wynne, and so many more. I'd also like to thank Dick Holway at the University of Virginia Press for his support of the project, and Mike Hudson and Lynne Bonenberger for their thoughtful edits of the manuscript. Most of all, I'd like to thank my lovely wife, Lynn, for keeping her sense of humor through too many years of hearing me grumble, "I've got to do research on the book." Thanks, Werner. And, of course: Ramsey, speak!

HOT
POTATO

ONE

In the Beginning

1905
1910

Jim Crowed One Night

History is silent on the exact date. But one evening in late 1907, as about a dozen white basketball players scuffed through their pregame tosses, two black men strode into the gymnasium of Washington's all-white Central Young Men's Christian Association, peeled off their overcoats, and settled into seats in the small gallery that ringed the wooden court.

Heads turned.

One of the men was Edwin Bancroft Henderson, a twenty-four-year-old local teacher and the first black man to teach physical education in an American public school.[1] Henderson, a tall, handsome man with wavy hair parted fashionably on the side, had spent the past few summers at Harvard University, where he studied under the most prominent names in American physical education.

While at Harvard, Henderson learned to play the newly invented game of basketball. It quickly became his favorite sport because of its delicate mix of brains, brawn, and teamwork. But in Washington, where sports was strictly segregated, whites were the only ones fielding organized basketball teams. To follow the sport, Henderson had no alternative but to walk into the games at the segregated Central YMCA and hope for the best.

Henderson, always proud of his race, didn't feel guilty about crossing the color line. He figured that if anyone could fathom the folly of

color lines, his warm-hearted Christian brothers at the Central YMCA
would be the ones. As Henderson had witnessed a week or so earlier
at the thirty-fourth annual international YMCA conference in Washington, thousands of men—most of them white—had joined hands to
sing hymns and embrace the organization's ideals of love, brotherhood,
and equality. "Love thy neighbor as thyself," Democratic presidential
nominee William Jennings Bryant had implored the overflow crowd.
"There is no question that this sentence cannot solve."[2]

On this evening, however, the leaders of the Central YMCA were
more interested in image than ideals. Having heard several members
complain about uninvited blacks' invading the club, the men decided to
strictly enforce their policy of segregation. If they didn't, some feared
the branch would lose members and miss the opportunity to inculcate
core Christian values in many young white men.

Spotting the two black men sitting in the stands, C. Edward Beckett,
the club's wiry young athletic director, whirled into action. He shooed
Henderson and his friend Benjamin Brownley from their seats and
warned them repeatedly in the blunt, racist invective of the day never
to return.[3]

Henderson and Brownley stormed out of the club—the word "Opportunity" displayed like a bad joke over the doorway—and headed into
the cold winter night.[4] How could a Christian organization whose motto
was "Honor All Men, Love the Brotherhood"[5] throw them out like the
kitchen trash simply because of the color of their skin? Henderson, enraged by the hypocrisy, vowed that if Beckett didn't want him attending
games at the Central YMCA, he would start a basketball league for his
own people.

And so he did.[6]

Henderson reserved a tiny basement armory in M Street High School,
today an abandoned, ivy-covered building about a half mile north of
Union Station, and opened training camp several nights a week for his
schoolboys. On the night after Christmas 1907, these students tipped
off a half century of segregated black basketball in the city at True Reformer's Hall on the corner of 12th Street and U Street N.W. In this
four-story brick building, designed by black architect John A. Lankford,
Duke Ellington would perform his first public concert ten years later.

The maiden game, which served as a preview of the upcoming basketball league, pitted students from Howard University, the nation's premier black college, against their rivals from local high schools. The

matchup was part of a much advertised winter athletic carnival that included a freestyle wrestling match, a fifteen-yard dash, and afterward, the toe-tapping tunes of the ten-dollar-a-night Lyric Orchestra.

But it was the game that stole the show. As the *University Journal* reported, "The basketball game was probably the most interesting number on the program. . . . The work of Warrick for Howard and that of Clifford of 12th Street received the most applause, while a goal by Russell from midfield brought down the house." The play was fast and apparently furious, but Howard's lackluster shooting spelled its undoing. The final score: high schools 12, Howard 5.[7]

Soon afterward, Henderson announced the formation of an eight-team basketball circuit, known in its first season as simply the Basket Ball League. The first mention of the league appeared in the *University Journal* on January 10, 1908. The eleven-line story, tucked away in the bottom right corner of page one, announced that the Howard University Athletic Association had voted to field a team in the new league. Soon thereafter, the *University Journal* ran an article listing the eight entries in the circuit: Armstrong High School, M Street High School, Howard Academy, Howard Medical, Howard College, Crescent Athletic Club, Oberlin Athletic Club, and LeDroit Park.[8]

Black Washington embraced the Basket Ball League. From late January until early May, hundreds of spectators shelled out two bits each to pile into True Reformer's Hall on Saturday nights and catch the league's weekly doubleheader. Henderson billed the games as can't-miss entertainment for the entire community. "Come out and enjoy an evening of excitement," coaxed one league advertisement. "You will never regret it. Basket ball is the recognized leading indoor game of the winter season, and when played by such men as those belonging to this league it is really fascinating."[9]

After each game, Henderson turned the lights down low, and the orchestra leader struck up the band. While the Lyric Orchestra thrummed through the numbered selections on the printed dance card, couples clasped hands and waltzed away their cares. When the clock chimed one, the house lights came back up and the bandleader motioned his men through the melody "Time to Go Home." Lined up outside along U Street, horse-drawn carriages waited to carry away the night owls and deposit them, like the morning paper, at their front doorsteps.

To those who like their basketball up-tempo, these early contests—featuring center jumps after every basket—no doubt would have seemed short on thrills. Teams fumbled their way to scores of 18-1, 5-4, and even 1-0—the result of poor offense born of inexperience and a relentless, bone-crunching brand of defense that sometimes bordered on manslaughter.

"Miller had so much foot ball spirit in him," wrote the *University Journal* of one game, "that it was a difficult matter for him to steady himself and [he] was as often on his head as on his feet, to the extreme delight of the crowd. Early in the game Miller and Cromwell developed a peculiar fondness for each other and lost no opportunity thereafter to show it, so much so that the referee would have to separate them from their friendly embrace and show them the ball."[10]

Having never witnessed Michael Jordan defy gravity or Shaquille O'Neal rattle a backboard, the fans knew no better than to cheer this rough-and-tumble action. After M Street topped Armstrong to claim the league's first championship, the *University Journal* predicted, "It is safe to say that basket ball among the schools and athletic clubs has won a permanent place."[11]

Washington Meets New York

The Basket Ball League launched its second season by January 1909. With the Howard teams boycotting the league for a larger cut of the profits, the circuit fielded five teams: Crescent Athletic Club, Colored High School of Baltimore, Armstrong Science, Armstrong Business, and the Spartans, an aggregation of M Street students that featured coach Ed Henderson at center.

On the court, teams entertained packed houses with generous doses of the comic and the sublime. In some cases, the fun was simply the sight of unlikely athletes trading barbs inside the clunky metal cage that circled the court, giving basketball players the nickname "cagers." As the *Howard University Journal* wrote of Armstrong Science's gangly big man George Fletcher: "The crowd fairly yelled itself into hysterics when this rare specimen delicately drawn out into two yards of living, breathing, yet inactive humanity, entered the wired court; for never before in the history of basket ball in Washington had such a lean, lanky, single-breasted, double fisted, left footed player been seen in the garb of basket ball."[12]

Like today, defense won ball games. Defenders suffocated their men from baseline to baseline. If their men got loose with the ball, defenders spared no pain in halting their path to the basket. "Basketball is a sissy game today compared to then," reflected Ed Henderson in the 1950s. "It was almost like football. If you knocked a man down in the game or ran into him, you might or might not be fouled."[13]

To avoid the defensive rush, offenses concocted intricate games of keep-away. The center, who served as the playmaker, often anchored himself at the top of the key and blindly whipped passes to spots on the floor where cutting men caught the ball and fired it to another pair of moving hands—and so on and so on. This weave of passes, which could last several minutes, was designed to stretch the holes in the defense and let offensive players slip inside for easy lay-ups.

When the passing game clicked, True Reformer's Hall roared. "On the toss up the Crescent center slapped the ball directly in the hands of one of his men, and from this until the time it dropped through the wicket the Spartans actually failed to touch the ball," wrote the *Howard University Journal* of one play in which each Crescent player touched the ball three times. "This was considered the cleverest playing ever witnessed in the court and brought forth vociferous applause from the galleries."[14]

News of these clever plays already had reached the Smart Set Athletic Club in New York. George Lattimore, the ambitious president of the makeshift African American club tucked among the immigrant neighborhoods of Brooklyn, had posted a letter the previous season to Howard University professor William A. Joiner to ask about Washington's interest in staging an intercity championship series.[15] Although a game was never arranged, Lattimore tried again in 1909, and by April of that year, arrangements were finalized for the first championship series of black basketball. In game one, Smart Set would visit Washington's league-leading Crescent Athletic Club. A week later, Smart Set would host Washington's Armstrong High School.

The word "championship" today implies outstanding teams and dazzling plays. This championship series offered none of the above. Smart Set easily topped the Crescents 27-11 in a dull, turnover-marred game before a large, enthusiastic crowd in True Reformer's Hall. A week later, in a snoozer before a crowd of five hundred, Smart Set blasted Armstrong 18-4 in Brooklyn's Pilgrim Hall.

The lackluster performances were due to several factors. The most obvious was that the black game in New York, like Washington, was still in its infancy. According to the *New York Age,* Smart Set organized the first black team in the city around 1905, though the club probably played few games in its initial season. Soon thereafter, the St. Christopher Club, operating under the flagship of the well-to-do St. Philip's Episcopalian Church, formed the second team.[16]

Smart Set, Crescent, and Armstrong also were poorly trained, a point accentuated when teams were more evenly matched and defense dominated. None had seasoned coaches calling the plays, and some may have had no coaches at all. Compounding the problem, most black neighborhoods had few, if any, functional gymnasiums. Those that existed were in great demand, making it difficult for most clubs to schedule practices. In fact, so limited was practice space in Washington that some teams scrimmaged in the abandoned wing of a hospital.

Also absent was the partisan, do-or-die atmosphere that today's fans expect of big games. "Victory is no great matter and defeat is less," read a statement on a basketball program from this period that echoed a cardinal tenet of the amateur movement, the prevailing philosophy of the early black game. "The essential thing in sport is the manly striving to excel and the feeling that it fosters between those who play fair and have no excuses when they lose."[17]

According to the amateur philosophy, basketball was a means to promote physical fitness and strong moral character. The sport was viewed only secondarily as entertainment—and then only grudgingly so.

The first championship series nevertheless marked a critical step forward for black basketball. No longer would players in each city compete strictly among themselves. The series established intercity basketball as a regional attraction, opening the door for the top teams to travel, play the best out-of-town clubs, and vie for greater trophies and prizes. The series also placed New York and Washington on the sports pages as the leading centers of the black game.

The central place of these two cities in early black hoops didn't necessarily come about because they had the first black teams. It's likely that black sporting enthusiasts in other cities organized teams in the years immediately following 1891, when James Naismith invented the game. In New England, the birthplace of basketball, African Americans might have cast their first set shots years before Smart Set or Crescent ever took the court. The same holds true for black neighborhoods and towns that began the twentieth century with decent YMCA buildings, such as Buxton, Iowa, and Indianapolis. In Philadelphia, the Wissahickon Boys Club and Stentonworth Athletic Club formed the first black quintets around 1907, and several cities in New Jersey also had teams at this point.

Who came first is less important than who exercised the greatest influence on the sport in the early years.[18] The "original" teams, if they existed, clearly were short-lived and were neither prominent nor influential in shaping the black game. The real question is: Where did the black game take root? Where was it first organized on a large scale, and where was it popularized? All the evidence points to Washington and New York. They were to black basketball what the Mississippi Delta was to the blues and New Orleans was to jazz.

Washington provided proof that basketball could thrive in black colleges and public schools. For the segregated South and the Midwest in particular, Washington provided the organizational blueprint that black interscholastic and intercollegiate leagues would follow for decades. These organizations would grapple each season with chronic money woes, petty disputes among member schools, and the erosion of amateur values.

Yet the Washington model weathered these problems and went on to enrich the lives of thousands of young black men. Not only did these student athletes keep alive and advance the sport, many apprenticed under now forgotten black coaching icons who served as mentors and role models for them on and off the court.

"I personally feel a great debt of gratitude to you," wrote the legendary physician Charles Drew, a graduate of Washington's Dunbar High School, in a letter to his coach and physical education teacher Ed Henderson. "You have set the pace continually, and we who have the privilege of coming under your influence cannot but feel just a bit 'chesty' when we say, 'Mr. Henderson, sure I knew him, he taught me in high school and you bet he's O.K.'"[19]

New York, meanwhile, provided the entrepreneurial push to popularize the black game as entertainment. During the teens and 1920s, every top black team from Chicago to Washington ran the gauntlet of New York's established club teams to earn their championship credentials. Black New York featured many of the best players and all the best halls, and generated the fattest profits.

New York also would serve as the inevitable battleground between Puritan amateur ideals and American capitalism. Over time, capitalism would prevail and New York would produce the first great black professional team, the New York Renaissance.

In April 1909, however, the organizers of the championship series were happy just to have given the sport a little extra exposure. "Permit me to offer congratulations upon the skill and clean work of your boys," wrote William Joiner to Smart Set's Lattimore after the first championship series. "It has been a pleasure to us to have them with us, and I believe a tremendous impetus to basketball in this city. I think it will also prove an inspiration to our teams to work harder for future seasons."[20] For Joiner and the others, the championship had been a victory for amateurism and a testament to black America's new embrace of the nation's physical fitness movement.

The Rise of the Black Physical Education Movement

At the turn of the century, sports had become an essential part of the fabric of American working-class neighborhoods. Fans bantered for hours on street corners about how to pitch Ty Cobb or swat the blazing fastball of Walter Johnson. "There is perhaps in all the world no occasion so eagerly anticipated, so numerously attended and so keenly enjoyed as the first day of the professional base ball season in the United States," wrote the *Washington Evening Star.*[21] When autumn came, fans debated the strategies of famed football coaches such as Amos Alonzo Stagg of the University of Chicago, Walter Camp of Yale, and Fielding Yost of Michigan.

Numbered among the nation's sporting icons were a small but growing number of black athletes. In track and field, John Baxter Taylor was the king of the four hundred meters. In 1904, as a freshman at the University of Pennsylvania, he smashed the collegiate record in the event with a time of 49.5 seconds. By 1907, Taylor had won the four hundred meters at every big meet in America and had represented the United States in European competitions. "He was a perfect judge of pace," wrote Ed Henderson, adding that he would "never forget" how several white sportswriters claimed that the dark-skinned Taylor was "a member of the then less advertised Nordic race, by comparing the rounded calf muscle, and well developed gastrocnemius muscle bulge to the leg contour of northern Europeans of rugged countries."[22]

In sprint cycling, one of the most popular sports of the day, an unheralded black teenager from Indianapolis named Marshall "Major" Taylor breezed to the American championship in 1898. The following year, he captured the world title in the one-mile event in Montreal, bringing home high praise for his race. "We were literally amazed to find [Taylor] better educated than the average foreigner who comes over and possessed of far better manners than our own riders," wrote a French journalist. "When we think of some of the harsh treatment to which this man has been subjected on account of his color, we cannot refrain from uttering the strongest words of disapprobation of such acts, nor from thinking that some parts of [the United States] must be in a state of savagery."[23]

While major league baseball toed the color line, many black semipro squads battled in mixed city and state leagues. There were the Philadelphia Giants, Royal Giants, Cuban X Giants, Wilmington Giants, Columbia Giants, and other truly large teams. But no band of black sluggers won more hearts than Chicago's Leland Giants, led by a pistol-packing cowboy from Waco named Rube Foster. Honus Wagner, the immortal Pittsburgh Pirates star, said of Foster, "He was the smartest pitcher I have ever seen in all my years in baseball."[24]

But the greatest success came in the boxing ring. For a people struggling to find an identity after three hundred years of legalized oppression, there was no greater hero than the legendary lightweight Joe "Old Master" Gans.

Gans's greatest moment came on Labor Day 1906 when he defended his world lightweight crown against the scrappy Danish immigrant Battling Nelson in the gold-rush city of Goldfield, Nevada. This rumble had all of the hype of a legendary Frazier-Ali bout of the 1970s. With no round limit to stop the fight, Gans eventually won in the forty-second round when Nelson was disqualified for throwing one too many low blows.

The bout brought in more than $67,000, then the largest single payday in the history of boxing. In these "separate but equal" times, the white challenger Nelson got $22,500; the black champion Gans claimed $11,000. But Gans didn't complain. He had been given $4,000 in Goldfield mining stock, and he stood to claim most of the royalties from the Gans-Nelson film that would play in cinemas across the land. With great fanfare, Gans also had wagered $10,000 of his own prize money on himself two days before the fight.

In the days and months following the fight, black folks across the nation rendered their own unanimous decision. "Could a colored minister, orator, or editor have accomplished in a few short hours in their separate or combined professions what Gans did in the same length of time?" wrote the *California Outlook*. "I think not." The *Indianapolis Freeman* rolled its sentiments into four words: "Keep on stepping, Joe!"[25]

Even black heavyweight hopeful Jack Johnson got into the act. "All that Joe needed, as far as I can see, was the chance to meet [top white fighters]. That is the same in my case," he said. Gans agreed, telling the *Boston Guardian*, "The point I want to bring out most strongly is the gradual closing of the gap that marks the difference in the athletic excellence of the white man and the black."[26]

But some worried the gap was actually widening. Millions of black kids, rich and poor, still received their athletic training on makeshift ball fields, tossing balled-up rags and flailing their mothers' discarded broomsticks. Black leaders feared that without an organized movement, African Americans would fall even further behind, fueling popular notions of black inferiority. As the *Indianapolis Freeman* lamented, "As a whole the colored athlete has gone back 50 per cent, unless young blood takes interest. The Negro race will soon drop out of the limelight if [it] is not up and doing."[27]

Blacks already had a lot of catching up to do. The white physical fitness movement, launched in the 1880s, was booming. In New York City, nearly ninety neighborhood recreation centers had sprouted by 1905, with the New York Athletic Club alone claiming more than ten thousand members. In the city's public schools, roughly two hundred thousand students suited up on scholastic teams. Building on this momentum, American Athletic Union president James E. Sullivan urged Gotham politicians to transform every public park into an athletic field with a clubhouse, gymnasium, and running track. "Athletics should be for the masses and not for the [upper] classes," Sullivan bellowed.[28]

The white physical fitness movement scarcely trickled down to black neighborhoods. Conrad Norman, a founding member of New York's black Alpha Physical Culture Club, recalled, "Although there were seventy thousand colored people in New York at that time [1904], and the big city fairly teemed with athletic clubs of all kinds, recreation centers, playgrounds, settlements, schools, Turn Verein halls, and colleges, each provided with a gymnasium, there was not a single one devoted to the colored people."[29]

Even the YMCA, a leader in the American sports movement that encouraged black clubs, hadn't made much of a difference. In 1906, the

YMCA sponsored more than 4,150 sports teams for some 30,600 Americans. The organization estimated that just six of these clubs belonged to black YMCAs, allowing just 88 people to take the field. Of the YMCA's 568 gymnasiums, three belonged to black YMCAs. None of these black clubs was in the South, where 92 percent of blacks still lived.[30]

Civic-minded black men began independently to build black sports clubs. In Savannah, a committee of twelve formed the Eureka Aid and Athletic Club in 1901. In New Orleans, the city's four black colleges cobbled together their own athletic association around 1903. In New York, John Morgan founded the Alpha Physical Culture Club in 1904 in a church on West 134th Street. In Indianapolis, barrel-chested Edward Galliard and others rolled up their sleeves in 1905 to help the Colored YMCA organize "an all-round athletic team to take in all sports." In Denver, Victor Walker opened the doors to the Rocky Mountain Athletic Association in 1910. And so it went, across the country.

But it was in Washington, with its large, educated black middle class and its thriving black school system and social clubs, that schoolyard games coalesced into a bona fide sports movement through a trailblazing organization called the Interscholastic Athletic Association.

Founded in 1906 by Ed Henderson and five other schoolteachers to promote the well-being of black students in Washington and Baltimore, the ISAA sanctioned the city's first legitimate black high school football and baseball competition, staged its first black track meet, and trained its first black referees. When Henderson founded the Basket Ball League in 1908, he launched the game under the auspices of the ISAA.

Black Washington Organizes

The story of the ISAA begins in 1904. That summer, Henderson returned to Washington after completing his first term at Harvard's Summer School of Physical Training. The twenty-year-old Henderson immediately landed a job in the District's black public school system, making him the first black man ever to teach gym in an American public school.[31]

Novelty did not beget privilege. Henderson spent his first two years on the job mounting his bicycle three mornings a week and, as he called it, "riding wheel" to schools nestled in the city's remotest neighborhoods. There, this future inductee into the Black Sports Hall of Fame taught youngsters the beanbag toss, run-sheep-run, and other children's games. Two afternoons a week, he wended his way through the busy downtown streets to M Street and Armstrong Tech, the city's two black high schools, where he instructed boys in the rudiments of exercise and athletics.

As Henderson directed his students through calisthenics each day, he looked past their waving arms and twisting torsos to fixate on the larger issues. It was no secret that Washington's black mortality rate stood at about double that of whites, with tuberculosis alone claiming nearly five hundred lives in the year 1900. This fact inspired well-meaning white public health officials to pontificate about the sickly city-dwelling black, which rankled many black leaders. "Even men of the scientific spirit and method, who are accustomed to sift, weigh, analyze, and balance facts and arguments before espousing a theory based upon them, rush headlong to conclusions upon the negro question, with heedlessness and avidity of school boys in an academic debate," wrote Howard University's Kelly Miller on the subject.[32]

Henderson knew blacks were not the only ones dying of tuberculosis, since the "White Plague" also "levied a tribute" of nearly four hundred whites in 1900. Henderson thought that black people's aches and pains owed more to Washington's cramped urban milieu than to some inherent physical defect. Borrowing a page from the white physical education movement, Henderson believed that urban life offered blacks neither the time nor the space to exercise regularly, destroying their natural vitality and making them susceptible to disease.

"It is unfortunately true that the vitality of the Negro youth is seriously undermined by the crowded city," Henderson wrote in 1910. "Many young men leave our secondary schools and colleges to engage in strenuous work, amidst varying conditions, with bodies unsound and but few, if any, hygienic habits formed for life. . . . To preserve present health and to insure the future welfare of the race it is necessary that we build up a strong and virile youth."[33]

Henderson dreamed of building an athletic association that would help breathe life back into the limbs of his city-weary students. He saw the association as a black version of the Public School Athletic League of New York City, widely hailed as the nation's model scholastic athletic association. Like the PSAL, the Washington association would be led by adult volunteers, each of whom would commit himself to building up a new generation of virile black youth who could compete with all races. But Henderson took the idea a step further. He wanted to establish a regional association that would control high school and college athletics not only in Washington but in Baltimore and other nearby cities.

In Henderson's mind, the association would build a pipeline to send forth the city's best black student athletes to Harvard, Yale, and other top white colleges in the North. The idea made sense. In 1904, M Street High School, the nation's premier black academic high school, had four of its graduates accepted at Ivy League schools, including football star Hugh Francis. Why not send more?

Henderson envisioned achievement in athletics as the best weapon for attacking and destroying Jim Crow. He believed that in sports, unlike politics, all races followed the same rules. Henderson reasoned that with formalized training, black athletes would have a rare chance to compete on equal terms with whites. They would have the opportunity to outperform them, capture the nation's imagination with their poise and talent, and debunk the stereotypes that stigmatized the race.

For an unproven young man like Henderson, these were radical notions. But Henderson had been accepting challenges all his life. Born on November 24, 1883, in Washington, D.C., Edwin Bancroft Henderson was the eldest of four children. His mother, Louisa, was a domestic and the daughter of a white slaveholder and his slave; his father, William, was a day laborer and the son of a Portuguese soldier and his part-Indian, part-black wife.

Like most poor kids, Edwin started to work soon after he learned to walk. After his family moved to Pittsburgh in 1888, he would slosh door to door in the Pennsylvania winter offering to light fires for a nickel in the fireplaces of Orthodox Jews, who were forbidden to labor on the Sabbath. The next morning, his mother would send young Edwin and his brother Charles out bearing hot rolls to sell to the nattily dressed men and women strolling home from Sunday services.

In 1894, Henderson's family moved back to Washington and settled in a racially mixed area in the city's southwest section, a largely undeveloped patchwork of brickyards, marshes, and barren fields. When he wasn't earning a few bucks, Ed could be found in the street tossing balls and bantering with his buddies. "There was no organized recreation," he remembered. "I played baseball games on the Washington monument lot and because there were no automobiles, no green and red lights, we played all sorts of games in the streets and on the vacant lots."[34]

Henderson's most cherished boyhood memories were cultivated during the summers he spent on his maternal grandmother's one acre of land

in rural Falls Church, Virginia, now a crowded Washington suburb. It was
there that Ed experienced one of the greatest thrills of his young life when
he saw a decorated black soldier—Major Charles Young of the Ninth
Ohio Infantry Battalion—cantering on horseback down the main street:

> I was seated on the steps of the village feed store one evening listen-
> ing to a white Virginia soldier boasting of his experience when Major
> Young rode past on his return to camp. I heard the white soldier say
> to his companion, "I'll never salute a damn nigger." I thought Young
> had not seen the soldier seated on the bench against the wall. In a
> great cloud of dust, Young whirled his horse around and yelled, "Get
> up! Salute!" There stood this soldier listening to as severe a tongue
> lashing as ever I had heard one adult give another. Young's final
> words were, "You're saluting the United States Army." That evening
> I went across the street to home a proud youngster.[35]

Like many bright teenagers, Ed grew enamored of books and ideas.
After school, he wandered the marble hallways of the Library of Congress soaking up theories from the world's great thinkers. On other occasions, he sat under the Capitol dome listening to the blustery words
of pinstriped congressmen. Amid this roil of ideas, Henderson started
to form definite opinions about turn-of-the-century America and his
place in it. He rejected grandstanding southern senators who attacked
his race and embraced the democratic ideals of liberty, justice, and dig-
nity for all people.

By 1902, Ed had graduated from M Street High School, where he
spent four years on the honor roll. He pitched four seasons on the
school's baseball team, anchored the offensive line of its first football
team, and participated in its first track meet on an oval that required
participants to run sixteen laps to log one mile. In 1904, Henderson
graduated No. 1 in his class from Miner Normal School, a small two-
year college that prepared students for teaching careers in Washington's
black public school system.

While at Miner, Ed had come increasingly under the wing of a thirty-
three-year-old trailblazer named Anita Turner. Turner, a New York City
native, was one of the first black women to graduate from Dudley Sargent's Summer School of Physical Training at Harvard University, the
nation's premier school of physical education. In the 1890s, she came to
Washington to teach the new subject of physical culture in the black
schools. Turner would serve in the public school system for forty-nine

years—of which thirty-eight were spent as the director of physical education in the black elementary schools.

Turner advised her athletic young friend to enter Harvard's summer school. Although he readily agreed, Henderson knew that he would be hard-pressed to pay the school's fifty-dollar tuition. "I had planned to work that summer [in Washington] being depleted of funds," Henderson recalled. "Miss Turner wrote Dr. Sargent asking him to get me a part-time job. I borrowed enough money for car fare, tuition and lodging, and waited on Dr. Sargent's table in his boarding house for meals."[36]

At Harvard (he attended during the summers of 1904, 1905, and 1907), Henderson was the first black male physical education student in the United States. There, among the red-brick buildings, with the urban silhouette of Boston rising above the Charles River, Henderson lost himself in a classroom world of theory. He navigated through exercise physiology, applied anatomy, the history of physical education, and other weighty subjects. He also enjoyed the company of some of the biggest names in American academia, including the philosopher William James, who was on the faculty.

In September 1904, having completed his first summer at Harvard, Henderson joined the staff at Bowen Elementary School, not far from the Washington Navy Yard. For a poor kid who used to hawk hot rolls on the street corner, Henderson enjoyed the eighty dollars that he earned each month. But the money brought him no intellectual satisfaction. He yearned to do something bigger. Henderson toyed with the idea of enrolling in the Howard University Medical School. But his meager bank account soon dimmed the idea.

Meanwhile, many of the old-time black educators smirked at Henderson's ivory-tower ideas about black athletics. For years, gym class had meant a visiting white teacher's marching the boys into a hallway once a week for fifteen minutes of toe touching and arm waving. When Henderson signed on as gym teacher at Bowen Elementary, these sessions were stretched to twice a week. For most teachers, this was more than enough aerobic exercise. With hardly enough money for schoolbooks, they believed colored schools could scarcely afford to fritter away resources promoting such foolishness.

This point was driven home one day when Henderson asked W. S. Montgomery, the superintendent of colored schools, to lobby the white superintendent to build a gymnasium at Armstrong High School. Montgomery, a dapper gentlemen with muttonchop whiskers, shook his head and chuckled, "My boy, they may build gymnasiums in our schools in your day, but not in mine."[37]

Henderson forged on. At Howard University, he found a sympathetic ear in William Joiner, a popular professor and a graduate of elite Oberlin College. Joiner, an adviser to the Howard Athletic Council, was an outspoken supporter of athletics. Once, during a school meeting, Howard professor Kelly Miller dismissed sports as a sidelight of academia. Joiner dissented vehemently. The two, he said, were one and the same.

At M Street, Henderson tossed around the idea of a sports association with a twenty-five-year-old teacher named Garnet Wilkinson, another graduate of Oberlin College. Wilkinson, a handsome Washington native with a passion for cigars, taught Latin by day and studied law by night at Howard University. No matter how hectic his schedule, he found time to serve as a volunteer coach for the M Street football team. As Wilkinson knew, several M Street graduates already had attended white colleges and starred in football and track. With proper training, more could shine in northern colleges.

Finally, at Armstrong, Henderson garnered the support of math teacher Robert Mattingly, a recent graduate of Amherst College. Mattingly, a short, dark-skinned twenty-two-year-old, taught mathematics and trained the school's football and military drill teams.

Eventually, a meeting was held on the Howard campus to discuss the athletic association. Present that evening were Henderson, Wilkinson, Mattingly, Joiner, W. J. DeCatur of Howard University, and Ralph Cook of Baltimore High School.

These men faced huge infrastructural problems. By the early 1900s, Washington had ballooned into a government boomtown of 275,000 people. As real estate developers replaced fields with asphalt and row houses, more than 100,000 children of both races were left groping for the few open play spaces left in the city. Most had only streets and vacant lots for playing fields.

Concerned citizens complained that teenaged toughs congregated on street corners and in the streets, hopping on and off passing streetcars like common hooligans. To remedy the situation, the city adopted a law in the 1890s that prohibited all children from playing or loitering on streets and in alleyways. If shopkeepers noticed children gathering in public places, they could invoke the unlawful assembly ordinance and have them carted off to the nearest police precinct. From July 1913 to June 1914 alone, nearly a thousand children were arrested for unlawful assembly and tried in juvenile court, with most drawing probation.

Newspapers described burdened youths who shuffled into corner saloons to cadge nickel bottles of beer. Others lounged around pool halls or in the smoky upper balcony of the Gayety Theater, hooting at scantily clad burlesque dancers.

Henderson had heard through the grapevine that even some of his best and brightest students spent their winter evenings on local nightclub stages performing ragtime dance routines for a fast buck. As a Howard student complained, "The greatest need of the University is something or some where for the young men to spend their leisure hours. . . . There is nothing or no place in the dormitory where they can go and indulge in an hour's liveliness."[38]

At the turn of the century, Washington followed the lead of several other American cities and began to establish public playgrounds. The first playgrounds were much different from today's communal backyards for joggers and dog-walkers. They were public finishing schools where specially trained adults scrupulously planned and supervised children's play.

Though some Washingtonians disputed the wisdom of spending public funds to teach children how to play, others welcomed the idea. The authors of the McMillan Report, a congressional plan issued in 1902 that would have a major impact on Washington's urban development, strongly advocated playgrounds in the nation's capital. Senator James McMillan, the leader of the plan, is said to have shelled out two hundred dollars for the purchase of swings, seesaws, and other equipment that were used on the city's first playground in 1902.

Even President William Howard Taft voiced his opinion. "Every city is under the strongest obligation to its people to furnish to the children, from the time they begin to walk until they reach manhood, places within the city walls large enough and laid out in proper form for the playing of all sorts of games which are known to our boys and girls and are liked by them."[39]

By 1910, however, the Washington playground movement had stalled. Inadequate appropriations chronically hamstrung the endeavor, causing the director of playgrounds to moan that the "ugliness" of the unfinished playgrounds "makes them uninviting elements in the landscape and creates opposition to them from those living around them."[40]

If white children were hurting for play space, black kids were in agony. In 1903, when the city turned a raggedy square near Ed Henderson's childhood home in southwest Washington into the city's first black playground, there were more than twenty-six thousand black children of school age. By 1911, the number of black playgrounds held steady at two for more than fifty thousand children. One of these playgrounds, Cardoza, was purchased for fourteen thousand dollars in 1908. The same year, the District secured two other playground sites, both for whites, at thirty thousand dollars each. While the Washington Playground Association planned to spend five thousand dollars the following year to improve one of the newly purchased white lots, Cardoza was neglected.

"The Cardoza ground is still bare and uninviting and should be surrounded with a hedge," reported Henry Curtis, the association's supervisor. "There is at present no place to keep the equipment on the playground, except a box which is placed on the ground, and balls, rackets, and other equipment are soon rotted from the rains."[41]

While the lack of play space presented an enormous problem, an even more pressing issue was the perennial neglect of the city's black school sports. At M Street and Armstrong High Schools, the football and baseball teams were driven by a few gutsy kids willing to cough up the bucks to pay for uniforms and equipment, including cleats. Although Wilkinson, Mattingly, Henderson, and a few others helped, these die-hard students often would play their games, which they scheduled themselves, on soggy fields with a single football or twenty-five-cent baseball at their disposal. Since most students were already strapped for cash, they typically could not afford to travel, making national or even regional competition impossible.

Athletics was not any better off at Howard University. From 1874 to 1906, students ran the show—forming teams, fielding games, and finagling uniforms without a penny of support from the university. While some professors volunteered to chart plays on the sidelines, most viewed sports as a distraction. Worried that the sporting spirit might pollute the study hall, university officials decreed in the 1890s that no more than five intercollegiate football or baseball games could be held on campus per year. Moreover, these games were to be arranged under the following conditions: They were to be (1) scheduled only on Saturdays and school holidays, (2) held with a faculty member presiding, and (3) conducted with no more than fifty spectators in attendance.

By the early 1900s, following the lead of white universities, football became all the rage on the Howard campus. A bit of doggerel published in the *University Journal* in 1904 attests to its popularity:

The football days have come again,
The gladdest of the year,
One side of Morton's face is gone,
Bill Bailey's lost an ear.

Heaped on the ground the players lie
And bite and kick and tear.
They punch each other in the eye
And gouge without a care.

O grand, O glorious football days!
How proud the maidens look
When they begin to make mincemeat
Of dear Alonzo Cook!

Now all the fair ones gather 'round,
And this alone they fear,
That there should not be limbs enough
For each a souvenir.

Each loyal Howardite must have
A trophy of football—
An eye or ear, a nose or thumb,
Preserved in alcohol.[42]

Howard football games were raucous events. W. H. Washington, captain of the 1902 team, wrote of the Bisons' 5-0 triumph over Shaw University: "Fully two thousand people witnessed that memorable game and when the sharp shrill of the referee's whistle sounded Shaw's last death note, that whole multitude broke loose. Hats were in the air, flags were kissing the breeze, white and blue streamers were dangling in the atmosphere, bugles were sounding. Gray haired grads and beardless undergrads vied with each other in doing all kinds of stunts. Some were two-stepping, some waltzing, some cake walking, and others were doing the buck and wing dance, while a band played 'Oh Howard, General Howard,' to the tune of 'Yale Boola.'"[43]

Although the students cheered, they neglected to pay for Howard's football and baseball programs. Without full university support, which

would come in 1922 following the establishment of the physical education department, students could take athletics only so far. "We are
aware that we have a few loyal students and we are proud of them but
it is a folly to suppose that they can support the athletics of the school,"
wrote the *University Journal* in 1904. "They are always ready with their
donations while a number of others meet the request with trifling excuses but can always find the price of a box of candy or the theatre, yet
these gallery gods are the first to set up a howl and wonder why we don't
have more games."[44]

Hoping to shatter these obstacles, Henderson and his colleagues
agreed that the time was right to rally public support for an amateur athletic association. They believed strongly that local black sports should
be broadened beyond the mainstays of football and baseball, and that
more students should participate in athletics. After further discussion,
the men named as the first president of the association the thirty-seven-
year-old William Joiner, a man of myriad talents who would win renown
during his lifetime as an educator, administrator, lawyer, poet, and author.

At the organizational meeting for the Interscholastic Athletic Association, the men decided that Howard University, with its quaint red-brick
buildings and beautiful hilltop campus, should be the hub of local black
athletics. They also agreed that a large running track should be con-
structed on the Georgia Avenue campus, and that Joiner and some of
the other men should lobby the university trustees for financial help in
laying the first four hundred yards of the future of local black athletics.

The Howard University trustees, when quoted the princely sum of
four hundred dollars to construct the track, balked at the idea. However, they agreed to let the men build a track on campus if ISAA members DeCatur and Joiner took personal responsibility for the endeavor—and if they promised to replace any uprooted sod should the
project go bust. It was a daunting financial proposition for a half-dozen
schoolteachers with holes in their pockets. Henderson, for one, was of
such humble means that he would have to wait six years to squirrel away
enough money to marry his college sweetheart.

The men passed the hat among themselves, scraping up enough
money to hire a construction crew to hack out the oval. Several members bled their bank accounts and fell into debt to keep the project moving forward. Roughly five weeks later, a permanent cinder track was
completed on the Howard campus.

With a final adjustment here and there, the ISAA staged the city's first black track meet on a sunny Memorial Day in 1906. The participants included eighty athletes from Howard, M Street, Armstrong, the Colored High School of Baltimore, Wilmington (Delaware) High School, the local Oberlin and Diamond Athletic Clubs, the Washington Colored YMCA, and an eager band of local eighth-graders. The ISAA officials also recruited more than twenty men to serve as timers, scorers, and marshals. They were joined by thousands of spectators bearing a multitude of colors representing their clubs and schools.

The meet began with the blast of the starter's pistol for the hundred-yard dash and proceeded through twenty-eight events, including the pole vault, the mile relay, a potato sack race, and even an exhibition basketball game between M Street and Armstrong. By sundown, Howard's track stars had logged fifty-five points—well ahead of second-place M Street's twenty-three points—to claim the meet's ornate grand trophy.

With their big day behind them, the men counted a total of $315.64 in proceeds. Since the track meet cost them $270, they now had $45 in seed money to introduce other sports.

The ISAA track meet was a defining moment in the history of black amateur athletics. Held on the campus of the nation's premier black university and in the city that so many prominent blacks called home, it was a showcase and an affirmation of the infant amateur black sports movement. It showed not only that organized athletics was thrilling to watch, but that African Americans had the leadership and drive within their own communities to develop athletics on their own terms.[45]

The Black Game in New York

By the turn of the century, skyscrapers had begun to dominate the Manhattan skyline. From most vantage points, one could locate the twenty-one-story American Tract Building and the thirty-story Park Row Building. Along "Newspaper Row," the tall headquarters of the major dailies dwarfed the once mighty facade of New York City Hall.

"As the sun drops low, it glares into the windows of the sky-scrapers all along the island, and they give back the light in a flare of rose," commented writer Will Irwin in the 1920s. "I know an artist who sometimes crosses the river just to revel in this effect. 'It isn't art perhaps,' he says, 'but it is glory.'"[46]

For African Americans, who comprised about 2 percent of the city's population, New York provided little personal glory. Costs were high, work was backbreaking, and discrimination was commonplace. Most had grown up in the rural South, emigrated to New York to fill service or factory jobs, and landed in squalid, multistory tenement houses. Tuberculosis was epidemic, and two of every seven black babies born in New York died before their first birthday.[47] Though living conditions were better for the middle class, in this overly cramped city of 3.4 million people, many complained of a lack of "race-friendly" gyms or open spaces in which they could exercise. Without regular exercise, many feared that the grime and grit of industrial New York eventually would rob them, in the language of the day, of their "natural vitality" and their resistance to tuberculosis.

Alarmed at these trends, scores of African Americans campaigned for the wholesale expansion of physical fitness programs. Unlike in Washington, where the leaders of the movement expanded existing programs in the city's black school system, New York's public schools were not segregated. The existing black YMCAs in Brooklyn and Manhattan were not equipped to promote physical education. With the black YMCA building boom of the teens and 1920s still a few years off, these makeshift clubs were little more than old brownstones converted into Bible study halls. None had the space to house a gymnasium.

Nor were the churches overly enthusiastic about helping the black physical education movement. "With the exception of the Episcopalians, the churches undertake little institutional work," wrote Mary White Ovington in her classic book of this period, *Half a Man.* "Money is lacking, and there is only a feeble conviction of the value of the gymnasium, pool table, and girls' and boys' clubs."[48]

With a boost from the Episcopalian diocese, fitness-minded African Americans followed the lead of their white neighbors and, starting in 1904, began independently organizing athletic clubs in Manhattan and Brooklyn. Black athletic clubs offered a sanctuary from the bustle of the city, an oasis of well-being where members could relax, tone their muscles, and exchange training tips. They also were important social gathering places. In some ways, they were like small-town men's clubs where members were on a first-name basis and often had grown up with each other's families and friends. In other ways, the clubs resembled college fraternities. Members preached a rah-rah fraternal spirit, displayed club emblems on sweaters and lapels, and actively recruited new pledges.

By around 1905, some of these original clubs introduced team sports into their athletic programs. The sports of choice varied, but most clubs eventually would dabble in one or more of the following: cricket, soccer, track and field, baseball, and basketball.

While New York wasn't the only American city with black athletic clubs, it was unusual in that it had so many of them up and running at such an early date. The clubs were plentiful enough that Manhattan's St. Christopher Club and Brooklyn's Marathon Athletic Club and Smart Set Athletic Club in 1907 founded the city's first black basketball league, called the Olympian Athletic League. Though the short-lived league attracted sparse crowds—a sign that games initially were promoted as exercise instead of entertainment—it nevertheless served as the organizational catalyst that spurred other clubs to try their luck at basketball.

The clubs in the Olympian Athletic League quickly established their own pecking order, based largely on their social and athletic reputations. At the top was the St. Christopher Club, part of the socially elite St. Philip's Episcopalian Church. St. Christopher had its own gymnasium and other training facilities in the large St. Philip's Parish House, a rarity that in later years would help the club attract the city's top black athletes, including many of the best basketball players.[49]

Running the show at St. Christopher was an athletic board headed by the Reverend Everard Daniel. Idealistic, uncompromising, and fearless, Daniel preached to his fellow board members that their raison d'être was to promote wholesome amateur sport and protect the club's teams from the taint of money and professionalism. St. Christopher's social status and Daniel's rigid stance regarding the amateur creed would establish the club as the overseer of New York amateurism, a position it would fill until the early 1920s.

Another popular organization was Manhattan's Alpha Physical Culture Club, founded as New York's first black athletic club in 1904. Despite its humble beginnings in the back room of a church, Alpha pooled enough cash by February 1906 to move into a more spacious locale that included room for a makeshift gymnasium to train a basketball team. The following winter, Alpha joined the Olympian Athletic League, and within a few seasons, its basketball team was among the best in black New York and the recognized arch rival of St. Christopher.

"At present, our membership numbers seventy—representatives of the best colored people in New York—physicians, dentists, lawyers, teachers, musicians, clerks, Government employees, real estate men, brokers, students, etc.," wrote Alpha's Conrad Norman in 1910, offering a glimpse into the upper-crust nature of an early black athletic club.[50]

Also in the early spotlight was Brooklyn's Smart Set Athletic Club, formed in 1905. Known for its young, trailblazing athletes, Smart Set was one of the first clubs in New York to sponsor large, interracial athletic carnivals for the public. These carnivals, like the first track meet at Howard University in 1906, became rallying points for black athletics in New York. "I remember how that meet, sponsored and managed by a Negro club, was one of the really big events on the metropolitan indoor program," recalled black track star Lester Granger. "Famous athletes from all over the East ran in those Smart Set meets, and yet colored lads regularly gathered their share of honors distributed."[51]

Smart Set also was renowned for its unbeatable basketball team. As a founding member of the Olympian Athletic League, Smart Set dominated its opponents, winning most of its contests by wildly lopsided scores and earning its teams the nickname "the Grave Diggers."

Other subsequent members of the Olympian Athletic League were Manhattan's St. Cyprian Athletic Club, which had its own small gymnasium and was overseen by the city's Episcopalian mission; Brooklyn's St. Augustine Guild; and the Jersey City YMCA, later the Mozart Athletic Club.

Why did the New York area have so many small black athletic clubs? A major factor obviously was the city's melting-pot society. In 1910, the five main boroughs had nearly two million foreign-born residents, accounting for 40 percent of all New Yorkers. Most immigrants settled into self-contained ethnic neighborhoods defined by race, religion, nationality, language, and class. Given this self-segregating immigrant culture, African Americans, particularly those in the working class, willingly settled into their own neighborhoods, where they socialized among themselves and largely ignored their white neighbors.[52]

Another factor was that the estimated ninety thousand African Americans in the New York metropolitan area had yet to coalesce into a single, defining neighborhood. The move to Harlem, though under way, would not reach critical mass until the late teens. Many African Americans were dispersed throughout Manhattan's midtown area, between 20th and 63rd Streets, while others were scattered in one- or two-block enclaves in the boroughs and northern New Jersey. These small black neighborhoods gave rise to a sense of community that in turn provided the impetus for the athletic clubs.

Another important factor was the cultural heterogeneity of black New York. Unlike black Washington, which was southern to the core, black New York even then consisted of a mix of native northerners, southern-born immigrants, a sprinkling of Africans, and a small but growing Caribbean community. As Ovington wrote: "These new-comers occupy many of the pulpits, are admitted to the bar, practice medicine, and become leaders in politics, and their wives are quite ready to take a prominent part in the social world. They meet the older residents, and the various groups intermingle, though not without some friction."[53]

The social friction extended to the athletic clubs. Fans judged athletes by their ethnicity or birthplace and labeled the clubs according to their predominant ethnic group, place in local black society, and neighborhood of origin. For instance, teams from Manhattan often belittled clubs from Brooklyn, a point that always raised the stakes in interborough play.

This tension infused early black basketball in New York with a contradictory personality. Rival clubs encouraged polite, often affected, tea-party sociability at their games. Many club leaders proclaimed it didn't matter which team won; what mattered was that all subscribed to the amateur ideal of sportsmanship and fellowship. But wins and losses did matter, and for some, winning became an obsession. Alpha had to beat St. Christopher, and St. Christopher had to beat Smart Set. "Rather than again face what would have undoubtedly been the worst defeat of the season, the St. Christopher Club forfeited to the Smart Set Basketball team," stated an article in the *Indianapolis Freeman* of a scheduled game in 1908, when the fraternal spirit of amateurism should have been at its highest. "Courtesy does not appear to be a factor in the organization."[54]

As basketball became more popular in black New York, some clubs disregarded the rules of amateurism and bickered over the financial arrangements of games, and most made heavy-handed attempts to embarrass or upstage rivals. This me-first attitude would rapidly pollute the amateur spirit and clear the way for money and professionalism to creep into black basketball by the early teens.

The Undefeated 12th Street YMCA

By 1910, amateur basketball's popularity had overwhelmed Washington's Interscholastic Athletic Association, the overseer of local black sports. In just two years, the ISAA had trained forty basketball teams and roughly a thousand players. With all these squads clamoring for court time, the ISAA canceled its league format and began almost exclusively to sanction games, in much the same way the National Collegiate Athletic Association today governs sports at the college level.

As the ISAA grew more powerful, some players and fans complained about its maze of rules and apparently steady flow of cash. The Howard Athletic Association, which rebounded from near bankruptcy in 1909 when the university tacked a one-dollar sports tax onto student tuition, began asking for handouts to aid its underfinanced athletic association.

"The Y.M.C.A. team and the Howard teams have played most of the games that this institution [ISAA] has pulled off and yet they were only able to get $3.39," complained an editorial in the *Howard University Journal*. "We are forced to believe that there is something radically wrong and that it is time to give up basket ball."[55]

Another problem was the association's rule that no students with failing grades could play in an ISAA-sanctioned game. This new approach to athletics was hard to swallow for students who traditionally had always had free rein to come and go as they pleased on school teams.

The association responded to its critics in a father-knows-best tone. "There has been some complaint and dissatisfaction on the part of the members of some of the teams, growing out of the restrictions put on them," wrote ISAA representative Robert Mattingly in 1910, "but the Association feels sure that when they realize the ideals toward which it is aiming, hearty cooperation will become the rule."[56]

All of the ISAA's talk would have been meaningless without a team that would embody these ideals and validate them with a championship. In 1910, the ISAA found such a team in the 12th Street YMCA, named for Washington's now historic black YMCA, which was then under construction and would open its doors in May 1912.

The 12th Street team was the creation of Ed Henderson. At age twenty-six, Henderson still competed on the basketball court, his heady play prompting a prominent *New York Age* columnist to name him the best black center in the game. As a competitive player, Henderson wanted to help Washington challenge New York's Smart Set for the black title. But he also must have realized that an unbeatable basketball team would generate a great deal of excitement for the sport in Washington.

Joining Henderson on 12th Street were some of the finest young black athletes in the city. They included Ed Gray, a Howard medical student and former All-American football player at Amherst College; Arthur "Doc" Curtis, also a Howard medical student and the son of one of the nation's most prominent black surgeons; Maurice Clifford, a teacher at Armstrong and a former star player in Cleveland; Henry Nixon, a popular Alabaman who attended Howard; and Hudson Oliver, a newly arrived Howard medical student who in 1909 had been one of the stars of Brooklyn's Smart Set.

Building on the 1909 championship series and its introduction of intercity play, 12th Street opened the season with back-to-back victories over New York's Alpha Physical Culture Club. This set the stage for an early showdown in True Reformer's Hall between 12th Street and black champion Smart Set. Now in their sixth season of basketball, the Smart Set Grave Diggers had rolled through the season undefeated and registered a huge victory over Brooklyn's white champion Sapphire Athletic Club, marking one of the first interracial contests in New York.

But none of that mattered on this night. "At the blow of the first whistle the ball was tossed from Henderson to Curtis, back to Henderson and shot into the basket from midfield," wrote the *New York Age*. "After a foul thrown by Henderson, and another goal from Curtis, the Y.M.C.A. boys were never headed."[57] Henderson and the 12th Street team defeated the Grave Diggers 24-15.

As so often happened in early basketball, when games were arranged weeks, not years, in advance, Smart Set wanted one more crack at 12th Street. This time, the Grave Diggers planned to meet Henderson and company in Brooklyn, where, legend had it, the team was invincible. With a victory, Smart Set would likely have the right to a third and deciding game for the title. If the YMCA notched the win, the team would enter the record books as basketball's first undefeated—and thus undisputed—black world champion.

The game was played on March 31 before nearly two thousand fans at Brooklyn's Fourteenth Regiment Armory. The game was the main attraction of a winter athletic carnival that was a combination track meet, basketball tournament, and public assembly. Smart Set officials were said to have forked over an eighteen-thousand-dollar security deposit to rent the armory for the day.[58]

During the first twenty-minute half, Smart Set had its way with Washington. Led by stars Charles Scottron and Chester Moore, Smart Set worked the ball masterfully, taking a solid 14-10 lead to the dressing room at intermission.

But in the second half, the 12th Streeters caught fire. With Henderson in his pillow-sized knee and elbow pads barking signals to his teammates, the YMCA "ran the home team off its feet" on offense and "covered with lightning speed" under its own basket. The YMCA cagers passed the ball from spot to spot, setting up open shots that pulled them ahead of their hosts. Smart Set bounced in a free throw and a lucky shot from the field to move to within three points of its opponents late in the game. But the Washingtonians wouldn't buckle. As the final seconds ticked away and the 12th Streeters clung to their 20-17 lead, the packed house "cheered the Y.M.C.A. lads to the echo" for their outstanding second-half performance and unbeaten season.[59]

At the final whistle, YMCA fans streamed onto the court, hoisting their exhausted heroes onto their shoulders and parading them across the hall. Smart Set coach J. Hoffman Woods forced his way though the crowd, motioning to the jubilant Ed Henderson. Woods shoved the game trophy into Henderson's hands, saying there would be no formal presentation of the trophy later that evening.

Smart Set's poor etiquette served only to solidify the 12th Streeters' image as irrepressible do-gooders. The *Howard University Journal* wrote of the trophy incident: "The Washington boys are so good natured and full-hearted that they soon overlooked such spirit and are now rejoicing over the fact that they are champions of the world."[60] Formalities didn't matter. What mattered was that the team had become the first undisputed champion of black basketball. The accomplishments of generations of black basketball players to come would be built on the foundation of that one magical season.

TWO

The Golden Era of Amateurism

1910
1918

The Howard Big Five Meets the
New York All-Stars

On a cold Christmas night in 1910, basketball celebrated its coming-out party as popular entertainment in black New York. A record-smashing two-thousand-plus spectators, including many prominent local black socialites, poured into Manhattan Casino's old-time spectator gallery to watch Washington's champion 12th Street YMCA place its unbeaten streak on the line against the Alpha Physical Culture Club.

That Alpha hosted this break-out promotion was in many ways predictable. Unlike St. Christopher, Alpha had no stabilizing financial ties to a wealthy church. The club kept afloat financially by throwing garden parties, gymnastics demonstrations, and other fund-raising events. So it was only a matter of time before Conrad Norman, Alpha's shrewd young president, milked his basketball team for all it was worth.

Norman had thrown the club's first "basketball party" during the 1909–10 season when Alpha entertained the 12th Street YMCA. Though the game drew twelve hundred fans, by far the largest crowd to date, Manhattan Casino still had been only half full. By touting his second intercity clash with 12th Street as a must-see holiday attraction and nearly filling Manhattan Casino to the brim, Norman and his crew awakened the other amateur athletic clubs to the game's financial possibilities. As time would tell, this awareness would slowly lead the amateur clubs down the road toward increased competition, greed, jealousy, and professionalism.[1]

On this record-setting night, however, all seemed right for the hometown Alphas, who wore a trademark "A" on the front of their blue jerseys. In these days when teams ran set plays off the mandatory jump ball after each made basket, the taller Big Babe Thomas toyed with 12th Street's Ed Henderson throughout the first half, slapping the basketball into play and allowing Alpha to fly back on the offensive, where it could dominate the ball, the clock, and the scoreboard.

Midway through the second half, Henderson realized he was fighting a losing battle with the octopus-armed Thomas. He voluntarily switched to one of the guard positions and let a tall but inexperienced player, George Gilmore, try his luck jumping center with Thomas. It was a risky proposition, like switching quarterbacks in the middle of a football game. The center was the playmaker who distributed the basketball, and as a newcomer on the YMCA team, Gilmore might be out of sync offensively with his teammates even if he outjumped Thomas. The concerns immediately proved unfounded. "Slender and gimletlike," wrote the *Washington Evening Star*, Gilmore rose to the occasion, winning the taps and teaming with Henderson and Hudson Oliver to move the basketball around the horn and send the YMCA on a gameending offensive blitz. When the smoke cleared, 12th Street had escaped with a tense 24-19 victory, pushing its unbeaten string to eleven straight.[2]

Afterward, the 12th Streeters huddled in their dressing room to savor the win—and to say goodbye. Captain Ed Henderson, who had married his longtime sweetheart, Mary Ellen Meriwether, the night before, informed his teammates that he would make good on his vow to retire after the Alpha contest. Without Henderson to navigate the team's affairs on and off the court, all players agreed: 12th Street had reached the end of the road.

The team's loss soon became Howard University's gain. YMCA players Gilmore, Oliver, Ed Gray, Henry Nixon, and Doc Curtis already were enrolled at Howard University, and they simply joined the college's basketball team. In one swoop, Howard went from a bit player on the black basketball scene to its defending national champion, a dramatic change of fortune for a college that still had no gymnasium.

After the Christmas holidays, the Howard Big Five continued its title defense without Henderson. College and club teams still had no intercity leagues or conferences, nor had anyone thought to organize a post-season tournament to crown a regional or national champion. Because the early teams functioned as independents, Howard's goal was to schedule and defeat the best quintets in the black game, particularly those in New York. If the team defeated all its opponents—including in a two- or three-game series, as teams often played in those days—public opinion would crown Howard the world champion of the black amateur game.

In game one of its six-game season, Howard traveled to Manhattan Casino to face the most controversial quintet in black basketball, the New York All-Stars. Formed in the fall of 1910, the All-Stars were the creation of former St. Christopher star Major A. Hart, a pudgy, light-skinned man who appeared to be in his thirties. Though he never said exactly why he had left St. Christopher, Hart clearly had grown disenchanted with the New York club scene, which he viewed as petty, two-faced, and disorganized.

"That this game has taken a firm hold on our people has been demonstrated beyond a doubt," wrote Hart. "Now it is up to the players and their friends [to advance the black game] by not only forming a basketball league among the teams, but playing good, fast, clean games, eliminating therefrom all petty jealousies, quarrels and the little meannesses that have a tendency to disgust the people who assemble to witness these contests.

"We want to play the game as our white friends play it. That is, in the spirit of fairness and for the benefits that the exercise will give us and the enjoyment we can afford to our friends."[3]

Hart clearly envisioned basketball as entertainment, not just physical education. Like Ed Henderson and the 12th Street YMCA team, he seemed to recognize that a winning team of all-star performers would help further popularize the game in black New York. But Hart took his plan one step further than Henderson could in Jim Crow Washington. Hart calculated that his all-star aggregation had enough talent and skill to compete against white teams. Whether Hart reached this decision for financial or idealistic reasons is unclear, but his scheduling of local white club teams to begin the season probably marked the first attempt by a black team in America to cross over into white basketball.

Hart's ambition immediately landed him in trouble with New York's black athletic clubs. It is hard to imagine an athletic club of this era that would not be morally opposed to the New York All-Stars' playing basketball primarily for its entertainment value. Nor could the clubs have been pleased when Hart raided their best players to stock his team. Hart made off with St. Christopher's muscular center Charlie Bradford and most of Smart Set's top players, marking the end of basketball for the small Brooklyn club and leading to its eventual demise in 1915.

Hart quickly became a reviled figure in local basketball circles, with most clubs refusing to play his team. He parried in a measured tone: "This team was not formed for any spirit of revenge or to hurt any of the good clubs that are in the game, as has been rumored. . . . Neither are we professionals and we feel that we can show that this team will be a 'top notcher.'"[4]

Having opened the season in October 1910, Hart's team had yet to prove it was a "top notcher" against white opponents. The All-Stars had logged a disappointing .500 record by early January 1911, an indication that the top black players in New York still had a lot to learn before they could compete against the best white teams. Still, the showdown between Howard and the All-Stars marked a key occasion for both teams. For Howard, it was a chance to defeat its top challenger for the title right off the bat. For Hart, it was the best attraction of the young season, one that would draw scores of local Howard alumni, and, ideally, convert them into fans of his much maligned team.

In the first half, Hart seemed to proved his critics wrong. Led by Bradford and forward Ferdinand Accooe, the All-Stars swamped Howard en route to an 11-2 halftime lead. But in the second half, Howard's fleet-footed Hudson Oliver stole the show, almost single-handedly tying the score at 16 apiece with just a few minutes left in the game and momentum squarely on Howard's side.

Then things got wild. According to the *New York Age,* the trouble started when an unnamed Howard cager got into a tiff with a now nameless All-Star. As the white referee Sam Melitzer stepped between the players, the Howardite called Melitzer a "short, mean name." Melitzer, with God and the Manhattan Casino crowd looking on, immediately raked a right cross at the Howard player, and a bench-clearing ruckus ensued. When order was restored, Howard's momentum had evaporated, and the All-Stars nudged ahead to claim a controversial 19-16 victory over the previously unbeaten 12th Street/Howard team.[5]

Melitzer's controversial right cross set the stage for a rematch in late February in Washington's True Reformer's Hall. The game was held on a Tuesday night, an odd choice since most big games coincided with weekend dances to fatten the profit margin. This wasn't the only unusual feature. The All-Stars pulled into town without the services of their top player, Charlie Bradford. Hart claimed his star was sick and bedridden back in New York. His enemies sniped that Bradford had turned in his uniform for good, igniting more finger-pointing between Hart and his accusers.

Without Bradford clogging the middle, the Washington team was in control of the game. Ahead 16-7 at the start of the second half, Howard stormed out and gave its fans one of the greatest displays of basketball ever seen in True Reformer's Hall. It started with a chip shot by Gilmore. Then came a deuce from Nixon. Then came another deuce and another and another. When the twelve-minute barrage abated, Howard had racked up a 25-0 run. As the clock ticked down, the Howard student body rocked the hall with applause. Gilmore ended up with twenty points, Oliver netted seventeen, and Nixon added fourteen. The final score: Howard 69, All-Stars 14.

While Howard fans cheered, the New Yorkers rained down a torrent of "bah, humbugs." Members of the team claimed that the floor in True Reformer's Hall was too small for basketball, an issue that would flare up again over the next few seasons. The All-Stars pressed Howard for a return match in New York. Folks already were billing it as "the greatest basket ball game of the season."[6]

That game was not to be. Howard closed out its season with a home-court pasting of Alpha and its second win of the season over Philadelphia's Wissahickon Boys Club, showing intercity play had spread to another eastern city. Because of Hart's checkered reputation and the season-ending rout of his team, few quibbled with Howard's claim to the 1911 championship. As soft-spoken Howard guard Ed Gray said, his team had spent the past two years battling "the most formidable teams of the East, and during these contests have had her colors lowered but once. This means that Howard in basket ball as in foot ball holds the championship among the best colored teams of the country."[7]

The New York All-Stars closed the season as they had begun it—in controversy. In what amounted to a major society event, Hart partnered with the *Amsterdam News* to have the All-Stars play the popular Tenth U.S. Cavalry band and basketball team. At issue was whether it was proper for the public to attend the basketball social and patronize Hart's team.

"This game . . . provoked a newspaper wrangle, pro and con; exhibited feelings blue, bitter, vindictive, and otherwise; caused arguments in the home and on the corners; explanations tangled and tangled again," went one account, showing how popular basketball had become in mainstream black New York over the past few months.[8]

In the end, about two thousand fans opted to watch the All-Stars defeat the Cavalry team. But Hart's reputation as a shady promoter lived on. By the next season, he had moved on to become, according to an advertisement in the *New York Age,* manager of the torturously named Missionary Committee of the Cathedral of St. John the Divine for the Benefit of the Home for Working Girls and Boy Scouts.[9] He left a watered-down version of his all-star team in the care of a local florist. The team would disband a few months later, marking the end of the first bold attempt to commercialize the black game.

Hart later rejoined the black game briefly with New York's Salem-Crescent Club. After World War I he moved to Buffalo, and during the 1920s he served there as a Prohibition officer. In July 1927, while on duty, Hart flipped his car. He died shortly thereafter from his injuries.[10]

Life in Segregated Washington

Black basketball bounced into Washington on a stretch of U Street N.W. from 7th Street, near Howard University, to 14th Street. Today, U Street is an eclectic avenue of decaying storefronts, trendy cafes, and vintage clothing stores. But for longtime Washingtonians, the street still invokes memories of the good old days when black culture and refinement was squeezed into a glittering half mile of shops, theaters, and restaurants.

In the teens, U Street had just come to life as the main thoroughfare for the blocks of middle-class, black-owned Victorian homes ringing Howard University. Locals referred to U Street as the Stroll, the Avenue, the Boulevard, the Rialto. Like Lenox Avenue would be during the heyday of Harlem, U Street was where the fashionable crowd came to put a swagger in its step, order a steak dinner, and blow smoke rings around the day's news. According to one longtime resident, the street marched to the beat of "gossip, sidestep, and spend."[11]

At night, U Street pulsed with the country's finest black entertainment. At the Hiawatha, which billed itself as the nation's first black-financed movie house,[12] a nickel bought a ticket to see silent whodunits with titles like *The Exploits of Elaine* and *The Clutching Hand.*

But the biggest shows in town—all the top acts on the black entertainment circuit—played the Howard Theater, a plush fifteen-hundred-seat venue just off U Street at 7th and T that catered to the cultivated tastes of high-society black folks. For some of these socialites, taking their box seats at the Howard was as much a part of their weekly ritual as sitting down to Sunday dinner.

While the good times rolled on U Street, a new day was dawning in the nation's capital. Once a backward federal town known for its dirt roads and stray cattle, the District had blossomed into a world-class city smitten with itself and its rising status in international affairs. The "New Washington" was a city of foreign diplomats and DuPont Circle mansions, Smithsonian masterpieces and State of the Union addresses. It was a genteel society whose leading citizens sauntered out of their homes each morning, socialized at tea parties and black-tie dinners, and retired to the beach when Congress recessed for the summer.

Folks flocked to Washington by the thousands. In 1905, the capital had swollen to 323,000 residents. By 1915, the number would top 437,000.

New neighborhoods sprouted like dandelions. On Pennsylvania Avenue, south of the Anacostia River, one dollar down bought a plot of land overlooking the city's many monuments and federal buildings. Near 16th Street, the tree-lined boulevard that some predicted would one day rival Manhattan's Park Avenue, a nine-room brownstone went for just six thousand dollars. In Chevy Chase, where land sold for as low as three cents a foot, high-hatted dandies boarded downtown-bound streetcars each morning at 7:45 sharp, puffing Cuban cigars and exchanging chit-chat. "Evidently the charms of the federal capital as a place of residence are beginning to make themselves felt," wrote the *New York Tribune* in 1905. "No city in the United States offers more to its inhabitants, and very few offer so much."[13]

But many griped that Washington was too provincial ever to rival the great European seats of power. While gentlemen of the aristocracy lounged at the National Theatre, drunken throngs hooted at busty showgirls in the latest burlesque revues. In Georgetown and other middleclass neighborhoods, the scruffy set congregated curbside, swilling Old Purissima whiskey and ogling young women. On F Street, the heart of downtown, panhandling waifs thrust grimy cardboard signs into the hands of unsuspecting shoppers and whined, "Mister, please give me something on me card." Even the president of the United States wasn't immune. He could peer from any back window of the White House and behold clapboard shacks announcing the sale of pigs' feet, oysters, and ice cream.

High-minded citizens petitioned Congress to vote in a new era of enlightened laws to cultivate the social graces. They prodded authorities to raze the hundreds of alley shantytowns housing the city's poor and destitute. The Anti-Saloon League, more than five hundred members strong, lobbied to shut down the corner taverns and make the capital city dry as a bone. In 1908, the police chief recommended the whipping post for wife-beaters.

Amid this public outcry, some reformers took potshots at a familiar target, African Americans. Declaring racial equality a failure, many conservative whites griped about the thousands of "colored deep water folks" who wandered into Washington each year clad in "Prince Albert coats, checkered pants, wearing 'old Marse' Henry's style of a beaver [hat]."[14] They cursed blacks who peddled moonshine in the alleys, bore children out of wedlock, and were prone to violence. Many whites took their prejudice one mental leap further. Since most had little or no social interaction with educated blacks living near Howard University, they adopted the opinion that all blacks were ghetto-dwellers at heart, and that the race was better suited to sweating in the field than toiling in the federal buildings.

As a result, Washington scrapped its experiment with racial equality at the turn of the century for the crude idiosyncrasies of word-of-mouth segregation. Stories circulated about Jim Crow restaurants, theaters, drugstores, and taverns popping up throughout the city. Other stories made the rounds about white shopkeepers' charging "Negro prices," which were always three to four times higher than the regular prices for white customers.

In 1913, newly elected president Woodrow Wilson paraded into Washington, according to one black newspaperman, "lugging his cracker cabinet and segregation policy" for the federal government.[15] Under President William Howard Taft, Wilson's predecessor, more than thirty blacks had held high-ranking federal positions. Under Wilson, a lone black appointee remained. With Wilson's blessing, government agencies began posting signs in their buildings declaring segregated workstations, bathrooms, lunchrooms, and even elevators. Those who disagreed with the policy found pink slips waiting for them. Uncle Sam had spoken.

"There is a whole lot of talent just going to shucks in the departments," wrote the *Washington Bee*. "Negroes who are as bright as a fresh-coined dollar and could eat up opportunities if they only had the nerve to cut loose from this segregating society. But they won't."[16]

Although full-blown protest was still years away, segregation stoked the smoldering embers of race pride in black Washington. From the podium of the Bethel Literary and Historical Association to the pulpit of the Shiloh Baptist Church, black leaders cried out for unity. "It is in this land that we are to work out our salvation, that we are to demonstrate to the world of what material we are made," proclaimed Francis J. Grimke, pastor of the 15th Street Presbyterian Church. "It is of the utmost importance that we make no mistakes here, for as a twig is bent the tree inclines."[17]

In this rigid, segregated society, Hudson Oliver and his Howard teammates labored with the same duality of being that burdened virtually all black men in America. On U Street, they were basketball players; in white neighborhoods, they were colored basketball players. On U Street, they were hailed as stars; in white neighborhoods, they were shunned as inferior athletes. On U Street, they were a team that others dreamed of playing; in white neighborhoods, they were a team that nobody could imagine playing.

But as black folks knew all too well, Jim Crow America hadn't been created in a day, nor would it be changed in one afternoon. The Howard Big Five played on, like the barnstorming black baseball teams that rolled through America every summer shrouded in varying shades of anonymity, simply for the love of the game. They had no other choice.

Snookered in Pittsburgh

By December 1911, the Howard Big Five returned to the court with more firepower than any team in the black game. Not only did Howard return intact its championship combo of Nixon, Oliver, Gilmore, Gray, and Curtis, it added another star athlete named Snake Sykes, who could score at will. By its sixth game of the season, Howard had a perfect record, had manhandled the top New York teams, and had outscored its opponents by a combined 251-59.

Then the champions ran into bad luck. The trouble started in late February 1912 when Howard traveled to Virginia to play Hampton Institute, its first encounter with a fellow college team and quite possibly the first black intercollegiate game ever played in America.[18]

Though Hampton had a large, brand-new, five-hundred-seat gymnasium, the men from the farm-and-trade school were muddling their way through their first season of organized basketball. On paper, this game would be no more than a tune-up before Howard embarked on its first trip to Pittsburgh to face the Monticello Athletic Association. Hudson Oliver and company would simply trot out, wow the crowd with their fancy passing, then call it an early night.

Hampton forgot to read the script. Fielding a squad of scrappy New Yorkers who had played basketball for a few years, Hampton clawed its way to an early advantage. Without regulars Doc Curtis and team captain Henry Nixon in the lineup, Howard couldn't dent the lead. Gilmore, coming off a gaudy, twenty-five-point effort against Alpha, clanked in just one hoop. Snake Sykes, who had scored an amazing fifty-four points in two games, was good that night for two baskets. Even reliable Hudson Oliver rattled through just one field goal.

Despite their shooting woes, the champions managed to pull within a basket of Hampton with under two minutes left to play. The champs got the ball back one last time and headed upcourt. Gilmore signaled a play. Whipping the basketball to and fro as they had done so many times before down the stretch, the Howard players sliced through the Hampton defense and trickled one through to send the game to overtime.

The newspaper accounts are unclear on what happened next. In the five-minute extra period both teams slugged it out. But it was Hampton that punched out the game winner for a 19-16 upset, pinning Howard with only its second defeat in two years.

With that loss, Howard's upcoming battle in Pittsburgh took on enormous meaning. If Howard shut down Monticello, the Hampton loss would be old news. If the champs choked in Pittsburgh, it would be the end of their 1912 championship bid.

The Howardites knew getting out of Pittsburgh with a win would be no easy chore. Monticello suited up the slickest black cager around in thirty-one-year-old Cumberland Posey Jr. The lean, light-skinned Posey had been a star forward on Penn State's 1911 team before he left school in a spat over grades. Posey's game was to bomb from long range, an unpopular tactic in most gyms in America. Coaches wanted high-percentage lay-ups, or chip shots. "Scientific basketball," they called it. But in the small, happy-go-lucky world of black basketball, Posey had the green light to step beyond the free-throw stripe and fire.

That season, Posey had been the star attraction on a top-flight basketball team at Pittsburgh's Colored YMCA. Though the YMCA club mowed down several white teams in Pittsburgh, the squad hadn't been a smash at the box office. By February, Posey and crew formed their own independent club team, which they named the Monticello Athletic Association after the street on which two of the players lived.[19]

With a few practices behind it, Monticello lured Howard to Pittsburgh for a game. If the team upset the defending black champions, Posey could make a strong case that Monticello deserved the 1912 black crown and, as a titled team, land games in the larger, more lucrative dance halls of New York. Posey planned to beat Howard—even if it meant cheating, as Hudson Oliver and his teammates soon would discover.

On March 8, 1912, the two teams tangled under the dim lights of Washington Park Fieldhouse, a tiny, city-owned gym. Though the venue lacked glamour, the stands brimmed with a fashionable, high-society crowd that had come to witness the first black intercity basketball game ever played in Pittsburgh. Gilmore shook hands with Monticello center Sell Hall, the ball went up, and the show was on.

The first half offered the standard fare of pushing and grabbing around the basket, but Howard managed to bang out a few hoops to take the early lead. Enter Cum Posey. With under five minutes left in the half, Posey let the laces fly. And fly. And fly. Even Howard's muscle-bound defensive ace Ed Gray, who had given up one basket all season on defense, couldn't cuff Posey. By intermission, Posey's aerial show had propelled Monticello to a 9-8 lead, and the second half promised to be a doozy.

Then things got weird. Having battled under college rules in the first half, Monticello manager Joe Mahoney let it be known the second half would be played under YMCA rules, one of four sets of rules then in use in men's basketball. Under the college rules, the Howardites were allowed to dribble around the court and, as in today's game, shoot at will. Not so under the YMCA rules. Players were permitted a single bounce to avoid a charging defender, and shooting off the dribble was strictly forbidden.

Being unfamiliar with the YMCA rules, the Howard players balked at Mahoney's demand. Mahoney persevered, claiming the college rules were all Greek to a club team like Monticello. Why should his team be handicapped for the entire game? After further squawking, Mahoney got his way. Fair was fair.

Or was it? Cum Posey, as a former college star, was clearly well-versed in the dos and don'ts of the college game. So were his teammates. Posey even fessed up in a newspaper article thirty years later that the Monticellos often pulled this stunt "to bewilder the opposition"[20] and gain the upper hand in the second half.

According to the *Pittsburgh Courier,* "Howard was completely dazed" under the new rules, and its "reputed team work was nowhere in evidence."[21] The Monticellos, sensing they now had the edge, went for the jugular in the second half. In no time, Posey's boys built a four-point bulge.

But as in the Hampton game, the Howardites came back one last time, YMCA rules or not. Gilmore, whose shooting the *New York Age* called "of the sensational order,"[22] kept nailing clutch baskets to keep Howard close. With under three minutes to play, Gilmore and his mates narrowed the gap to a single point, 20-19. Howard, as the more veteran ball club, smelled victory, and all it needed now was the ball and a game-winning basket.

Once again, enter Cum Posey. With the over-and-back rule still twenty years down the road, Posey darted into the backcourt on Monticello's next possession, well over twenty feet from the hoop, and found some open space. He took a pass, squared, and fired. Nothing but net. He now had fifteen points on the night. Monticello 22, Howard 19. After the center jump, Monticello forward Sell Hall found himself open at midcourt clutching the basketball. He measured and "pulled a Posey," arching the ball through the hoop for his only points of the evening. Monticello 24, Howard 19. It was all over.

Posey and his teammates uncorked the postgame celebration, belting out speeches like politicians on election night. "The backers of Monticello feel safe in claiming the colored basketball championship of the country and stand ready to defend it against all comers," declared the *Pittsburgh Courier* in a front-page story.[23] Posey and company even told the *New York Age* which teams they deemed worthy opponents for a championship game, omitting Howard from the list.[24]

Howard finished the season on a tear. It routed Lincoln University, its second intercollegiate game, then twice thumped its old nemesis the New York All-Stars. But in the end, public opinion would crown Monticello the champion. "As this is Howard's third defeat in three years [counting the record of the 12th Street YMCA team], the colored basketball world will be forced to recognize Monticello as one of the fastest of colored quints," wrote the *New York Age,* a measured but clear declaration that Monticello had won the title.[25]

The sudden turn of events opened the Howardites' eyes to the dangers of playing independent club teams. Because these clubs were accountable only to themselves, as Monticello had shown, some played fast and loose with the rules to win games and build their reputations.

Those who sat on the Howard Athletic Council hoped more black colleges would develop competitive basketball teams. Ten years earlier, such hope might have seemed unrealistic. But a month before the Monticello game, Howard had joined the Colored Intercollegiate Athletic Association, or CIAA, the first large black collegiate conference in America. With a little money and luck, the CIAA would organize black college sports and place them on track to one day compete against white colleges.

The Birth of the CIAA

The story of the CIAA began in early September 1909 as the dozen or so members of the Howard University football team trained on campus for the upcoming season. Cheering the squad from the sidelines was its new coach, Ernest Jones Marshall, a tall, twenty-year-old college graduate and recent addition to Howard's chemistry department.

Though Marshall was younger than some of his players, in this era of volunteer faculty coaches he was the logical choice to try to reverse the fortunes of the underachieving football team. Marshall had been a star offensive tackle at Exeter Academy and Williams College, both highly regarded white institutions in Massachusetts. He also had spent a year studying at the University of Michigan, where he observed how a well-funded football program could produce outstanding student athletes and generate thousands of dollars in profits for a university.

At Howard, Marshall discovered the football team was more an afterthought than the centerpiece of campus life. The problem wasn't talent; the team featured several outstanding athletes. The trouble, according to Marshall, was the perennial head-in-the-sand neglect of sports by university administrators. In particular, he cited their failure to build a fence around the football field, which would have forced students to purchase tickets instead of watching games for free, and their inability to secure the requisite funds to pay for team equipment, travel, and competent referees for games.

"Our athletic tax is too small," he wrote, referring to the one dollar each student paid, or twelve hundred dollars total, that financed Howard's six teams: football, basketball, baseball, track, cricket, and tennis. "The men who engage in the sports at Howard are put to great personal sacrifices on this account and cannot be properly equipped. We are endeavoring to support too many branches of sport with the small revenue which comes from the tax."[26]

By the fall of 1911, Marshall had seen enough of the second-rate conditions at Howard and its rival black colleges. In one of the seminal moments in the history of black collegiate sport, Marshall posted a letter to every black college in America inviting them to join him in forming the first black intercollegiate athletic association. Marshall hoped a dozen or so colleges would answer his letter, adopt a standard set of eligibility rules, and impose a sense of order on black collegiate athletics, including basketball.

Marshall received just four replies: Hampton Institute in Virginia; Lincoln University in southeastern Pennsylvania; Shaw University in Raleigh, North Carolina; and Virginia Union College in Richmond. For Marshall, a good-natured, idealistic young man, the number of replies hardly mattered. His idea was timely, and he intended to forge on with it.

On February 12, 1912, Marshall and the delegates from the four other institutions held a planning session on the Hampton campus. "For two days these delegates met in morning, afternoon and evening sessions, their deliberations being largely guided by the letter sent out by Mr. Marshall which suggested a permanent organization, the introduction of a 'four-year [eligibility] rule,' a 'scholarship standing rule,' and a rule for 'time for matriculation of new students,'" wrote Hampton's Charles Williams, who attended the session and who, by the late teens, would be the leading voice of the new organization.

Black collegiate athletics had always been as unpredictable as the weather, Williams knew. "During the early period of athletic development in our schools, some men were known to have played football for twelve years," he wrote. "On one of the teams at that time it was said that every man had played at least eight years and some even more. . . . There were no transfer rules and players often went from one school to another, playing continuously on athletic teams."

Nor were the referees always on the level. Williams recalled a game in which a team "carried the ball over the goal line four times. Each time the referee brought the ball back for some infraction of the football code. When it was carried across the goal line for the fourth time there was such a threatening demonstration on the part of the enraged football fans that after consultation with officials it was decided that the play was good and the touchdown counted."

Betting on games was common, and fans sometimes couldn't contain their emotions. In one case, Williams wrote, "the center recovered a fumbled punt and was on his way to a touchdown when a spectator stepped in the field of play near the goal line with a board and dared the runner to cross the goal line."[27]

At the start of their two-day session, the delegates voted to approve the formation of the Colored Intercollegiate Athletic Association. The delegates elected Marshall as their president, a post he held until 1915, and formed a three-member committee to draft a list of proposed rules and a second committee to develop a constitution and bylaws. In May the committees presented their recommendations and all delegates ratified the CIAA constitution. "By this fall it is hoped that other institutions will join the association, and that the work of putting intercollegiate athletics on the highest plane possible will be pushed forward."[28]

Marshall and his colleagues already had committed to paper a plan to expand the CIAA into a national regulatory body, a smaller black version of the National Collegiate Athletic Association. During their second meeting, the delegates passed a resolution declaring that "the country be divided into sections as follows: (a) Georgia, Florida, and Alabama; (b) North and South Carolina; (c) Ohio, Kentucky, Tennessee; (d) Texas; (e) Louisiana, Arkansas, and Kansas; and that an active man be secured in each district to push the association."[29]

But the plan fizzled for two reasons. Most colleges, already on shoestring budgets, feared that joining the CIAA would commit them to mandatory league schedules and increased travel costs. As many no doubt asked, why should they travel eight hours to play Howard, a trip that the school and most of its fans could not afford, when a Saturday afternoon game with a rival local high school club cost them nothing? Second, many colleges worried that with the competition improving and athletic talent in short supply, the CIAA's eligibility rules would leave them with no players.

"The first objection is based on a misunderstanding," wrote Marshall, referring to increased travel costs. "The members of the Association are not required to play with one another unless they find it convenient to do so.

"The second objection has more weight, especially with those institutions whose work is, by necessity, mostly for preparatory departments," he wrote. Most black colleges of this era included college preparatory schools, and many prep students played on the varsity football and basketball teams. This meant prep students conceivably could enroll at an institution for eight school years: that is, high school and college.

"In such institutions it does seem a hardship to limit a player to four years," Marshall continued. "The proper solution of the difficulty, however, does not consist of nullifying the four year rule, but in the elimination of preparatory school pupils from teams called 'University,'" a controversial proposal that the CIAA would not adopt for several years.[30]

Given the continued cool response to the league, the CIAA might have died a nearly instantaneous death. As it was, the association operated almost exclusively under an intercollegiate honor code in its early years, not as the competitive league that one sees today. Its five member schools voluntarily enforced the four-year eligibility rule and other lesser prohibitions. That was it. The only practical advantage of membership was a list of CIAA-approved referees who agreed to provide their services for a reduced rate. Besides that, CIAA schools had nothing to lose but their honor in breaking a rule. The CIAA had no two-year probations to hand down, like the NCAA does today, and even if it did, the sanctions would have been meaningless. The association still operated no competitive league schedules in its sanctioned sports, including basketball, and neither did it award championships.

How did the CIAA survive? One reason is the high quality of the founding schools. Howard, Hampton, and Lincoln were among the most prominent black colleges in the country, and all were already bitter arch rivals. In a sense, the lack of a competitive league schedule was irrelevant, because these three schools would have played each other in football and basketball regardless. Moreover, Shaw was known for its fine football teams, and the weakest link, Virginia Union, benefited from playing nearby Hampton and Howard.

Another factor was the commitment and high character of the CIAA's founding fathers. In addition to Marshall and Williams, they included Shaw's Charles R. Frazer, W. E. Watkins, and H. P. Hargrave; Virginia Union's J. W. Barco and J. W. Pierce; Hampton's Allen Washington; and Lincoln's George Johnson. These men refused to compromise their principles for personal gain. Brotherhood seemed to rule the day, not petty jealousy, as was sometimes the case in early black sports.

Just as important, did these schools really have an option? Marshall and Williams had been trained in white northern colleges, and they realized, in Marshall's words, that black colleges "should begin to run their athletics on strict business principles, and at once do away with loose and disorderly methods which are now in vogue."[31] At the same time, the founders of the CIAA believed, like Ed Henderson before them, that the race could use sports to its advantage, and that they had a responsibility to organize intercollegiate athletics for future generations.

"The manner in which the Negro has forged his way to the front of Northern colleges is sufficient to cause us to believe that in the near future the athletes of our Colored colleges of the South will rank among the best in the country," wrote Marshall in an interesting reversal of Henderson's theme of developing black athletes in the South to send to white colleges in the North. "When our schools and colleges begin to give attention to the physical as well as the mental and moral development of the youth, we may expect to see the Negro reach a high mark in the athletic world."[32]

The emergence of the CIAA, however, had little impact on black college basketball during the teens. The Howard Big Five, for instance, was comprised of students enrolled in either the university or its medical school, meaning the CIAA's four-year rule was a moot point. Because Howard already had athletic ties with Hampton and Lincoln, the CIAA offered no other viable competition. Shaw and Virginia Union had horrible basketball teams, and Howard continued to round out its season schedule with the top club teams on the East Coast.

Still, the CIAA represented an escape hatch for the Howard Big Five. Though the trips to New York and Pittsburgh were the buzz of the campus in the winter, Howard officials had tired of their dealings with Cum Posey, Major Hart, and those of their ilk. They longed for the uniformity and organization that the CIAA promised. Howard just had to wait for other nearby colleges, such Morgan in Baltimore, to develop quality teams. That wouldn't take place until the 1920s, when eligibility and transfer rules, personal jealousies, and the meddling of fraternities in sports would divide and nearly destroy the association.

By then, Ernest Marshall, the driving force behind the CIAA, would be gone from Howard. Marshall joined the army at the outbreak of World War I, and upon his discharge he enrolled in medical school at Northwestern University in Chicago. He was awarded his M.D. in 1927, then performed his residency in Kansas City's General Hospital, where Howard's Ed Gray had interned. Marshall opened a doctor's office in Kansas City, where he would live and work for the next thirty years. He died in August 1959 after a long illness.

Today his contributions to the CIAA are largely forgotten. But his vision of organized black intercollegiate athletics lives on, with the CIAA now in its ninth decade of operation.

A Season of Revenge

By the 1912–13 season, intercity competition had become a staple of the black game. No longer did facing the best teams mean making a three-day trip to Washington or New York. Intercity competition had grown in just four seasons into an expanding network of towns and cities that also included Philadelphia, Pittsburgh, Newark, Baltimore, and Atlantic City, and the college campuses of Howard, Hampton, and Lincoln. In a few more seasons, the network would extend into the Midwest and New England.

The black game also had begun to develop a deeper pool of talent. At Harlem's St. Christopher Club, where teams were said to have the luxury of practicing "two hours a day regularly," the seeds already had been sown for the next great New York team.[33] At Hampton, under the direction of Harvard-trained physical educator Charles Williams, another outstanding college team was in the making. At the same time, a boom in the construction of YMCAs for black men was under way, which would have a profound impact on the training of young players in cities throughout the country.

But in 1913, the black game's two best teams remained the Howard Big Five and Pittsburgh's champion Monticello Athletic Club. Howard clearly had the more talent and cohesiveness as a team, with most of its stars having played together for four years. George Gilmore now was the best center in the black game, Ed Gray was the best defender, and Hudson Oliver was probably the second-best player overall.

The title of best player overall belonged to Monticello's thin, sandy-haired Cum Posey. According to some, Posey stood shoulder to shoulder with Paul Robeson, Henry Lloyd, Oscar Charleston, and other great black baseball and football players as the finest athlete of his generation. "Giants crumpled and quit before the fragile-looking Posey," recalled the *Pittsburgh Courier*'s W. Rollo Wilson in the late 1920s. "He was at once a ghost, a buzz saw, and a 'shooting fool.' The word 'quit' has never been translated for him."[34]

With the hot-shooting Posey on its roster, Monticello stood a decent chance of repeating as the black champion in 1913. But as in his first showdown with Howard, Posey didn't want even odds; he wanted to stack the deck in his favor by weaving a series of special requests into the contract negotiations. Posey always seemed to get the better end of the deal, a point that irked his competitors and became an element of his popular legend.

Posey's prickliness was in full force in 1913, when Howard's Henry Nixon, a business major, attempted to arrange a title series with Monticello. Problems began around New Year's Day, when Nixon assumed he had finalized a three-game championship series with Monticello, with the first battle set for January 17 in True Reformer's Hall. Nixon already had mailed a contract for the final signature of Richard Garrison, the new Monticello manager, and as far as Nixon was concerned, the two teams had reached an agreement.

A few days before the first game, no doubt after consultation with Posey, Garrison and his assistant J. A. Norris returned the contract—unsigned. They said Monticello would never put its title on the line in an old sardine can like True Reformer's Hall, with its cranky rims, low ceiling, loose floorboards, and crazy obstacle course of iron poles ringing the court.

With the game just a few days away and signs plastered along U Street touting the championship showdown, Nixon and Howard assistant manager Clarence Richardson felt the squeeze. The two men scoured the city for an alternate site, but with no luck. Finally, the leaders of the white YMCA agreed to let Howard book its new gymnasium for the contest, a small miracle in these early days of segregation. There was only one hitch—the YMCA was a private club, and no nonmembers would be permitted to enter the gymnasium. Or, in the racial shorthand of the day, no colored patrons would be permitted to attend the game. It was a lot to swallow; but still, it was a large, neutral court, and a frantic Richardson clicked off a telegram to Pittsburgh proposing Plan B. The Monticellos responded with one word: "Unsatisfactory."

Richardson was outraged. He fired off a letter to the *New York Age* in which he derided the Monticellos, denounced their championship, decried YMCA rules, and denigrated club teams. This diatribe sparked a nasty exchange of letters in the newspaper between Norris and Richardson:

> Norris: "[T]he thing that touched me most was not his dastardly attack on Monticello or his unprincipled comment on the game last year;

it was his bold intimation that they regretted playing city teams. . . .
This slur does not stop with Monticello; it includes the host of other
city teams that has entertained Howard."

Richardson: "He calls on all clubs in Christendom to resent the
bigotry of Howard. I do not question (as he insinuates) the moral,
the social, or the intellectual status of the Monticello or any other
club. . . . What I do question is their sportsmanship, and on this point
I need no modification."

Norris: "We told Mr. Nixon in the middle of December and continued to tell him that we would not play in True Reformer's Hall.
But Howard . . . goes on with this arrangement certain in the end the
social glamour would ensnare us against our best interest; for it is a
well known fact that Howard slaughters every team she plays in True
Reformer's Hall, not so much on account of the inability of the
enemy as the disadvantage of the hall."

Richardson: "If he will carry his investigation a step further, he
will find that every team, save one [Monticello], that Howard has
'slaughtered' in True Reformer's Hall she has beaten by a larger margin in the team's own home town. The one—as Mr. Norris well
knows—would not give us a return game."[35]

It took the intervention of two New Yorkers to finally bring together
the teams from Pittsburgh and Washington. Romeo Dougherty, sports
editor of New York's *Amsterdam News* and a dyed-in-the-wool basketball fan, already had gotten the go-ahead from Howard's Henry Nixon
to try to stage the game in New York. To coax the matter forward,
Dougherty joined forces with New York sports promoter Nat Strong, a
white, middle-aged wheeler-dealer who bankrolled some of the top
black professional baseball teams on the East Coast. Dougherty and
Strong urged the teams back to the bargaining table, and within a week
or so both sides had hammered out an agreement. They would settle
their differences on Thursday evening, March 13, in a winner-take-all
match in New York's Manhattan Casino.

"The morning of the 13th found both teams on Manhattan Isle in
good physical condition and after each team in turn had taken an hour's
work-out on the casino court, they each went to bed in their respective
quarters to sleep and dream the matter over," wrote the *Howard University Journal.* "At nightfall they rose to meet in the contest which was
to decide which way the championship should go."

At 10 P.M. sharp, the two teams gathered at midcourt. Gilmore and Posey shook hands in the center circle, scuffing their sneakers and eyeing their teammates. "When referee Zinovoy of New York University blew the whistle as a signal to start and tossed the ball into the air," wrote the *Howard University Journal*, "twelve hundred anxious spectators involuntarily rose to their feet to see what would happen."[36]

What happened was magic. Gilmore tapped to the streaking Snake Sykes, who flipped the ball over his head for Hudson Oliver; Oliver speared the pass out of the air and zipped the ball across court to the waiting Ed Gray. Howard looked untouchable, and the irony was the first half was being played with the same YMCA rules that had hamstrung the team a year ago in Pittsburgh.

At the other end of the floor, Posey looked lost. Matched against tall George Gilmore to start the game, the five-foot-ten Posey couldn't get a good look at the hoop through Gilmore's octopus arms. Frustrated, Posey switched to Hudson Oliver, who clung to the Pittsburgh superstar as tenaciously as Gilmore had. On one possession, Posey dribbled downcourt with Oliver bumping him toward the sideline, blocking his path to the hoop. When Posey reached the far baseline boxed in with nowhere to go, the catlike Oliver batted the ball away, grabbed it, and bounded back downcourt. Oliver looked up and flipped the basketball to a waiting Snake Sykes. The Snake Man set and flicked—two points.[37]

So it went. After a few early miscues to start the second half, Howard pushed its lead into double digits playing under the more familiar college rules. Five minutes later, Oliver, Gilmore, and company had busted the game wide open, cruising to a 33-15 final. "I think I speak in all fairness to Pittsburgh when I say that her trouble was, not that she was not playing to form, but that her form was inadequate," crowed Clarence Richardson in celebration of the school's second championship in three seasons.[38]

Back in the locker room, Oliver, Gray, Nixon, and the other members of the Howard Big Five yanked off their soggy blue-and-white jerseys for the last time. Each was scheduled to graduate in the summer, and as they changed back into their street clothes, they had to have been pleased that they had had the last say in their year-long war with Cum Posey.

With the NBA still forty years off, none of the graduating Howard stars was concerned about finding agents or signing multiyear deals. They collected their diplomas and went on to spend their lives giving back to the black community that had claimed and nurtured them.

"To say that he will be missed is putting it mildly," wrote the *Howard University Journal* of the popular man-about-campus Henry Nixon. "His unassuming manner, his cordiality, yes, even, his ponderous olfactory passage will be longed for by many."[39]

Nixon, a native of Alabama, accepted a position teaching science at Louisville's black Central High School. While there, he brought basketball to black Louisville, coaching and even playing on the high school team for several seasons until his untimely death in the 1920s.

Gray, who played for Howard in the days when medical students were eligible for varsity sports, set off for an internship at General Hospital in Kansas City. By the summer of 1916 he had opened a doctor's office in Cincinnati, where he would spend his career as a pillar of the black community, helping to establish a hospital and a chain of drugstores. "My father was a quiet man," recalled his daughter Corolynne Branson. "But he was very generous and would lend people who were in need of money. I thought the sun rose and set with him."[40] In 1943, at age fifty-three, he died after a brief illness.

Oliver, also a medical student, eventually opened a practice at 257 West 139th Street, not far from Manhattan Casino. There, he treated the sick for the next thirty years, until his death in 1955 at the age of sixty-six. Throughout his professional career, Oliver was feted as a pioneering basketball star, the speedy forward who led the Howard Big Five to victory over the great Cum Posey.

Perhaps the biggest complement of all came in 1928 when *Pittsburgh Courier* sportswriter W. Rollo Wilson, a friend of Posey's, heaved a sigh and wrote, "Howard never had a greater team than Gilmore, Sykes, Gray, Nixon, and Oliver. And never did anyone else."[41]

Ed Henderson: Fighting the Good Fight

Back in Washington, Ed Henderson forged ahead with his dream of nurturing black student athletes. By December 1910, at the behest of Roscoe Bruce, the head of Washington's black school system, Henderson had mobilized a small army of volunteers to launch his latest weapon in the war on flabby schoolboys. He called it the Public Schools Athletic League, or PSAL. The league was a vast network of organizing and promotional committees modeled after the PSALs in eighteen other U.S. cities that promoted athletics in white schools. The ISAA remained intact, but it now served as the official sanctioning body for black sports in the Washington region.

The new PSAL was not only the first in Washington, it was the first of its kind in any black public school system. In just over four years, Henderson, Garnet Wilkinson, and scores of others had come together to build a cradle-to-diploma system of physical education in the city. No other black community came close to matching this degree of organization—not in New York, Chicago, Richmond, or Philadelphia. And Henderson knew it: "I predict that Washington will be the greatest competing center in athletics among Negroes."[42]

With no stereotypes yet in place defining the so-called "black sports," most kids lined up for just about anything the PSAL had to offer. Newspapers carried word of an intracity soccer league, a forty-team grammar school baseball tournament, and high school cross country meets winding through the streets of Washington. No sport was too obscure to organize. Henderson lobbied in the 1920s for black colleges to take up lacrosse, rowing, swimming, handball, tennis, golf, boxing, and gymnastics.[43]

Like the ISAA, the PSAL featured basketball as its big-ticket item of the winter. On Saturday nights, a parade of people shuffled into the True Reformer's Hall, climbed the well-worn stairs to the second floor above Doc Gray's drugstore and soda fountain, and settled in for a quadruple header of three basketball games and dancing afterward.

On a typical Saturday night, the action began at 7:30 sharp with the grade schools, divided into lightweight (under one hundred pounds) and heavyweight (more than one hundred pounds) divisions. New to basketball, the youngsters scooted around the court, hurling, hooking, and heaving the ball at the hoop. After the final buzzer sounded, out trotted the high school boys for their match. When they finished, as an added attraction, Hudson Oliver and the Howard Big Five came out for the nightcap.

The PSAL worked wonders in popularizing basketball across Washington. In 1911, the league fielded eight grammar and four high school teams. Two years later, the lineup expanded to more than forty grammar and eight high school squads. Just about every black schoolboy had picked up a basketball at one time or another, and a local newspaper ran headlines declaring, "More than 800 Boys in Basket Ball Teams" and "Basket Ball Booms in Colored Schools."[44]

"Over 300 boys assembled at the gymnasium of the Armstrong School last night to practice basket ball," wrote the *Washington Evening*

Star. "The scene was very similar to a crowded recreation center in New York City, and the system employed enabled every boy and all teams to get in some floor work on the big court."[45]

This rapid growth exposed a serious problem in black school sports—a lack of experienced coaches. In a great show of school spirit, textbook-toting teachers—men and women alike—signed on to coach the boys. Most didn't know a thing about basketball. But that didn't stop them from pretending to be experts and twisting the rule book to their school's advantage.

The PSAL made adjustments. Its leaders appealed to the teachers to focus on helping the children rather than on school rivalries, and Henderson sent out a weekly bulletin explaining the whys and wherefores of proper training, sportsmanship, diet, and even grooming. To get the grammar school kids up to snuff on the court, the PSAL assigned Howard players to various elementary schools, where they instructed the boys and their teachers in the nuances of the game.

The adjustments worked. By the 1920s, the PSAL had become an assembly line for top-flight basketball players. Having learned the game under a coach's eye rather than free-lancing on a playground, these stars stuck to the fundamentals. They were drilled to play a tight team game in which suffocating defense, snappy footwork, and well-timed passes won the day.

But as Henderson watched his years of labor pay off in more healthy black schoolchildren, he also saw his life change. In 1910, he had married his sweetheart, Mary Ellen Meriwether, and with some of his teaching buddies had purchased a sixty-seven-acre farm across the Potomac River in rural Falls Church, Virginia, where he had spent his summers as a boy. By 1914, he had finished building his family a house on a few acres he had purchased near his father's home in Falls Church, and two years later he had two young sons to feed on his five-hundred-dollar-a-year teaching salary.

Henderson loved the wide-open feel of the country. After hustling in the city by day, he now took refuge by night on his farm. He slogged through the mud, grooming his horse, feeding his Rhode Island Red roosters, and tending to the nearly eight hundred trees growing in his orchard.

But country life came at a cost. The city-raised Henderson couldn't abide the small-town traditions that he said stifled the hopes of black people. It seemed as though black folks couldn't get ahead here. They had the worst of everything—the worst schoolhouses, roads, stores. Like a settlement of nineteenth-century sharecroppers, most black families still fetched their water from wells and burned oil lamps instead of using electricity.

These injustices and hardships weighed upon Henderson and ate away at his self-respect. He said he even found himself having to perpetuate the racist system that he loathed. "One day my son and I were sitting in the back of the car when he and I noticed a little white boy in front of us who wanted to play with my son," he recalled. "Naturally, that was not allowed so I had to explain to my son why he couldn't play. That was an extremely painful and terrible thing for me to have to explain to him."[46]

Henderson began to fight back. In January 1915, the all-white town council, reportedly miffed at the wave of educated blacks moving into town and threatening their control of local affairs, decreed that all blacks must live within a defined area of Falls Church. Henderson and other black residents owned property outside this arbitrary boundary, and they vowed they weren't going to be pushed around.

Blacks in Falls Church marched to town hall and denounced the mayor and town council, then stalled the measure in the local circuit court. The nation's highest court was on their side. That year, the U.S. Supreme Court ruled in a similar case (Harris versus City of Louisville) that forced residential segregation was illegal, pulling the plug on the Falls Church ordinance. Henderson was ecstatic. He wrote: "In all we are proud of the fight we made in interest of our own self respect and feel that we have added a drop to the tide that we hope will soon, in light of world events [World War I], bring us into our own in the country and on earth."[47]

Some of Henderson's legal skirmishes hit closer to home. One morning at the Falls Church train station, his father, William, stepped aboard a commuter train through its rear door, the customary entrance for blacks in those days. As he hoisted himself onto the train, a hand grabbed his shoulder and tossed him like a sack of potatoes into the rear of the car. The hand belonged to a conductor, who had cleared the way for a white woman to enter the car. The conductor, scowling like an old bulldog, barked for William to get the hell off. The train groaned out of the station, and William Henderson was still waiting for the next one an hour or so later when his son bumped into him. William recounted his ugly encounter, and Ed stormed to the police station and filed a warrant against the conductor. The charge: assault on his father.

A few weeks later, the case went to trial. Henderson would remember what followed for the rest of his life: "Colonel Jacob De Putron, formerly of the Union army, who had witnessed the incident, consented to represent my father as counsel," he recalled. "When the case was tried in the Falls Church courthouse, Captain Bethune of the Home Guards [a local white militia that kept black people in line], the defendant's attorney, brought into court with him enough of the uniformed Home Guards to fill half the room. Colored citizens occupied the balance of the space. After the conductor and others had refused to testify, Colonel De Putron had himself sworn in as a witness. His account substantiated our case, and the defendant was fined $20 and costs. On the following morning De Putron, in effigy was seen hanging from an electric light pole."[48]

Henderson described his civil-rights battles as "my second career." He would spend the next forty years leading a crusade to integrate sports and entertainment in Washington, D.C. It was an unpopular cause that would make him many lifelong enemies. For his entire professional career, he kept an unlisted phone number to shield his family from crank calls and racist threats, including the venom of the Ku Klux Klan, which threatened "thirty lashes" if he didn't obey the white status quo.[49]

Henderson and his ideals did win respect among enlightened whites. As William Gay Thompson, a white physical educator in Virginia, said of Henderson: "In conversations with him, he in a constructive fashion pointed out that the black man could through [mutual participation in sports] learn to know his brother better and eventually live together in peace and harmony. He was not militant, but wise, persevering and unbending in this philosophy."[50]

New York Takes Center Stage

With the start of the 1913–14 season, the balance of power in black basketball shifted to New York. Howard had graduated most of its players from the 1913 championship team, and Pittsburgh's Monticello Athletic Club had hit hard times. According to Posey, for reasons that aren't clear Monticello abruptly split into two clubs before the season—Monticello-Delaney Rifles and Leondi, later known as Loendi.[51] The rift left Posey temporarily with a subpar lineup.

Filling the power void was New York's improved St. Christopher Club. After nearly a decade of fielding losing teams, St. C. defeated its arch rival Alpha twice in 1914 to claim the undisputed black championship of New York for the first time.

St. C.'s emergence as the top black team in the city puffed up the club's rabidly pro-amateur athletic board. Its members, led by the Reverend Everard Daniel, spent nearly a decade preaching self-sacrifice, dedication, teamwork, and clean play to any neighborhood kid who passed through St. Philip's Parish House. As former board member George Clayton recalled of these years, the club's leadership was "devoid of vanity and a desire for personal gain. . . . There is bound to be misunderstandings, but as long as there is faith, nothing can stop one's efforts to do good."[52]

Ironically, the board members placed their faith—and their basketball team—in the hands of the unscrupulous Will Anthony Madden, the former ball boy of the loathed New York All-Stars. A tiny, loquacious young man who looked to be in his late twenties, Madden could be as charming as a peacock in his silken suits with a fresh white carnation pinned to his lapel. But when challenged, Madden could explode into a raging volcano who, many joked, was the spitting image of baseball manager John "Little Napoleon" McGraw of the New York Giants. Thus the shared nickname "Little Napoleon."

Little Napoleon built St. C.'s championship team largely out of sight of the slow-moving athletic board. He hired Jeff Wetzler, an experienced white coach from a nearby recreation center, to teach the "wonderful Wetzler system" of basketball.[53] He also brought on board two former members of the now defunct New York All-Stars, Charlie Bradford and Ferdinand Accooe, to form a veteran club that most likely was better than the original championship Smart Set teams. Or at least Madden thought so. When his "Red and Black Machine," as he proudly dubbed the team, trotted out for pregame warm-ups, he ordered the team band to belt out the popular song "Hail, Hail, the Gang's All Here," suggesting the finest basketball team on earth had just made its entrance.

After the Red and Black Machine defeated Alpha for the New York title, the self-promoting Madden took the extra step of arranging a season-ending title game against the defending champion Howard Big Five. True to Madden's growing reputation for controversy, the game would go down as one of the craziest encounters in the history of early black basketball.

The trouble started when Madden scheduled the championship game and dance for the first night of Lent, a public-relations disaster for a pious, church-run club. Some spectators also openly wagered on the contest, a common practice at baseball games and a growing menace at amateur basketball events. The stigma of wagering prompted the Reverend Hutchins C. Bishop, pastor of St. Philip's Church, to write a front-page denunciation in the *New York Age*.[54] Bishop's harsh words no doubt rankled the freewheeling Madden, who seems to have accepted, if not welcomed, gambling as good for building public interest in the sport.

Then there was the bizarre ending of the game itself. With about fifteen seconds left to play, Howard was clinging to a 16-15 lead. The Red and Black Machine secured the basketball after a jump ball and raced downcourt for one final shot to win or lose the championship. The ball landed in the hands of St. C.'s sure-shooting Fred Lowry, who squared to shoot with one tick left on the clock.

What happened next nobody knows. The timekeeper blew the whistle on cue to end the game, and believing Lowry had failed to shoot in time, the Howard fans erupted in celebration of their team's improbable third title in four seasons. Out on the court, referee Big Tom Thorpe motioned for a foul against Howard precisely as the whistle blew. Or was it after? The St. C. players, too, had burst into cheers after watching Lowry drain his two-handed heave. This raised the additional question of whether Lowry had released the ball before or after the whistle. Or had Thorpe's foul call stopped play and canceled out the basket altogether?

With no instant replay to help sort out the final second, pandemonium ruled. Thorpe huddled with both teams at the scorer's table, listening to each side plead its case. Howard's Clarence Richardson, who was sitting in the stands, later wrote, "In the midst of the excitement members of the fairer sex unconsciously embraced male onlookers, men threw away their hats, and a number of younger women found slits in their skirts and waists not in evidence before the game started."[55]

One hour later, the jury was hopelessly deadlocked. Having heard every possible permutation of the events, Thorpe ruled the game a tie. The championship would have to be replayed.

On April 17, Howard and St. Christopher tried again, in what proved to be a much different game than the first one. St. C. dominated the action from the opening tap, and Madden's Red and Black Machine walked away forty minutes later with an easy 29-17 victory and a silver-plated trophy that had been donated by William Hunt, United States consul of St. Etienne, France.

While Bradford, Accooe, and the other St. C. players hoisted the Hunt trophy, Madden let loose a roar of hyperbole. "St. Christopher outplayed Howard in every department of the game," he bragged, "and the score does not indicate how completely the visitors were at the mercy of the whirlwind play of the New Yorkers."[56]

That would be Madden's final public declaration as a member of the St. Christopher Club. In October 1914, he hastily left St. Christopher to protest the athletic board's tighter control of "his" team. As further payback, Madden declared that he owned the name St. Christopher Red and Black Machine.[57] To prove it, he went to the trouble of filing the paperwork to legally incorporate his new men's social and athletic club as the St. Christopher Club of New York, Inc.—or, as the club would soon be known, the Incorporators.[58]

Madden also contended the new Red and Black Machine, not St. Christopher, should wear the mantle of defending black "champions of the world." The St. C. athletic board scoffed at the claim; after all, just three members of its championship squad had defected to Madden's new club. But Madden refused to relent, and he soon dispatched his right-hand man, Harold Harding, to Howard University to propose replaying the title game.[59] Harding told the Howard Athletic Council that Madden would front Howard $250, then a hefty sum, to cover its expenses in New York. The Howard officials, apparently unconcerned about the Madden–St. C. feud and in need of cash, snapped up the offer.[60]

And why not? New York, with its spacious halls and sell-out crowds, was the one place where Howard could turn a nice profit. True Reformer's Hall, with its rickety rims and rackety floor, might have been fine in 1909 when Howard sparred on weekends with small-time Washington club teams. But no more. Professor E. P. Davis, a member of the Howard Athletic Council, wrote that every one of Howard's home games over the past three seasons had grossed less than a hundred dollars, most of which went toward renting True Reformer's Hall. So dire had the team's finances become, Davis was considering booking all Howard's games on the road in 1915 to help the team make ends meet.[61]

On December 15, 1914, more than a thousand fans assembled in Manhattan Casino to watch the replaying of the championship game. James Reese Europe's Lady Society Orchestra concluded its final pregame number, and a voice boomed out the customary "Ladies and gentlemen, may I have your attention, please." The crowd hushed. All eyes focused on the court, where the esteemed nephew of the former mayor of Cleveland stood poised to throw out the ceremonial first basketball.

Then, in a rare glimpse of the offstage wrangling over money that sometimes unfolded before basketball games, the Howard team didn't appear. With anxious fans shifting in their seats, word reached Madden that the players were holed up in their locker room, and they weren't coming out. The *New York Age* later reported that Howard, long resented by the New York club teams for demanding one-third of the gate for its appearances, refused to play "until all 250 simileons were counted out and passed over"[62] to the team up front. After an hour of wrangling, Madden reluctantly forked over the cash. The game was back on.

After the Howard squad trotted onto the court, it didn't take long to see the delay had been more like a brief stay of execution. The team, which still featured its star center George Gilmore, didn't play worth a dime. The Incorporators held Howard to just one field goal on the night, while Madden's Machine racked up points at will en route to an impressive 33-13 victory. Leading the way for the Incorporators were former St. C. tossers Ferdinand Accooe, James Hargrove, and Perky Perkinson, plus talented newcomers Walter Cooper and Harry Williams.

Having succeeded in stealing St. C.'s identity and championship, Madden sought next to embarrass his former club. He booked St. C.'s arch rival Alpha Big Five for a New Year's Day contest, then billed the game as a "who is who in basketball in New York,"[63] implying the original St. Christopher Club no longer mattered now that Madden had left its employ. As Madden well knew, St. Christopher had battled Alpha on New Year's Day for the past few years in what many considered the top social event of the basketball season.

On December 25, St. Christopher announced it had obtained a court order blocking the Alpha-Incorporators game on the grounds that St. C. usually played Alpha on New Year's Day. To tweak Madden further, St. Christopher booked Manhattan Casino, the site of the proposed Alpha-Incorporators game, on New Year's Day afternoon to play Lincoln University.[64]

Madden hit the roof. He stormed off to Manhattan Casino and rebooked the Alpha game for New Year's night. But Madden soon discovered he wasn't the only one out to upstage the St. Christopher–Lincoln game. The *New York Age* reported that Smart Set, Spartan Field Club, and another New York team had scheduled games in the city that day to grab "the prestige and support of the public" from the reigning champion.[65]

Why the sudden power grab? There was money and social prestige in basketball. The game certainly wasn't as lucrative as baseball, which had tradition and mass appeal behind it. But basketball was "king of the winter," and as sportswriter Romeo Dougherty wrote, the black game generated thousands of dollars each season in New York, making it a major source of revenue for the local athletic clubs.[66] With the well-heeled Nat Strong promoting only college games in 1915, Madden and the other team managers smelled an opportunity to move in, put together a championship season, and laugh all the way to the bank.

What worried fans was that the athletic clubs, long self-described bastions of fine breeding and fellowship, now were willing to make money at each other's expense. This angered many, because the bell-wether white American amateur movement seemed to be succeeding in its mission of promoting physical fitness. Whether accurate or not,[67] this popular perception of the movement's success was embraced as fact by most Americans, and many black New Yorkers feared that if money overtook their basketball games, it would leave the race lagging behind in this important national trend.

"Never before in the history of athletics in New York has there been so much keen rivalry for leadership, and Will Anthony Madden has become the central figure in what will prove to be a devastating conflict for some big organization when the smoke of battle has disappeared," wrote Dougherty.[68]

On New Year's night, before a packed house, Madden's Incorporators rallied from a five-point deficit in the final two minutes to steal a 21-20 thriller from Alpha. Afterward, Madden praised both teams like a true statesman, before his mouth again got the best of him. "At the next time . . . I am positive that the result will not be so close," he crowed—meaning the Incorporators could thump Alpha any day of the week.[69]

His gaffe didn't matter this time. Probably tired of the bickering and unable to book local games, thanks to a decree by St. Christopher to other clubs, Madden blew out of Harlem with his players for more than two months. On the road, the Incorporators dominated just about every team they faced, black and white.

When Madden's men came home on March 19 to meet the Boston Gladiators, they returned as conquering heroes. The Incs sported at least a 10-1 record, and the original St. C. club recently had lost both games of a road trip to Philadelphia's Southwest YMCA and Hampton University. The 1915 crown was Madden's, unless St. C. beat the Incorporators—and there was no chance the antagonists would ever agree to set foot on the same court.

In Washington, meanwhile, Howard's glory days had come to an end. George Gilmore left the team after the 1914–15 season to play center for the Alpha Big Five. The departure of the top center in the black game meant U Street began to fade as a prominent address on the intercity club basketball scene. Briefly attempting to fill the void was Washington's Cardinal-Hiawatha, a second-tier team led by former Howard players Joe Holland and Charles Henderson. Henderson and his Hiawathas pulled off an improbable home upset of Madden's champion Incorporators in December 1915, but the team's lack of manpower soon became apparent. The Alphas and the Incorporators trounced the Hiawathas in the new year.

With no hometown teams in the hunt for the 1915–16 world championship, U Street fell eerily silent on the subject of basketball in the latter months of the season. The poor showing wasn't due to a lack of talent, as the District's public schools rolled out some of the smoothest black scholastic players in the country each year. The problem hinged on space. "Washington, D.C. is another great basketball center, but [the city] lacks facilities for the staging of large games," wrote Will Madden. "Whenever a game is given in True Reformers Hall the place is generally packed, but there are hundreds and hundreds of people who would like to witness the game but cannot on account of the lack of accommodation. True Reformers Hall is alright for a home attraction but is hardly adequate for the making of enough money to cover the expenses of a team from New York or places of like distance."[70]

Without an adequate space for games, U Street's problems on the court compounded over the next decade. No respected local promoters stepped forward to sponsor an all-star contingent to replace the Howard Big Five, and the smaller club teams that emerged had to make do without the year-in, year-out stability that big-time managers in New York and other eastern cities brought to their squads. As a result, Washington fell behind in the experience, teamwork, and overall spit and polish that an improving black game now demanded of its top teams.

By the midteens, that meant the best New York club teams were starting to look beyond the Potomac to earn their stripes. They looked to Pittsburgh, where Cum Posey taunted all comers, white, black, and all shades in between. Or to nearby Philadelphia, where club basketball was on the rise as the city's black population mushroomed. Or even out west to Chicago, from where rumblings of deadly South Side set shooters had made their way to Harlem.

But for many New York and nearby New Jersey clubs, unlike black teams elsewhere, there was no driving financial reason to hit the road. With its large, money-making dance halls and many high-quality teams, the New York metropolitan area was the "Black Mecca" of basketball. Even the proud Cum Posey made a personal pilgrimage each season to see the sights and make a grab at the thick wads of cash that games in New York brought.

But Black Mecca, like other sacred realms, had its feuding factions with definite and distinct ideas of good and evil. In the midteens, these differences in ideology would explode into a bitter clash for control of New York basketball and its worldly possessions. When the war was over two years later, the body count had reached just one—Will Madden.

Little Napoleon Meets His Waterloo

Ira Lewis, a reporter with the *Pittsburgh Courier,* noted that during the midteens, "the word[s] 'Incorporators,' 'Red and Black,' and 'Will Madden,' were synonymous with SNAP, DASH, EFFICIENCY, and CLASS." Many were the times, Lewis recalled, when the Incs' bony center Walter Cooper lifted into the air during center jumps, tapped the ball to the outstretched hands of a teammate, and then, cool as a breeze, "turned his back and walked away, as the scorer marked up one for the Incorporators."[71]

In the autumn of 1915, however, Cooper and his teammates should have been watching their backs, not turning them. The athletic council at St. Christopher was on the warpath again, turning its feud with Incs manager Will Madden into a full-fledged campaign to break up his team and run him out of basketball. As its opening act of hostility, St. C. struck a deal with two rivals, Alpha and the Spartan Field Club, to boycott the Incorporators during the 1915–16 season. These three influential clubs, later nicknamed the "Triple Alliance," then spread the word around New York that other black teams should refrain from booking games with Madden's championship five. The defending world champions of black basketball had been blackballed by their worthy challengers.

Madden, now tapping out a weekly basketball column for the *New York Age,* used four of his first five assignments to rail at his shoddy treatment, hoping that he could shout the boycott out of existence be-

fore the height of the season. "Playing imported teams is all right but
the real attraction to the fans are the meetings of the big local fives,"
he wrote. "Unless these teams meet, the interest never reaches its
height. So, Alpha, 'Incorporators,' and St. Christopher when will it
be????????? The people want these games."[72]

Madden might just as well have been mumbling to himself. While
basketball fans still gathered en masse for the big weekend games featuring St. C. and Alpha, the Incorporators had been scratched perma-
nently from the dance card. That meant Madden had to import his entertainment, often leaving him with mediocre opponents whose cash
advances to travel to New York each week he could not afford to pay.
The great Incorporators often had to make do in 1916 with, in Madden's
words, second-rate[73] black club teams such as Washington's Cardinal-
Hiawatha and Atlantic City's Vandals.

Not only did Madden have to pay more for less, he also had to work
harder to push his product. Though he peddled pins, pennants, and
other promotional puffery to boost his team's image, he couldn't sell out
Manhattan Casino by singing the praises of the Hiawathas, a team little
known in New York. One way around this problem would have been to
start booking local white clubs. White teams were always big draws in
Harlem, and the alliance would have been powerless to halt such high-
profile interracial games. But for whatever reason, Madden balked at
the idea.

Though the newspapers are quiet on the subject, the Triple Alliance
likely crowned the Alphas as the champions of Harlem in 1916. The
men with the Old English "A" displayed proudly on their chests had
compiled the best season record, and Madden's Incs still remained in-
visible as far as the Triple Alliance was concerned.

Madden, defiant to the bitter end, crowned his Incorporators repeat
black champions of the world based on the pretzel logic that there were
only six other big-draw teams in black basketball that qualified for the
title: Hampton, Alpha, Lincoln, Monticello-Delaney Rifles, St. Christopher, and Howard. As reigning champions, the Incorporators had to lose
to a big-league team to relinquish their crown. Because the Incs defeated Pittsburgh's Monticello-Delaney Rifles—the only elite team they
faced—Madden's boys retained the title. One game, one championship.
There is no record of whether the Triple Alliance mocked or disputed
Madden's championship claim. Suffice to say there was no agreement
on the identity of the true champions.

According to Cum Posey, the following season, 1916–17, probably marked the zenith of amateur basketball in New York.[74] Thousands of loyal fans spent the cold winter months waving the blue and white banners of Alpha, the red and black of St. Christopher, and the green and gold of the Spartan Field Club.

With Madden still under boycott, the Alphas emerged as the clear favorites to claim the 1916–17 title of New York. The club was top-heavy with talent, size, and experience, including former Howard star George Gilmore and Alpha mainstays Big Babe Thomas, Sing Goode, and Little Babe Wiggins. But Alpha failed to bring home the championship. The A's dropped five games by March, including two narrow losses to St. Christopher and one to Cum Posey's improved Monticello-Delaney Rifles.

"The game was played at Manhattan Casino before a packed holiday crowd, Washington's Birthday," recalled Posey of the latter Alpha loss. "After a little bit of everything which included a scrap between Cum Posey and the referee and the subsequent removal of the official at the end of the first half, the game ended 16 to 15, when the new official decided M.D. [Monticello-Delaney] had fouled as the final whistle blew."

In these days when a team could select the player it wanted to shoot any free throw, like a technical foul today, Posey offered a glimpse of the bedlam that sometimes ensued when a referee whistled a foul. "Gilmore ran from the court to get Eddie Mathews, a member of Alpha's second team, to change clothes and shoot the foul," he wrote. "Eddie was 'the shark.' While Gilmore was gone, Scott, the [overconfident] Alpha guard, shot the foul and missed it. 'Scottie' was Alpha's bad man and no words were said that night, but the next day everybody that passed Scotty in Harlem said behind their hand: 'There goes Bob Lee.'" (According to Posey, Bob Lee was a mouthy Harlem boxer who talked a good fight but who had once crumpled to the canvas when his opponent delivered a benign pat to his rear end.)[75]

With Alpha pulling its own "Bob Lee" that season, St. Christopher seemed poised to capture the title. Though probably not as talented as Alpha, player for player, the Red and Black Machine hit on all cylinders as a unit that season. Powering the on-court combustion were former New York All-Stars center Charlie Bradford; the Jenkins brothers, Harold and Fat; and the legendary Paul Robeson.

On March 16, 1917, Robeson and his Machine mates topped off their season against the Spartan Field Club in one of the wildest Friday-night games on record. The Spartans had been on a season-long roller coaster

ride—up one game, down the next, but never quite up enough to compete basket for basket with St. C. or Alpha, their Triple Alliance brothers. That night, however, the young Spartan players rose above medi-
ocrity and shut down the St. Christopher juggernaut with a series of
well-timed shoves, blocks, and holds—the kinds of tactics that passed
for defense in those days.

By halftime, the upstart Spartan defense had limited St. C. to a total
of two free throws en route to a 10-2 lead. Will Madden, covering the
game for the *New York Age*, wrote that the first half had brought "one
of the most spectacular reverses of form ever shown by two basketball
teams. . . . St. Christopher's exhibition of basketball was so poor that the
fans could hardly believe their own eyes; while on the other hand the
game played by Spartan was truly wonderful."[76]

St. C., well-known for its miracle finishes, would be true to its reputation in the second half. Though still butting their heads against a tough
Spartan defense, the St. C. boys somehow whittled the Spartan lead to
13-11, with about nine minutes left in the game. For Spartan fans, it was
time for the nail-biting to begin.

But luck would be on the Spartans' side. At the eight-minute mark,
the referee whistled a foul on St. C. star Fat Jenkins. Jenkins and his
teammates, frustrated by the rough Spartan defense, exploded at having a call go against them and mobbed the referee. Working himself into
a froth, Jenkins demanded that the ref reverse his call. The official refused. He tooted his whistle and motioned for St. Christopher to accept
the foul call and get on with play or else forfeit the game. As the sworn
enemy of the St. C. club, Madden no doubt reveled in this salty exchange. He described what happened next: "As the referee refused to
reverse his decision, the St. Christopher team walked off the floor amid
a bedlam of hisses and cat-calls from practically everybody in the
house."[77] After the hissing ceased, the game went into the books as a
2-0 win by forfeit for the Spartans.

Dissecting the drama from the sidelines was the first-year manager
of the Spartans, thirty-six-year-old Robert Douglas. Though none of the
fans could have known it that night, Douglas would one day land in the
Naismith Basketball Hall of Fame as the man who became the leader
of black professional basketball on the East Coast. But on this deliri-
ous night, Douglas was still a card-carrying amateur man, still a St.
Christopher supporter, still hell-bent on running Madden out of town
on a rail.

At least for the moment, Madden was doing well on the basketball court. In the 1916–17 season, his Incorporators had battled in first-rate promotions against Chicago's Wabash YMCA, the Pittsburgh Independents, and football star Fred Pollard's Providence Collegians, and had defeated two big-league clubs, Lincoln and Howard. During the latter game, Madden, once an aspiring singer, even arranged for the Howard Glee Club to assemble on the floor and belt out spirituals.[78]

With these two wins and no losses against big-league teams, Madden felt compelled to crown the Incorporators the 1916–17 world champions of black basketball. For Madden, that made three world titles in a row, a point he proceeded to flaunt like the white carnation ever present in his lapel.

"The 'Incorporators' *originated* the title of 'world champions' and have always held it and will continue to hold it until one or more of the seven big teams register a victory over them," wrote Madden. "St. Christopher's refusal to play and its continual hiding behind technicalities and imaginary principles will do them no good. The great basketball public in New York don't [sic] care anything about St. Christopher and its feeling toward the 'Incorporators.' . . . The game is *the thing* and nothing else matters *one iota*."[79]

But some things did matter more. In April 1917, the United States declared war on Germany, hurling the nation into World War I and sending some of Madden's players marching off to serve Uncle Sam.

Blackballed, his roster depleted, and with wartime rationing slowing the economy to a crawl, Little Napoleon made one last stand. In 1918, Madden assembled a makeshift team and, with great pomp, headed for Chicago—and straight into fresh controversy. Madden arrived in town with two white players in his lineup, prompting a near riot during and after the game. The reason: The game had been organized as a show of racial unity, pitting Chicago's South Side against New York's Harlem. Once again, Madden had failed to go along with the program.

After the war ended, unlike his foes Alpha, Spartan, and St. Christopher, Madden never gassed up his Red and Black Machine again. Why he didn't remains open to speculation. In the 1920s, some commentators claimed that Madden's volatility and thin finances had alienated his players. Some also blamed the blackball for forcing Madden out of the game. Another possibility is that Madden, the frustrated singer and showman, followed his muse elsewhere. The answer is maybe all of the above.

During the early 1920s, Madden briefly managed the slumping Manhattan Casino. He then relocated to Greenwich Village, where he would spend much of his life. As the years passed, Madden opened a small theater in New York. He also launched a one-man traveling show and reportedly landed a brief gig at Carnegie Hall. In 1959, Madden was named poet laureate of Greenwich Village, and he later published several plays, poems, and short stories.

But before Madden ever took his show to Greenwich Village, he offered a final prophecy about the troubled state of black basketball. "The real issue on the future of the game is whether it will be controlled by real amateurs, fake amateurs or professionals," he wrote. "It looks as if the professional forces will undoubtedly control the game in time to come and public support will not be denied, because the public wants first-class basketball and is willing to pay for it, and it is just this kind of ball that will be produced by the professionals owing to their being in the position and having every advantage to do so."[80]

Madden's belief in the inevitability of professionalism would be the defining issue and battle of the 1920s.

America Marches to War

June 5, 1917. All across America, able-bodied men aged twenty-one through thirty queued outside their neighborhood polling places to register for the military draft. America had joined the Great War raging overseas, and Uncle Sam needed a hand to stick it to the German kaiser.

As the newspapers said, serving one's country was the American way, the democratic way, the only way. "Don't wait hoping that the lightning will strike elsewhere," a small-town newspaper in West Virginia wrote. "Do your bit to uphold the traditions of American patriotism."[81]

On the other side of the tracks in segregated America, whether or not to march off to battle was a tough decision for some young black men. Many grappled with an unyielding question: What had Uncle Sam done for them? Washington had ladled out promises about equality and racial uplift. None had amounted to much. Woodrow Wilson, the president of these United States, had turned a blind eye while his "cracker cabinet" segregated the government and supported back-of-the-bus Jim Crow legislation.

"The negro feels that he is not regarded as a constituent part of American democracy," wrote Howard University scholar Kelly Miller in an open letter to President Wilson. "It is the fundamental creed of democracy that no people are good enough to govern any other people without consent and participation."[82]

"The Colored Man has been in every great war in which this country has participated, and today he is no better off than he was when he first started," wrote the Sage of the Potomac, the folksy gossip columnist for the *Washington Bee.*

But two generations after slavery, black citizens were still hopeful about their prospects in America. The Sage added in his next breath: "The day will come when the Colored Soldier will be a necessity. . . . I have never known any ungrateful act to succeed, no matter how small. Meanness and ingratitude may last for a while, but there is a turning point."[83]

So off they marched, three hundred thousand black men, toward the turning point that would bring the race equal rights and justice.

THREE

The Decline of Amateurism

1919
1923

Welcome Home

After three nights of marching all night without any food but hardtack and beef we went over the top and advanced fourteen miles on one of the worst fronts of the entire war. I have never heard anything like the barrage that was carried on that night. Every gun from Metz to the North Sea was firing. More than two million allied soldiers went over the top at a given time. We were marching on Metz when the last shot [of World War I] was fired on the 11th day and the 11th hour in the 11th month. Where we were going the government had planned to lose 1,000 men an hour for 72 hours, so you can imagine our joy when we turned and started back from the Hun. Everyone sang, "I have laid my burdens down by the riverside." As we were marching alongside we passed a field as large as that camp at Fifth and Florida Avenue [in Washington], where [soldiers] were digging graves as fast as they could, anticipating the long-heralded drive on Metz, so you can see how God has blessed us.

George W. Askew, 368th Infantry, in a letter home,
reprinted in the *Washington Bee*, Jan. 18, 1919

On November 11, 1918, the final shots of World War I were fired. The bloodiest conflict the world had ever known was over. All across America, the streets rang with cries of victory and resolutions for the future. It was like New Year's Eve in November.

Back in Europe, black American soldiers celebrated victory. They were headed home, and nobody now could doubt their patriotism. Thousands had hunkered in foxholes for weeks, dodging enemy artillery and inching back the hated Hun. It hadn't been easy. Like the old gospel hymn, they had come up on the rough side of the mountain, and now that they had reached the top, they were going to get their reward. As one black war correspondent put it: "Each and all of them feel that when they return the Statue of Liberty in New York's harbor will bespeak universal liberty and equality before the law."[1]

But when the soldiers arrived home, they found that their bravery abroad had changed nothing in Jim Crow America. A loaf of bread still cost less than a nickel, and a black man still had better remember in which part of town he belonged. In Hickman, Kentucky, a white mob dragged Charles Lewis, a black veteran, from the town jail and lynched him for allegedly resisting arrest. Lewis had been home from the front only a few weeks. His story was not uncommon.

"It is a sad picture to look upon," wrote the Sage of the Potomac, a columnist for the *Washington Bee*. "There are many returning, to be greeted with the shotgun and the ku-klux. I understand that the South is being organized [with the threat of violence] to greet the colored soldiers on their return home. This is what you call American democracy."[2]

The rage simmering inside many black folks reached the boiling point as the warm spring of 1919 turned to a hot summer. Race riots erupted across the land, from South Carolina to Chicago to Omaha.

In mid-July, Washington erupted. A white lynch mob numbering in the hundreds rampaged through the streets of the capital in search of two black men accused of snatching the umbrella of a nineteen-year-old white woman. White hell-raisers pummeled innocent black men plucked at random from streetcars and shops. With no police protection to speak of, roving bands of black men battled back. Two days later, when order was finally restored, five people were dead and dozens were bruised and battered.

Weeks passed. Summer faded to autumn, then winter. All across the country, people reflected on the new decade dawning. What would the 1920s bring for black America? More lies? More lynchings? Or would blacks rise above their troubles and self-doubt and let their voices resonate across the country?

With a new wave of migration, the black enclaves of the North now acquired the complex flavor of urban melting pots, and nowhere more so than in New York's Harlem. Within roughly one square mile of Manhattan, the cultural seeds that had drifted across the ocean during Africa's three-hundred-year slave diaspora found a common ground and took root. On Lenox Avenue, unlike anywhere else in the world, one could hear the chatter of northern blacks, southern blacks, West Indians, and Africans. They spoke French, Creole, Dutch, Spanish, Portuguese, Arabic, lilting English, drawling English, broken English, Queen's English.

In this seedbed of African culture, the racial pride that had been beaten out of many blossomed anew. Black intellectuals said Harlem was the site of a burgeoning cultural renaissance that would break the psychological chains of slavery and set the people free.

"In Harlem, Negro life is seizing upon its first chances for group expression and self-determination," noted Alain Locke, a writer and Harlem resident. "Harlem has the same role to play for the New Negro as Dublin has had for the New Ireland or Prague for the New Czechoslovakia."[3]

In this age of worldwide social unrest, the great black melting pot of Harlem stewed with rebellion. On the streets and in the left-wing, Harlem-based press, black voices fumed with newfound cynicism and rage. "In a country whose government and resources are completely controlled by the white man, the Negro plays the game of life against a rival whose every cast is with loaded dice," growled the socialist *Crusader Monthly.*[4]

"Brothers we are on the great deep," declared W. E. B. Du Bois in the Harlem-headquartered magazine the *Crisis.* "We have cast off on the vast voyage which will lead to Freedom or Death."[5]

Woven through the rhetoric was a common thread of faith, faith that if God could lead Moses to the Promised Land, He surely could lead the race to freedom in America. But as the Good Book also says, faith without works is dead. Black people in all their anger, diversity, talent, and self-doubt would have to join hands across the land and confront white aggression. They would have to rise up with one mighty voice and, as in the old tale of Jericho, shout down the walls of segregation.

During the 1920s, that one mighty voice never thundered forth to capture the attention of white America. There were many small choirs of protest, but as Howard University professor Kelly Miller noted, the voices never harmonized into a larger movement. "Strange to say, the war has not made the Negro more progressive and assertive of his rights, as has been the case with all other suppressed races and classes in all parts of the world," Miller wrote. "Our militant organizations are, if anything, less radical than their ante-bellum prototypes."[6]

Lacking the will, leadership, and unified voice to reshape American public opinion in the 1920s, blacks faced a growing tide of racism. The catalyst for this new round of anti-black sentiment was the migration of some 1.7 million blacks to the North between World War I and 1930. White southerners feared they were losing control of a cheap source of labor, while white northerners watched black neighborhoods swell and worried in the racist terms of the day that they had inherited their own "Negro Problem," with the widely rumored threats to public safety, property values, labor unions, and local politics.

Whites responded to this show of black self-reliance with mockery, condescension, and rage. Though historians sometimes focus on the rise of white hate groups such as the Ku Klux Klan to highlight this point, Jim Crow rarely needed to hide beneath a hood. The white mainstream continued routinely and nonviolently to weave a self-interested web of state laws, city ordinances, and neighborhood covenants, each aimed at segregating African Americans and keeping them out of sight, out of mind, and out of touch.

Despite such rigid views on race, white America took a sharp turn for the progressive during the 1920s, particularly in its opinions of public morality. Young whites disillusioned by the war rebelled against the status quo. Women clipped their hair scandalously short, hiked their hemlines, puffed shamelessly on cigarettes, and professed an addiction to the wild gyrations of modern dance. Their brothers and boyfriends, meanwhile, wore their hair greased to a patent-leather sheen, their trousers devil-may-care baggy, and their progressive opinions on their sleeves.

"I would like to observe that the older generation had certainly pretty well ruined this world before passing it on to us," wrote one young person in the *Atlantic Monthly*. "They give us this Thing, knocked to pieces, leaky, red-hot, threatening to blow up; and then they are surprised that we don't accept it with the same enthusiasm with which they received it."[7]

Still, the mutual distrust and inability of the races to discard hateful stereotypes precluded any meaningful dialogue to improve black-white relations in 1920s America. As Swedish sociologist Gunnar Myrdal later noted:

There is no doubt . . . that a great majority of white people in
America would be prepared to give the Negro a substantially better
deal if they knew the facts. But to understand the difficulty the Negroes have to overcome in order to get publicity, we must never forget the opportunistic desire of the whites for ignorance.

It is so much more comfortable to know as little as possible about
Negroes, except that there are a lot of them in Harlem, the Black
Belt, or whatever name is given to the segregated slum quarters
where they live, and that there are more of them in the South; that
they are criminal and of disgustingly, but somewhat enticingly, loose
sexual morals; that they are the happy-go-lucky children of nature
who get a kick out of life which white people are too civilized to get.[8]

These opinions were especially prevalent in American professional
sports during the 1920s. One reason was the stigma of Jack Johnson, the
flamboyant, break-all-the-rules former black heavyweight champion
boxer, whose volatile rise to national stardom during the teens had convinced many white promoters never again to mix race with business. Another reason was, in this age of rising consumerism, professional sports
had indeed become big business.

The Golden Age of American Sports

Shortly before 10 A.M. on July 9, 1921, the iron gates groaned open at
the federal penitentiary in Leavenworth, Kansas, sending about three
hundred reporters and well-wishers who had assembled outside scrambling to attention. Seconds later, a large, smiling black man wearing a
tan hat and a blue pinstriped suit ambled out.

"Hey, champ," a reporter shouted.

"How does it feel to be a free man again?" yelled another.

Jack Johnson, the former heavyweight champion of the world who
had spent the past ten months locked up at Leavenworth for transport-
ing a white woman over state lines for sex, flashed his famous gold-
toothed smile. "I'll never forget this day," answered Johnson, now forty-
three years old, as the cameras rolled and the flashbulbs popped. "I
came in smiling, and I'm going out the same way."

"What are your plans?" a reporter hollered.

"First, I'm going to Kansas City for a visit and to fill a movie contract,"
he replied. "Then I'm going to New York to arrange for my appearances

in the ring. I'm going to resume fighting just as soon as possible. I'll be ready for my first appearance in four or five weeks. Right now, I weigh 220 pounds. I'm in splendid condition and only need a grind of final training to be fit."[9]

Big Jack answered a few more questions before he and his controversial white wife, Camille, escaped into the back seat of a luxury automobile that had been parked outside the gates. The engine clicked into gear and the car turned east toward Kansas City, whisking the world's most famous black athlete onto the comeback trail and one final assault on stardom.

Johnson spent the next several weeks touring from city to city, drumming up support for a title bout against white champion Jack Dempsey. At most stops, Johnson mauled a punching bag to evoke images of his former dominance in the ring and guaranteed, in the most ominous tones, a sure victory over the younger, less experienced Dempsey. But as the months passed and no offers materialized, Johnson and his fans had to face the facts. The white promoters who controlled prizefighting in America had taken a collective pass on Johnson. One of the greatest fighters of all time was washed up.

Today, from a purely financial standpoint, the Johnson blackball makes no sense. Johnson and Dempsey were two of the most recognizable faces in 1920s America, and a promotion involving them would have covered all the angles: black versus white, North versus South, old school versus new school, counter puncher versus stalker—and, for many, good versus evil. True, Johnson had two strikes against him: his advanced age for a prizefighter and his admission—whether true or not—that he had taken a dive five years earlier to lose his title. Still, any promoter daring enough to stage the fight could have made a fortune for himself and everyone involved.

What happened? Johnson had defended his heavyweight title on American soil during the teens. Now he couldn't even get in line to face Dempsey.

For those familiar with Johnson's career, the obvious source of the blackball would seem to be public opposition to the fight. As Johnson biographer Randy Roberts wrote:

> Johnson had become, in the language of the day, a Bad Nigger,
> that is, a black man who chose a different attitude and station
> from the ones prescribed by white society. . . . Starting in 1909,

the American public began to see . . . his flashy clothes and brightly colored fast automobiles. They saw the way in which he challenged white authority in his numerous brushes with the law. They heard stories of his night life, the lurid tales of his week-long drunks and parties. Tales of his sexual bouts were also told, and his shaved head came to symbolize the sexual virility of the black male. But most shocking of all were the times he appeared in public with white women.[10]

In short, Johnson was the black man white America loved to hate.

As tempting as it is to buy into this argument, popular white opinion did not directly dash Johnson's title hopes. He had faced the same overt racism during his early career, and it is unlikely that the average man on the street would have opposed a mixed-race heavyweight championship bout in the 1920s. For instance, when black heavyweight Harry Wills became the top contender for Dempsey's crown in July 1920, the white *New York World Telegram* reported in an informal survey of its readership that just 35 out of 750 respondents opposed the fight. Even in working-class Buffalo, a white sportswriter admitted, "[T]here is not now the great prejudice that one time existed to black-and-white contests. The time may be nearer than thought when the sporting public, which believes in giving the best man his chance, be his color white or black, will call on the title holder [Dempsey] to pick up the challenge."[11]

Though the sporting public may have been willing, the promoters with the deep pockets needed to stage the big fights were singing a different tune. Take Tex Rickard, the shrewd manager of New York's Madison Square Garden and the mastermind behind Dempsey's major title defenses. When a reporter suggested Wills should be next in line to meet Dempsey, the usually gruff Rickard responded in his Texas drawl, "Yes, you're right, Harry is the toughest of all the boys who are knocking on the door of the champion. A bout between Dempsey and Wills would be a great one. But I will not stage it, nevertheless."

Rickard continued, "Listen, if I gave no thought for tomorrow, I would put on a Dempsey-Wills match and would make just as much money out of it as I did out of last Saturday night's great contest [the Dempsey-Carpentier title fight]. I probably would make more, for the gate would be almost as large and the expense not one-third as much. But, I'm in boxing as a permanent business. My future depends on the future of boxing."[12]

TOP: *Alpha leader Conrad Norman.* BOTTOM: *Smart Set's George Lattimore, who helped organize the first New York–Washington championship game in 1909. (Moorland-Spingarn Research Center, Howard University)*

Brooklyn's Smart Set Athletic Club "Grave Diggers," the first black champions of New York. (Ed Henderson Collection, Moorland-Spingarn Research Center, Howard University)

The Interscholastic Athletic Association games committee at the seminal 1906 track meet. Ed Henderson is in the front row, holding a straw hat. (Author's collection)

Manhattan's Alpha Big Five, 1911–12. (Ed Henderson Collection, Moorland-Spingarn Research Center, Howard University)

The undefeated 12th Street YMCA team, 1910. Ed Henderson is holding the basketball, and Ed Gray is directly to his right. Hudson Oliver is No. 5, Henry Nixon is No. 2, and Doc Curtis is No. 9. (Author's collection)

Hudson Oliver as a member of the Howard Big Five. (Moorland-Spingarn Research Center, Howard University)

The Monticello Athletic Association team, 1910. Cum Posey is second from the left in the front row. (Basketball Hall of Fame, Springfield, MA)

Will Anthony Madden, wearing his trademark tailored suit and white carnation. (Moorland-Spingarn Research Center, Howard University)

The St. Christopher Red and Black Machine, c. 1925. Fat Jenkins is holding the basketball; George Fiall is to his left. (Photographer James Van-DerZee, © Donna Mussenden VanDerZee)

Ernest Marshall in his twenties. Marshall was a key figure in organizing the Colored Intercollegiate Athletic Association. (Moorland-Spingarn Research Center, Howard University)

The Renaissance Big Five in 1925. Left to right: Fat Jenkins, George Fiall, Pappy Ricks, Harold Mayer, Six Garcia, Hilton Slocum, Stretch Saunders. (Photographer James VanDerZee, © Donna Mussenden VanDerZee)

Washington's Carlisle Big Five during the late 1920s. Benny Hill is the player at the far right. (Author's collection)

The fast-talking Ewell Conway, manager of Washington's Carlisle Big Five. (Wallace Conway)

Washington's Dunbar High School basketball team, 1922. Dunbar's star player, Charles Drew, is third from the left in the front row. Drew went on to coach some of the great Morgan College teams of the 1920s and later won worldwide recognition for his contributions to modern blood banking. Ed Henderson is at the far right. (Scurlock Collection, Archives Center, National Museum of American History)

Bob Douglas in his office. (Basketball Hall of Fame, Springfield, MA)

Newspaper advertisement for the Commonwealth-Loendi showdown of 1923—"The Game You Have Been Waiting For." (Author's collection)

The Original Celtics. Left to right: Joe Lapchick, Chris Leonard, Dutch Dehnert, Pete Barry, Nat Holman, identity not confirmed (John Whitty?), Johnny Beckman, Eddie Burke. (Author's collection)

The World's Basketball Champions

NAT HOLMAN
The perfect player

DUTCH DEHNERT
-guard-

JOHNNY BECKMAN
-forward-

PETE BARRY
-guard-

Those Nonpareil Celtics have started a run of victories that has the fans very much enthused —

Bob

Boddington of the Brooklyn Daily Times Tells Us That This Combination Is One of the Hardest to Beat, but the Renaissance Five Appear Not at All Dismayed and Will Try to Stop These Famous Celtics at Manhattan Casino New Year's Night

The Nonpareil Celtics, a later version of the Original Celtics, still featured all the greats. As this 1926 cartoon from the New York Age indicates, Harlem rallied to the task of defeating the white world champs. (Author's collection)

The Palace Laundry Five, Washington's first outstanding white team. Horse Haggerty is at the far left. (Author's collection)

The Rens during their glory years in the 1930s. Left to right: Fat Jenkins, Bill Yancey, John Holt, Pappy Ricks, Eyre Saitch, Tarzan Cooper, Wee Willie Smith. (Basketball Hall of Fame, Springfield, MA)

Ed Henderson, still fighting the good fight, speaking at a dinner in 1954. (Ed Henderson Collection, Moorland-Spingarn Research Center, Howard University)

What did Rickard have to fear? An unpleasant memory, that's what. In 1910, while moonlighting as a boxing promoter in Nevada, he had bankrolled the controversial heavyweight title fight in which Jack Johnson humiliated white hero Jim Jeffries. Rickard remembered the chaos that followed Johnson's thrashing of Jeffries. He remembered the accusations that he had betrayed the Caucasian race, the bloody race riots, the red-faced politicians pushing for laws against mixed-race boxing, and the shame-on-you social reformers demanding that the sport be outlawed in the United States. At that point, Tex vowed never again to mix race and business—not for Wills and certainly not for Jack Johnson.

As the abrupt end of Johnson's career illustrates, the twenties began with a triangle of interests, both pro and con, that greatly influenced the integration of professional sports. At the top of the triangle were the politicians. They worried about reelection, feared scandal, and in general opposed mixed-race athletics on the grounds that nothing good could come of it. Pointing to Jack Johnson's tumultuous title reign, they said mixed-race sports would lead to violence, racial disharmony, and the loss of votes. The lingering threat that boxing promoters would renew mixed-race bouts was one of the main reasons some states created regulatory boards to control the sport and keep it in line with the political agendas of the governor or the dominant party.

Below the politicians was the general public with its core American values and sometimes deeply conflicted opinions about right and wrong. Unlike the politicians, the public viewed sports as entertainment, not public policy. The ballpark offered pleasure, identification with a team or favorite athlete, and a welcome diversion from the rigors of the workweek. Like today, most fans openly cheered the best athletes, regardless of color. True, some whites turned violent at the implications of integration, but lost in history is the fact that many grumbled but accepted without incident the sight of black athletes in their gyms or ballparks.

At the third corner of the triangle was the burgeoning sports industry, with its money-mad players, management, and promoters. When asked about the prospect of mixed-race sports, most in this whites-only club retreated to the pat answer: The public will never support it. The implication was that the races coexisted peacefully with their separate leagues and champions, and, as the nation already had learned the hard way from Jack Johnson, segregated sports was the safest policy for everyone.

Behind this well-practiced line, however, resided a dilemma for the sports industry. Many feared that if they lowered the color barrier or allowed more than a few African Americans into the fold, as the new National Football League had done, trouble was sure to follow. Management, seemingly always spooked by the worst-case scenario, feared wholesale player revolts, public boycotts by whites, political meddling, and pending bankruptcy.

But if they refused to abolish or lower the color line, they risked periodic agitation from equal-opportunity sports fans, civil-rights activists, and politicians in search of black votes. This was no trivial matter. If the agitation grew intense, the public looked first to the sports industry, not the politicians, to right the wrong.

That's what happened to Tex Rickard. When Harry Wills arrived on the scene in 1920 as the top-rated heavyweight challenger, Rickard was the only boxing promoter in America with the resources to stage such a high-profile fight. As has been seen, he refused. But Paddy Mullins, Wills's gruff white manager, clamored for a Wills-Dempsey title fight before the New York State Athletic Commission, which had the authority to force Rickard's hand. The three-man commission, appointed by and beholden to the governor, at first thwarted Mullins. But Mullins's one-man crusade drew attention in the newspapers, grew politicized, and quickly turned into a national referendum on civil rights: Did a black man have the right in America to fight for the heavyweight title?

By the mid-1920s, all eyes were turned to Rickard for the answer. In New York and probably most of the country, the popular consensus was Wills deserved his rightful shot at the title, thereby disarming Rickard's excuse that "the public will never support it." In times past, the politicians in Albany would have ridden to Rickard's rescue. Not this time. The ruling Democratic Party, faced with competing election-day objectives on the local and national levels, opted to play both sides of the fence. On the local side of the issue were those linked to Tammany Hall, New York City's notorious Democratic machine, which wanted to control the vote in Harlem, long a Republican stronghold. Hoping to score points in Harlem, Tammany forced Rickard to stage mixed-race bouts in Madison Square Garden and no doubt had a say in the State Athletic Commission's very public demand that Dempsey either fight Wills or forfeit his title.

On the national side of the debate was New York governor Al Smith, a former Tammany man who outgrew his famous brown derby, a hat that symbolized his humble upbringing on New York's East Side. Smith planned to seek the Democratic nomination for president, and he could not afford to be perceived in the South as pro-black, a signal that a Wills-Dempsey fight would have sent. According to Rickard, Smith's advisers warned him behind closed doors not to even think of staging the fight. "Them fellers in Albany are playing me for a sucker, all the way down the line," Rickard reportedly complained. "They're crucifying me in the eyes of the public!"[13]

One could dismiss this triangle of interests as unique to liberal New York, a soap opera with no broad application beyond the Hudson River. The facts, however, don't support such an assumption. Professional sports came of age in the East and Midwest, and New York was the most dominant city in the business. It had the most powerful media, the largest stadiums, and the most resourceful promoters, and its two baseball teams won more World Series by far than all other cities combined.

Neither was the situation unique to boxing. Major league baseball was subject to the same social forces as boxing and the other major sports. Jackie Robinson's shattering of the color line in the 1940s clearly shows it to be the case. The big difference was baseball had no tradition of equal opportunity, having drawn its color line in the early 1890s. That was not the case in boxing, which had crowned numerous black champions. "In the fighting business with me there is no creed, no color," declared sportswriter Hype Igoe, expressing an opinion that would not have been heard in baseball stadiums. "Fighting men are fighting men."[14]

As a result, major league baseball was largely immune to the race issue during the 1920s. Its customers expected all-white teams and had no reason to push for integration on their own. This meant the baseball moguls were not under government watch and were free to uphold or break their voluntary color line at any time. The choice was theirs.

The most direct threat to baseball's color line came from the sports industry itself. If a popular sport like boxing lowered its color line and reshaped public opinion on the subject, the baseball moguls had to take notice.

The great push to integrate professional sports originated in the 1920s on two fundamentally different, but complementary, levels. The first involved the politicalization of Harry Wills's quest to fight for the heavyweight title, which today is one of the most seminal and overlooked events in black sports history. Though Wills never landed the fight—and according to most experts, he probably would have been pummeled by Dempsey—the issue forced many whites to get over their dislike of Jack Johnson in the name of fairness. It was a sign of evolving public opinion that began in New York and, with the help of the New York media, filtered throughout the country.

The Wills saga also spawned the first organized protest against a color line in American sports. The public and, to some extent, the politicians put sports promoters and owners on notice: The line was not unbreakable. There would be significant support for anyone who had the courage to face down Jim Crow in sports. They just had to dare to do it—and then deal with the vocal minority of whites who might try to rally against integration.

"Would their predominantly white audiences 'accept' Negro stars, and 'identify' with them?" wrote Leonard Koppett in his classic book about the rise of professional basketball, *24 Seconds to Shoot*. "Today these seem to be naive, simplistic or insincere questions, but they generated real doubts at the time. Whatever else the sports promoters were, they were not social-engineering heroes, eager to take what they saw as a risk in their already shaky enterprise."[15]

The second level of progress came from amateur athletics. Unlike professional sports, where promoters were motivated by the bottom line, the amateur world remained mostly free of the taint of money. College athletics celebrated rivalry and school spirit and portrayed its heroes as all-American kids who embodied socially valued ideals such as fitness, discipline, bravery, and toughness. In this more idealistic environment, though many white coaches opted not to antagonize alumni and faculty by recruiting black athletes, a few dared to give blacks a chance, an opportunity that had been a main source of Ed Henderson's call to physical education at the turn of the century.

This opportunity to excel in the white world opened another door that Henderson had not, at least publicly, championed: the U.S. Olympic team. Black athletes who earned a spot on the team had a rare opportunity to represent their country and all Americans. Any black athlete who conquered the world for Uncle Sam became a national hero worthy of acclaim and admiration.

In the 1920s, DeHart Hubbard of the University of Michigan became the first of a stream of black athletes to bring home gold medals from the Olympics. Though Hubbard's triumph was less celebrated than Jesse Owens's legendary performance at the 1933 games in Nazi Germany, it nevertheless warmed the hearts of Americans of all races. "Imagine how proud I felt when I saw the two [American] flags go up on the score board and knew that it was our two boys, who had put them there," wrote a black journalist, referring to Hubbard and silver medalist Ned Gourdin, a former star at Harvard University. "Oh boy, what a grand and glorious feeling."[16]

These glorious feelings overseas and the protest stirring at home provided blacks with a vital stage from which to make their case for equality. Ironically, not all of them seemed to care about the big picture. Many students and alumni of black colleges wanted the next DeHart Hubbard to represent Howard, not Michigan.

"The competition between colored colleges is growing so keen that the scouts and alumni comb secondary school fields for likely material for their alma mater," wrote Ed Henderson of a trend that ran counter to his original vision of sports as a means to create national African American heroes and praise for the race.

"This search has pulled the star prep athletes from New England and the Middle States' schools into colored colleges far into the southland who otherwise might have matriculated in Northern universities," Henderson continued. "Let's sacrifice some local college pride and encourage such boys as [basketball star George] Gregory of Dewitt Clinton, other Drews, Hubbards, Marshalls, Morrisons, and Martins to make for Amherst, Michigan, Illinois, Penn, and Harvard to carve athletic marks. The battle may be harder but the glory will be the larger for the individual and the race."[17]

The glory, as Henderson knew, was more tangible than ever during the 1920s. Once the exclusive domain of gamblers, thugs, and the unsophisticated masses, sports had become a respectable national obsession. "Until the 1920's the general public regarded professional athletes as crude, muscular muggs engaged in activities hardly worthy of attention from gentlemen of breeding and culture," recalled writer Stanley Frank. "Amateurs were accepted with more tolerance, but it was founded essentially on the snob appeal of the social sports, and even the football players were looked upon as strange species in the human zoo.

"The crazy, turbulent twenties brought an abrupt and radical change in viewpoint," Frank wrote. "Whether it was an emotional hangover from the war or merely the firing of imaginations by the most colorful and compelling stars any decade has seen is a moot question. Whatever the cause, America suddenly became sports-mad and its athletic heroes were canonized one cut below sainthood."[18]

Part of the attraction was the big money now associated with the major professional sports. All the major league baseball teams except the Boston Red Sox made money during the decade, driving player salaries to a level that captured the imagination of many fans. Another attraction was the way nationally syndicated sportswriters lionized the greatest athletes of the era in larger than life prose.

Then there were Tex Rickard and the other promotional geniuses of the era. "No one knew more about the money fever that infects men," recalled Teddy Hayes, Dempsey's longtime trainer, of Rickard. "Each of his promotions had the marvelous, 'maybe-it-will-happen-to-me' spirit. The enormous sums involved, the huge guarantees he offered, generated so much excitement that his shows were virtually irresistible. *One million dollars.* The words tolled like a great bell through every one of his promotions."[19]

Experts agree white professional basketball lagged behind baseball and boxing in popularity. How far? A good gauge is the popularity of the Original Celtics, pro basketball's equivalent of the New York Yankees during the 1920s. According to sports historian Robert Peterson, the Original Celtics ranked as "hardly a household name." "By the middle of the decade," he wrote, "they were well enough known that they could compete for newspaper space with fencing, amateur boxing, and small-college football."[20]

A closer look, however, shows that Peterson might have misjudged the Celtics' popularity. The *New York Times,* an upper-class newspaper, paid little attention to professional basketball; its readers preferred baseball, golf, racquet sports, and even boxing. The story was different in working-class newspapers. The Original Celtics received a great deal more coverage in papers aimed at the masses, and the team's reputation as unbeatable preceded it in cities up and down the East Coast.

"The Celtics are the greatest basketball players that ever showed their stuff in this town," went a typical example in the *Washington Evening Times.* "Every fan who helped jam the Coliseum would do it again to see the Celtics, judging by the approval they bestowed on the Gothamites last night."[21]

Though popular in some circles, the Celtics and pro basketball in general suffered from a lack of organization that might have helped popularize the game on a greater scale. Unlike baseball, basketball had no national league to showcase the premier teams and players. This meant Americans had no annual pennant race to follow, no dramatic championship series, and no basketball stars to rival Babe Ruth in the national spotlight. Neither could basketball promoters wow the public with spectacular, million-dollar matches—not when games were played indoors, often in small dance halls.

Basketball was a work in progress during its early years. The drive to speed up the game and boost its entertainment value didn't begin until the 1930s with the elimination of the center jump after each basket. Until then, basketball was slow, rough, and low scoring. "The halves were 20 minutes; there was a center jump after each score; and there was no compulsion to bring the ball to the forecourt, within 10 seconds," according to sportswriter Tom Meany, who grew up attending pro games in working-class Brooklyn. "A team which was physically spent could stall in the backcourt with the ball. The courts averaged 60 feet by 40. They were bandboxes compared to the 90 by 50 courts prevalent today."[22]

Many games still were played on courts surrounded from ceiling to floor by a metal or rope cage. These clunky edifices helped keep the ball in play and prevent fans from interfering with the action. The court sometimes had the feel of a gladiator pit.

When no cage was present, the working-class fans that attended games often revealed their dark side. "I used to wonder how they could get so many people into the place," recalled one player of Brooklyn's Prospect Hall, which was nicknamed "Bucket of Blood." "It seemed as though they were hanging from the rafters. And the guys in the rafters thought nothing of shying a bottle at you when you were trying to shoot a foul.

"That was bad enough," the player continued, "but the fellows sitting on the sidelines would trip you up when you were going down the court. Once a fellow stuck a lighted cigarette into the back of my legs as I was trying to pass a ball in from out of bounds. They were holy terrors."[23]

What professional basketball had to sell in the 1920s was the speed and teamwork of the more talented teams that could negate the rough play. But with no national league, there was an unevenness to the quality of play from city to city. Washington, for instance, had no tradition of pro basketball, and its white semipro teams were generally weak. New York and Philadelphia, however, had fairly thriving, though undercapitalized, pro scenes.

New York's West Side produced the best white team of the era: the Original Celtics. Managed for much of 1920s by a small-time wheeler-dealer named Jim Furey, the Celtics were the smartest and best-drilled team in the business. They played more than a hundred games each season and rarely lost more than a dozen of them. "What made them so truly great was the Celtics literally won as they pleased most of the time," Meany wrote. "They rarely poured it on—first, because rolling up the score was bad business and had a deleterious effect upon the gate for a return game, and second, because it was exhausting. Some of the few defeats the Celtics sustained in a season . . . occurred because a team with which the Shamrocks were toying suddenly got hot in the closing minutes and poured through enough points to erase the Celtics' lead."[24]

Furey also was one of the first managers to sign his players to exclusive contracts, often for generous flat salaries. Needing to recoup his expenses, he began sending his often seven-man squad on brutal, month-long road trips up and down the Eastern Seaboard. According to Meany, the Celtic players "wore their uniforms for weeks on end without laundering them, simply because they never had time to have them laundered. Each man carried his own equipment in a small hand grip. The soiled, sweaty uniforms were stuffed in after each game, never to see daylight or feel fresh air until the following night when they were pulled out of the bag for the next game on the schedule."[25]

Team members used homespun remedies to fight the bumps and bruises that accumulated on these road trips. After center Joe Lapchick's arm was badly clawed by an opponent, the scratches quickly became infected. Veteran guard Johnny Beckman, seeing his center in terrible pain, pulled out his medicine bag. "He soaked a Turkish towel in steaming hot water and wrapped it tightly around Lapchick's arm," wrote Meany. "Then he proceeded to rub the scabs from Joe's arm with the towel. The final step was to pour a bottle of bootleg brandy over the open wounds. 'You'll be okay for tomorrow, kid,' said Beckman, lightly."[26]

Lapchick knew that he had no choice but to be okay. Each Celtic player took too much pride in winning to miss a game because of a mere bruise or infection. "We played together as a team and talked over plays and techniques between games hours at a time," Lapchick recalled. "Later we would work out the plays on the courts. When a fellow made a mistake, the rest of the Celtics hollered at him and chewed him out until he got it right. No floor instructions, just hints."[27]

The Celtics, unlike their white counterparts in major league baseball, did not draw the color line. As the black game entered the 1920s, particularly in New York and Pittsburgh, where the commercial forces were greatest, it would be only a matter of time before the top black team in America gained a rare opportunity to measure its skills against the top white team in the world. "Beat the Celtics" would become a common chant in Harlem, one that would eventually ring true. First, however, Harlem would need to return to a persistent question: Who would control the future of basketball—the amateurs or the professionals?

The Amateurs Tighten Their Grip

Now that Will Madden, the great purveyor of professionalism, had been browbeaten to an early retirement, St. Christopher and its fellow amateur basketball clubs seemed to have resolved their moral crisis. Henceforth, they only would field and play teams that fostered the ideals of brotherhood, teamwork, discipline, sportsmanship, and above all, racial uplift. Money and professionalism would play no part in the equation—supposedly.

By the start of the 1919–20 season, all eyes were on the St. Christopher Red and Black Machine, the two-time defending black amateur champion of New York. The Machine still operated its triple-turbine offense, featuring George Fiall and the athletic Jenkins brothers, Fat and Harold. Running interference for them was burly Paul Robeson, who recently had graduated from Rutgers University and was launching his career in the theater.

Most teams understood that they had no chance against this powerhouse. Bob Douglas and his Spartan Braves weren't intimidated, however. Douglas was known around Harlem as "Smiling Bob" for his sunny, why-worry disposition. But behind his jolly facade was a ferocious competitor who wanted nothing more than to knock the defending champion off its pedestal.

Over the past two years, Douglas had pounded the pavement in hopes of assembling a team that could sabotage the Red and Black Machine. By the fall of 1919, Smiling Bob believed he had succeeded, with a lineup that, as the *Crusader Monthly* wrote, "must have made many a manager tremble."[28]

The Spartan Braves featured some of the jazziest names ever—Hooks Wallace, Hobey Johnson, Hilton "Kid" Slocum, George "Head Ache Band" Capers, Strangler Forbes, Big McDonald, and Sammy Gumbs.

The Spartan–St. C. showdown came on January 21, 1920, in the first postwar contest between the two teams. But on this cold Wednesday night, a black cat named Tabby crossed Douglas's path. Or so the story goes. Tabby was a stray that resided somewhere in the bowels of Manhattan Casino and usually had the good sense to stay to itself. But on this night, with both teams still in the locker room and yell leader Charles Garland waving the St. C. faithful through pregame fight songs, Tabby skulked up from the netherworld and padded onto the floor, looking as out of place as a skunk at a Fourth of July picnic.

The crowd, giddy over the sight of a cat on the court, shouted for Tabby to dance, meow, or sing. It was all good fun, but when the fans finally fell silent, the darn cat wouldn't shoo. A few uneasy minutes passed, then a handful of Spartan faithful swaggered onto the floor and rushed the feline like defensive linemen ready to pounce on a loose football. But the cat burst through the Spartan line, tail high, and disappeared into the dark recesses of Manhattan Casino, allegedly spewing a mysterious curse on the Spartan Field Club.

Sound crazy?

Well, an hour later, the Spartans couldn't get their hands on St. C. forward George Fiall either. After a tight first half with the Machine ahead 19-13, Fiall flew out for the second frame and fired in two baskets and a free throw, then a flurry of points. "The crowd by this time was in an uproar," wrote the *New York Age*. "[E]very person in the house seemingly was trying to yell some instructions to one player or another."

On the court, Spartan defensive ace Strangler Forbes slumped to catch his breath. For three quarters he had tried in vain to stop Fiall, and the Strangler now looked like he was about to faint. Douglas, knowing Forbes needed a break, ordered Sammy Gumbs to get in there and shadow Fiall for a while. Gumbs hopped off the bench and immediately fired a pass to a player on the wrong team. That player was five-foot-seven Fat Jenkins, the St. C. deadeye, who raced downcourt for an easy breakaway layup before Head Ache Band Capers lunged after him and shoved him out of bounds. St. C. converted the free throws, and Douglas surveyed his bench for one last Hail Mary. "Big McDonald subbed for Capers, but was of no avail for the 'Machine' continued to pile up the score, only stopping when the final whistle announced the end of the game." Fiall finished with twenty-one points, and St. C. closed out the rout 40-23.[29]

For Douglas, the defeat was devastating. His hand-picked team had gone AWOL for the biggest game in the history of the Spartan Field Club. Douglas, by nature not prone to self-doubt, had plenty to think about that night. Like most coaches, he could replay a game in his head again and again. Make an adjustment here, try a substitution there. Yet he had to know his team might not get a second chance to beat the Red and Black Machine. Having buried the Spartans once, St. C. was under no obligation to risk playing them again. Unless the Machine lost a few games in February to force a rematch, Douglas would have to wait another year to get his next shot.

As it turned out, the road to a rematch was short. In early February, soon after the St. C. loss, Douglas and his Spartans bottled the lively Lightning Five from the Brooklyn YMCA 37-25, then left town for a two-game set. Game one sent the Spartans to Washington, D.C., to face the Carlisle Field Club, followed the next night by a meeting with Philadelphia's Southwest YMCA. Two tough opponents, two golden opportunities to reclaim their good name.

The Spartans proved too big and athletic for Carlisle. After a close first half, they busted the game open midway through the second stanza, and Douglas cleared his bench for mop-up duty. The final: Spartans 29, Carlisle 17. The next night in Philly, the Spartans fell behind early to the young, over-achieving Southwest YMCA team. But riding Kid Slocum's twenty-plus points, the Spartans got out of town with a solid 41-31 win.

By the time Douglas returned home, cries for a Spartan–St. C. rematch had reached fever pitch. Writing under the headline "Spartan Braves Fit Opponent for St. C.," the *New York Age* declared: "No more hazardous task has been undertaken by any club this season than that recently performed by the Spartan basketball squad in its invasion of the South."[30] The *Age*, clearly aboard the Spartan bandwagon, failed to mention that St. C. had performed the same road feat in February, hammering Hampton in Virginia and squeaking past the Vandal Athletic Club, probably tougher opponents than those the Spartans faced. Still, by the end of February, the Spartans seemed deserving of another shot at the Red and Black Machine. They boasted a 13-1 record and, aside from the St. C. debacle, hadn't been challenged all season.

The same could not be said of St. Christopher. Despite its impressive southern road trip, the once infallible team had fallen three times since the Spartan game—twice to Posey's Loendi and once to the Brooklyn Athletic Club. In the Brooklyn loss, St. C. manager Charlie Bradford had sent out his second string to start the game, a decision that had some wondering if St. C. had become too cocky for its own good. By March, Bradford seemed resigned to the fact that his team now needed a face-saving win over Spartan to bag another eastern championship and quell the rumors of his team's demise.

The Spartan–St. C. rematch was played on March 5, 1920, one of the stormiest nights in memory. Still, about two thousand gallant souls fought their way through the lashing rain to Manhattan Casino to witness the game of the year. Though it was billed as the championship of the East, many figured that the national title also was up for grabs that night. That's because Loendi, probably the best black quintet in the country, had run afoul of the American Athletic Union a few weeks back when it played a white team that employed known professionals. The AAU, which frowned on mixing pros and amateurs, immediately branded Loendi as professional, disqualifying the team from vying for the national black amateur title.

At the appointed hour, the white referee J. J. O'Brien tooted his whistle. St. C.'s Harold Jenkins shook hands with the Spartans' Kid Slocum, and O'Brien lofted the leather ball high into the air. Jenkins, one of the best leapers in the black game, stretched up, flicked the ball to one of his teammates, and the show was on.

Both teams worked the ball on offense like engineers, flipping passes with a precision that brought the crowd to its feet. But neither team could seem to get its shots to fall. Even George Fiall, the architect of Bob Douglas's nightmare in the first meeting, seemed out of sorts. The usually automatic Fiall was shaky from the free-throw line, nailing one and then, to the crowd's shock, bombing on the next.

For the Spartans, their opening jitters degenerated into a rash of costly mistakes. In a flashback to the January meeting, Head Ache Band Capers stepped onto the court after a time-out and almost immediately threw a pass to a player on the wrong team. That player once again was Fat Jenkins, a one-time New York City high school sprint champion, who raced downcourt for an easy two. But the Spartans eventually found their poise, and behind forward Hooks Wallace and quick, eel-like center Kid Slocum, they rallied to finish the half trailing 15-14.

"The team went off the court for their ten minutes rest period and the second string men entertained the spectators by warming up," wrote the *New York Age*, offering a glimpse of the Plain Jane halftime shows of the day. "Few fans left their seats fearing that they would lose points of vantage for the second [half]."[31]

Those vantage points would allow the spectators to witness one of the most bizarre finishes in the history of basketball. It started with thirty-four ticks left on the clock and the score knotted at twenty-seven all. The Machine snapped into gear, clicking off a series of passes that worked the ball into the hands of a wide-open Red and Black player, forcing Hooks Wallace to rush out in desperation to stop the game-

winner. Hooks, a step too slow, instead lunged after the jersey of the
St. C. player in what amounted to an intentional foul. Referee O'Brien
whistled Wallace for his fourth foul, then the requisite number for dis-
qualification, setting the stage for Fiall to step to the line for the lead
with under thirty seconds on the clock.

But the ball would never leave Fiall's hands. Capers, the Spartan captain, rushed toward O'Brien and commenced to throw one of the worst
temper tantrums in the history of Manhattan Casino. Some later claimed
it was a calculated outburst, a psychological ploy designed to buy his team
time in selecting a replacement for Wallace. Calculated or not, Capers's
tantrum sent the crowd over the top in an ear-splitting point/counterpoint
of boos and cheers that was one insult away from erupting into a brawl.

"At the height of this demonstration, a small figure strode out on the
court," wrote the *Age*'s Ted Hooks. "He did not go far—to the referee's
mind only seven feet. Nevertheless that was far enough for Captain
George Capers of Spartan. George fairly hugged both officials in his ea-
gerness to call their attention to the small man's presence."[32]

The small man, as Capers and just about everybody in the house
knew, was Eugene Williams, a local dentist and high-ranking St. C. official who was the club's delegate to the AAU. What Williams hoped to
accomplish on this diplomatic mission, nobody knew. But it put a whole
new spin on the final thirty seconds. Capers, dropping his argument
over the foul, now demanded that O'Brien call the mandatory technical foul on St. C. for Williams's illegal entry onto the court. O'Brien and
his partner at first refused. "But so sure was the Spartan leader of his
knowledge of the rule that he had the officials consult the rule book.
There in black and white his contention was borne out and the referee
was forced to call a foul on the St. C. team for their officer's transgres-
sion," wrote Hooks.[33]

Williams, Bradford, and the entire St. Christopher contingent went
berserk. After about fifteen minutes of hand-waving, chest-thumping,
rule-book-rapping chaos, O'Brien strode to the loudspeaker and informed
the frenzied crowd that both teams each had a free throw coming.
What's more, St. C. had two minutes to accept the technical foul—or
else forfeit the championship game. O'Brien set down the microphone,
and the clock commenced to tick.

But Bradford and his players already had dug in their heels along the
sidelines. They weren't going to accept the technical, and if not accepting it meant forfeiting the championship, so be it. Right was right.

For Bob Douglas, winning on a technicality wasn't the fairy-tale finish that had obsessed and animated him for so many years. A twenty-
point blowout or a last-second shot would have been a more convincing
denouement. But after all he and the Spartans had endured, Douglas
had to be grateful just to come out on top for once.

As the clock ticked and the fans rained down their disapproval of
St. C. for cheating them of an overtime period, few in the stands could
have guessed that from the ashes of this near riot would emerge the first
outlines of a new dynasty. Not just any dynasty, but arguably the greatest dynasty in the history of black basketball—a team that one day would
defeat the greatest white teams of the era, a team that one day would
win eighty-eight games straight, a team that would be the great ambas-
sador of black basketball for nearly three decades.

A few more ticks, and O'Brien waved his arms to signal the end of the
game. Fair or foul, it was now official: The Spartan Field Club reigned
as the black amateur basketball champion of the world for 1920.[34]

Later that night, with the crowd gone and the hall hushed, Bob Douglas stepped out into a downpour that still pounded 142nd Street like
pebbles on a plate. Douglas instinctively hurried ahead through the rain,
but his thoughts lingered back inside the casino. For the first time since
he started the Spartan Field Club fifteen years ago, Douglas was the
king of black basketball in New York. Despite the downpour, Smiling
Bob wanted to savor the moment.

Smiling Bob Douglas

For Douglas, the road to a championship had been unusually long and
winding. Born in 1882 on the sleepy Caribbean island of St. Kitts, Smiling Bob emigrated as a teenager to New York City, where he eventually landed a job as a night watchman. One night, according to Douglas, he wandered into an old attic-turned-gymnasium on 59th Street in
Manhattan, where he noticed two teams of men whipping around an
oversized leather ball. It was a moment he would never forget.

Back on St. Kitts, soccer was the game everyone played, Douglas
once recalled. "But when I saw that basketball game, I thought it was
the most remarkable game ever."[35] About 1905, Douglas and two
friends, George Abbott and J. Foster Phillips, pooled their money to
start the amateur Spartan Field Club. The small club, which catered to

the tastes of its West Indian clientele, featured the traditional Caribbean fare of cricket, tennis, soccer, and track. But thanks to Douglas and his friends, the club also slapped together an American-style basketball team.[36] From the first set shot, Douglas and his soccer-happy mates struggled to master the nuances of this newfangled game. Shouting out plays in their sing-song island patois, the original Spartan teams probably shot better with their feet than their hands. But the Spartans stuck with the sport, and when basketball became a fashionable attraction at Manhattan Casino in the early teens, this band of West Indians began searching for ways to break into the action.

The break came in the fall of 1914 when Harper Richardson, a former railroad worker turned entrepreneur, opened a big barn of a dance hall called the Palace Casino at 28 East 135th Street in Harlem. Richardson, eager to keep his place hopping, let the Spartans mount a pair of baskets in the hall and, over several weeks, stage games before the late-night dancing commenced.

Douglas and his teammates must have thought they had hit the jackpot. The dance floor at the Palace Casino measured 176 feet by 40 feet, or nearly twice as long and nearly as wide as one of today's NBA courts.[37]

To match their new home court, the Spartans lined up for their debut game the biggest team in Harlem, the defending champion St. Christopher Red and Black Machine. Though the Machine had been weakened by the sudden departure of manager Will Madden, nobody gave the Spartans a prayer against the champs. But on December 14, 1914, the Spartans—with Bob Douglas and J. Foster Phillips at the guards, George Abbott at center, and J. Abbott and Jimmy Ross at the forwards—yanked off their wool warm-up tops to the cheers of a small but boisterous crowd and gave it a go.

Maybe it was the adrenaline, or maybe St. C. was just plain rusty after a long off-season, but the Spartans stayed close before fading in the fourth quarter. Though the game was rough and degenerated into a dull parade to the free-throw line, the Spartans had to feel good about challenging the almighty Red and Black Machine, a feat that had Douglas and company thinking this just might be their breakthrough season.[38]

But as so often happens with young teams after an impressive outing, the breakthrough turned to bust. In January 1915, the Spartans suffered a rash of terrible defeats, and club manager Jimmy Ross had no choice but to unleash the team's secret weapon. His name was Tischinsky, or Tish for short, and he was a local Jewish kid who had signed on as the new coach, starting center, and Great White Hope for this all-Caribbean club.

Tish wasn't the first white player to appear in the black game. The crafty Cum Posey once flaunted a pair of white ringers on Loendi, and St. C. played a white kid named Irving Rose. But Tish was controversial just the same, not so much for his skin color as for his reputed links to professional sports. However, the alleged links soon proved to be false— or at least undocumented—and Tish took his place in the Spartan lineup for the next several seasons.

One of the game's original long-range gunners, Tish was by all accounts a decent basketball player. But he was no twenty-point-a-game savior. When he stepped beyond the arc and pulled the trigger with defenders draped all over him, more often than not he fired blanks. And so, too, did the Spartans.

Will Madden, after watching Alpha butcher the Tish-led Spartans early in the 1915–16 season, offered the following scouting report on the losers: "There wasn't much team work and if there had been Tisch [sic] would have broken it all up with his crazy long shooting. Ross is a tender[foot] while Phillips and Douglass [sic] are ordinary guards[.] Abbott at center though will probably some day develop into a mighty formidable man."

Finding the team more comical than threatening, Madden wrote, "The Spartans have a good organization and are progressive and hard workers but they cannot be forced on the public but must bide their time in the regular course of events the same as any other organization has had to do in the past."[39]

With the 1916–17 season, Bob Douglas took over as manager of the Spartans. Though he might have appeared "ordinary" on the court, Douglas possessed an eye for talent and an easy affability that coaxed top players into the Spartan camp. That autumn he added two coveted local players to the lineup: hard-nosed guard Sammy Gumbs and former Alpha forward Ardneze Dash, a young speedster who had played at New York's DeWitt Clinton High School and possibly at the City College of New York with Tish.[40]

The transformation of the team was immediate. In early December, the Spartans beat a makeshift but still reputable Howard University team in Manhattan Casino. Will Madden, who eight months before had smirked at the Spartans, was now using kinder words. "As to Spartan's team, I must admit it was a revelation," he wrote. "They showed such a vast improvement over last season that they surprised the fans."[41]

Though the remainder of the 1916–17 season was a gut-wrenching ride of ups and downs, the club's late-season upset of St. C. placed the once ridiculed name of Spartan on the short list of top teams in Harlem. Ever the competitor, Douglas saw no reason to stop there. He seemed to figure that with a few more top players in his fold, Spartan could be the best team in Harlem.

After the war, although Dash left to attend dental school in Washington, Douglas added several former members of Madden's now defunct Incorporators to his team, including Strangler Forbes and Hobey Johnson. The new quintet eventually clicked during the 1919–20 season, and with an assist from St. Christopher and Eugene Williams, Spartan now was the defending black champion of New York.

Picking Up the Pieces in Washington

Thanksgiving 1920. Possibly feeling as stuffed as the turkeys they had just consumed, hundreds of basketball fans crammed into Manhattan Casino for the latest installment of the oldest intercity rivalry in the black game, Washington versus New York.

On the floor for this early-season matchup were the Spartan Braves, the defending black champions of New York, and their challengers, the Carlisle Field Club, veterans of Washington's wartime YMCA league and now the capital city's ranking black team. When the two teams had battled once before in Washington, the Spartans had dominated Carlisle, leaving many in the sell-out crowd to groan that they hadn't gotten their money's worth.

But on this night, the New York fans got their money's worth and more. With the champion Spartans clinging to a 20-19 lead late in the game, Carlisle forward Benny Hill toed the free-throw line, where he had one charity toss coming to tie the contest. The five-foot-six Hill had stolen the show in the second half, darting in and out of the Spartan defense to take his two-handed nibbles at the hoop. From ten down at halftime, Hill had led the charge to pull Carlisle within a point of the champions and, more important, within one lucky basket from heading home with the greatest upset victory in the team's history.

Hill eyed the rim fifteen feet away. With one careful flick of his wrists, he lofted the ball into the air and sent it clanking in, then out of, the hoop. In the mad scramble for the rebound, the ball was batted back to Hill, braced by the midcourt stripe. He measured from about twenty-five feet dead on, fired, and clipped the cords for the lead.

The Thanksgiving crowd rose to its feet to cheer Benny and his Comeback Carlisles. To salute the crowd, Hill then drained another ringer, boosting the Washington lead to 23-20 with the final whistle about to blow.

But the game wasn't over yet. Sensing defeat for the hometown Spartans, Harlem referee Chris Hinsmond quickly whistled a Carlisle player for a foul. Spartan forward Hooks Wallace dropped in the free throw, and the champs moved to within two points, or one easy basket, of sending the game into overtime.

That was the cue for the timekeepers to come to the rescue. The men who controlled the game clock refused to end the contest until Spartan tied the score. The pro-Carlisle crowd, smelling a rat, shouted for the men to blow the blasted whistle. Some fans trickled onto the court in protest; others stormed to the scorer's table in vain attempts to blow the whistle themselves. Nevertheless, 2:40 seconds after one fan reckoned the final whistle should have sounded, Spartan star Kid Slocum finally stuck the ball through the hoop to tie the score, followed by the shameless tweet of the timekeeper's whistle.

In the overtime period, the crowd and the champion Spartans regained their composure. Led by Slocum and Head Ache Band Capers, the champs caught fire and, with the help of a few hometown calls, coasted to a 32-28 victory.[42]

Carlisle had learned the hard way what many visiting clubs already knew: Basketball games in Harlem could be crooked affairs. As some players later remembered, in close games the home team always seemed to get a little help from its friends in the striped shirts.[43]

Despite the bitter defeat, Carlisle had shown that a Washington team could compete with the best black quintets in the country. To prove it, Carlisle turned around and blasted the tough Philadelphia YMCA team 31-21 in Washington on Christmas Day. Benny Hill again was a one-man show, thrilling the crowd with a run of circus shots and outscoring the visitors from the field by himself.

Just when Benny and the boys looked like the second coming of Hudson Oliver and the champion Howard Big Five, trouble blew in from Baltimore. The problems had started about a week before the Philly game when Carlisle was supposed to square off in Baltimore against the city's new hotshot team, the Athenian Athletic Association. The Athenians manager, hoping to attract a handsome crowd for his team's inaugural contest, had talked up Carlisle in larger-than-life superlatives.

But when game time rolled around, the Carlisle Big Five was nowhere to be found. Rumor had it Ardneze Dash, the former Spartan star who coached Carlisle while he attended dental school at Howard University, couldn't find anyone to fill in for center Ralph Tibbs. Rather than risk defeat, Dash decided at the last minute to take the night off, forcing the Athenians to cancel the contest. "Should the rumor prove to be true, athletic relations will be severed with the Carlyle's [sic] and a letter sent broadcast advertising their actions," the Athenians warned in the Baltimore Afro-American.[44]

Dash's excuse sounds credible. The greatest stumbling block for his team, as with most rising amateur club teams, was getting players to show for games. As the revolving names in the box scores suggest, most Carlisle players had full- or part-time jobs that took precedence over the team.[45] Many simply had to beg out of games that fell during their regular work shifts, sometimes leaving gaping holes in the lineup.

A few days passed without incident, then the Athenians—or the "Greeks," as the team was nicknamed—were back pounding on Dash's door. This time it was the manager who came calling, rueing the day he had agreed to play his team's next scheduled opponent, the Ohio Collegiates. The manager explained that with just hours before game time, the Collegiates had sent word they weren't going to honor their contract to appear in Baltimore. No doubt worried about the public outcry at a second cancellation in a row, the Athenians manager told Dash he needed a favor. If Carlisle would fill in on short notice, he would forgive Dash and the past would be forgotten.

Dash faced a tough decision. Though Baltimore never had been much of a basketball town, the Athenians looked solid on paper with veterans Bill Harris, Ev Butler, and Elmore "Scrappy" Brown. Dash could try to assemble his starting five with a few hours' notice, knowing full well he'd never succeed. Then again, did he really need all his big guns against a new team that had yet to play a game or hire a coach? If Dash could just get Benny Hill and another regular or two to Baltimore, he could fill in around them with kids from the YMCA who could tag along for the trip, helping out on defense and staying out of the way on offense.

He was taking a chance. But if Dash could ease out a victory in Baltimore, he'd add to his team's growing reputation and, just as important, get the Athenians off his back.

Dash said yes. And for the first several minutes against the Greeks, it seemed he'd made the right move. Benny Hill, taking up where he had left off against the Philadelphia YMCA, roamed the Big Market Armory in his usual style. In the first four minutes of play, Hill pocketed two baskets and a free throw—a wild run of points in these low-scoring times—placing Carlisle on the fat side of a 7-3 count.

Then, at about the five-minute mark, disaster struck. An Athenians player caught up to Hill and walloped him, sending the Carlisle star thudding to the hardwood floor. Not even smelling salts could bring him back to his senses, and after a few minutes it was clear Benny was finished for the evening. So was Carlisle.

"The final score of 30-21 was like a revelation to the vast crowd that jammed the big armory," noted the *New York Age*. "The team that played Spartan to a tie in New York and decisively defeated New York 'Y' and Philadelphia 'Y' was trimmed by a team that had not played a game this season."[46]

For Carlisle, life only got worse after the Athenians debacle. Though the club rebounded with a dramatic 28-27 road victory over Hampton Institute, won on a miracle shot by a Carlisle player with no time left on the clock, the remainder of the season was a series of disappointments. In January Carlisle traveled to Atlantic City to face the Vandal "Blue and White Machine." The Vandals, on their best night a good but beatable club, built a first-half lead and then completed a 31-21 shellacking.

A few weeks later, the Carlisle players gave their fans more cause to groan when a so-so Brooklyn Y club ran them off the floor in Murray's Casino, a new U Street dance hall. Then came the crowning humiliation, when Carlisle lost the district title to its bitter rival, Alco Field Club.

How had a season that had started out so right ended so wrong? Blame the weaknesses that had been with the team from the start—a lack of manpower and experience. After the Athenians game, Benny Hill's name disappeared for the rest of the season from the few subsequent newspaper accounts of Carlisle games, an indication his tumble had lingering effects. No Hill meant no offensive spark. The power drain grew worse with the departure of Ralph Tibbs. Tibbs, the top pivot man in Washington who early in the season had parceled out his services, probably for a fee, to both Carlisle and Alco, defected to the Athenians in February. The loss of the two top Carlisle players, mixed with the regular run of no-shows and fill-ins for each game, destroyed team chemistry by the end of the season.

Disappointing though the season ended, Carlisle could look to the future with hope. The main reason was U Street. With the war and its lousy, cornbread-and-cabbage times no longer cramping its style, U Street had erupted like never before with all-night, oysters-on-the-half-shell gaiety. True, U Street during the 1920s would never rival in scope the nighttime rompin' and stompin' of Harlem or Chicago's South Side. But if you liked to dance and raise cain, there was no better spot in Washington to while away the wee hours. "Colored Boulevard Alive— Theaters Full and the People Happy," wrote the *Washington Bee* in 1921.[47]

In these rollicking times, Carlisle stood to make a killing at the box office. An entire generation had been raised on basketball in the Washington public schools, and no promoter had stepped forward with a dynamite independent team to claim its money and affections. Neither was there a dominant social club, such as St. Christopher in Harlem, already standing guard over the Washington basketball scene. The field was open for a motivated club to push its product, and Carlisle seemed like the logical product to push. Despite its late-season collapse, it still boasted the best record of any team on U Street over the last four years, and as an added attraction, its women's team was among the best on the East Coast.

Like the old 12th Street YMCA and Howard teams, Carlisle would need to recast itself as a dominating, sure-fire winner that would swell the hearts of U Street with pride. From a marketing standpoint, this meant three things. One, the club needed a wealthy owner or backer to pay the bills. Two, in a time when many amateur clubs had begun to slip a few bucks on the side to their top players, it needed to outbid rival teams for the best talent. Three, it needed a well-known athlete on its roster, such as a beloved baseball or football personality, as an added attraction to help sell seats.

On paper, it sounded easy. In reality, it was anything but. Successful promoters tended to throw their money behind basketball games, not basketball teams. Sticking to individual games meant promoters faced no long-term financial risk from dabbling in a sport many believed was a rotten investment. Sure, the amateur clubs had succeeded for years in using their basketball teams to fund-raise, like a church today uses bake sales. But compared to the more lucrative field of baseball, black basketball still had no nationally known teams or stars, played in smaller venues before smaller crowds, and had no track record of turning a comparable profit. Without solid financial backing, aspiring teams were left groping to find that magical player or irresistible showman who would allow them to survive and see another season.

The Rise and Fall of the Metropolitan Basketball Association

For weeks prior to the Carlisle game on Thanksgiving 1920, Bob Douglas had faced a question that has consumed every coach who has ever won a title: Could he win the same title for a second time in a row? While Douglas tried to wrap his fingers around this new concept, many of the faithful who had stomped in the stands that crazy night in March when the Spartans won their first title on a technicality already had begun badgering Douglas to work his magic a second time.

The strain of shouldering these expectations apparently didn't bother Douglas. In fact, he seemed to welcome the attention. After years of trying to palm off a two-cent Spartan club for fifty cents, Douglas had to be thrilled that he finally had placed a product on the floor that was worth the price of admission. Slocum, Wallace, Capers, Forbes, and their teammates had developed an uncanny sense of each other's movements on the floor that comes only from scrapping together for a few seasons. And much of the credit for creating that chemistry went to Douglas.

"Bob Douglas [is] one of the greatest managers the game has ever produced," wrote the *New York Age*. "Doug's managerial skill is backed up by a thorough knowledge of the game gained from years of play with the pioneers of the clan which he now manages. He is wonderfully blessed in being able to keep in tact [*sic*] and in harmony such an aggregation of stars as sport the green and gold."[48]

Douglas also seemed to have been bitten by the entertainment bug off the court. According to the *New York Age,* he began managing a popular Harlem song-and-dance troupe called the Bon Ton Boys. Among those on the troupe's steering committee were several prominent basketball players, including St. Christopher's George Fiall and Johnny Capers, a sign of Douglas's popularity and connections on the Harlem basketball scene.[49] With Douglas now trying his hand at show business, one had to wonder whether he also might begin to see financial possibilities in basketball, a sentiment that would put him at odds with St. Christopher and the other amateur clubs.

The 1920–21 Spartans tipped off the season in Manhattan Casino by walloping the Philadelphia YMCA. Two weeks later on Thanksgiving, the Spartans looked nothing like champions, eking out a 32-28 overtime win over Carlisle with a little help from the referees. The *New York Age* railed at the antics,[50] but Douglas could live with the bad press. He had bigger fish to fry, and that whopper dangling from the end of his line was Cum Posey, who was about to sign a contract for a home-and-away series between Loendi and Spartan. Game one would be staged on January 7 in Manhattan Casino, and as Bob Douglas knew, the winner of the two-game battle likely would be crowned the champion of black basketball for the season.

But before Posey pulled into town, Douglas had a more serious mess dropped onto his doorstep. The mess in question was professionalism. Many of the larger black athletic clubs in New York had begun subsidizing player expenses such as meals, time lost from work, and medical costs due to injury.[51] The clubs regarded the payments as legal, a necessity to entice players to show for games, not to commercialize the sport. However, passing cash from club to player set a dangerous precedent that soon left the amateur game teetering on the brink of professionalism.

That November, the St. Christopher Club had seen enough. According to Romeo Dougherty, the veteran Harlem sportswriter, St. C. officials exploded when some now nameless rival clubs allegedly offered to pay bonuses to their players if they could deliver a win over the Red and Black Machine. It was a sign of the prestige that a win over St. C. could bestow upon a struggling club.

In addition to banning bonuses, St. C. wanted to run all of the so-called "tramp" athletes out of town. A tramp athlete was a one-time loyal amateur club player who, now greedy for money, shopped his services around New York like a hired gun, jumping from team to team, handout to handout. Al Atkins, the longtime manager of the Alpha Big Five, told the story of how when he returned home from the war in 1919, all the members of his once mighty quintet had either resigned from the team or been voted out of the club for demanding payment for their services.[52] "Extortion," some called it, a sloppy shakedown that made kings of the cynical amateur teams, paupers of the law-abiding ones.

For Will Madden, the shamed poster boy for professionalism, the latest crisis was nothing more than a case of "I told you so." Madden believed that despite all the catchy slogans and feel-good ideals of the amateur movement, the commercialization of basketball would assuredly come to pass. He wrote:

> Amateur basketball is alright for young boys in schools and colleges when the spirit of organization exists and everything is done for the benefit of the institution as a whole, but in the social clubs, athletic clubs, and independent teams scattered everywhere across the country where men play the game it is entirely another proposition . . . the reason for this is due to lack of co-operation among the clubs. Each club is an independent institution and works only for itself, making it possible for the strongest organizations to hold the "whip hand" of power over the smaller clubs. This condition develops with a bitter antagonism, and, because basketball is the biggest source of revenue for the upkeep of the clubs, all efforts are centered on the perfection of teams.[53]

Madden's critics countered that the issue wasn't so much about who had the upper hand as it was about upholding high moral standards. To condone cheating, they contended, betrayed the sacrifices of St. C., Alpha, and the other original athletic clubs. These clubs at the turn of the century had every reason to bypass basketball for a lack of time, money, and space. But they didn't. The clubs saw an opportunity and, according to Dougherty, ran with it for the greater good of the race. "Here in Greater New York and New Jersey basketball has meant more to us than baseball," wrote Dougherty, "for the latter sport among colored people has been so closely allied to the saloon and underground dives the majority of sport writers passed it up in behalf of the game which is fostered by religious and other institutions working for the uplift of our people."[54]

At first, St. Christopher's latest declaration sparked only controversy, perhaps rightfully so. St. C., despite its ecclesiastical ties, had no right to speak as the moral voice of New York basketball. The club was just one voice—albeit a very influential one—among many, and its declaration from on high, wrote Dougherty, "threw colored athletic circles into an uproar. For a time it stunned the players and followers of the game and none could understand why St. Christopher acted first and called in consultation [with] the other clubs after."[55]

To calm its critics, but still consumed with a sense of urgency to preserve the amateur game, St. C. convened a special meeting of the old

Triple Alliance (St. C., Alpha, and Spartan) to discuss the state of basketball in the New York area. From this initial session emerged a wish list of reforms dubbed the "Treaty of the Parish House."[56] Scribbled into the text was a provision calling for the outlawing of "under cover professionals," a first step toward banning professionalism.

St. C. was just getting started. Within days, the club's athletic council severed its ties with George Fiall and Fat Jenkins on the grounds that both played professional baseball during the summer, which, according to a strict reading of the amateur rules, was taboo. The athletic council didn't stop there. In what amounted to a public dismantling of its beloved Red and Black dynasty, the council dismissed Paul Robeson, Johnny Capers, Fabby Robbins, and other longtime St. C. stalwarts for alleged infractions of the amateur code. When the council members finally laid down their battle-axes, the only cog still left from their once mighty Machine was Harold Jenkins. Everybody else was gone.[57]

St. C. meant for these blunt blows to serve notice that the other amateur clubs had better put their houses in order. That led to a pivotal meeting in late November 1920 to consider deputizing the old Triple Alliance as the watchdog of black amateur basketball in the New York area. Alpha, distrusting of St. C., dismissed the proposal as a ploy that somehow would benefit its longtime rival. Those in the room grew quiet, no doubt sensing that the basketball equivalent of a civil war was about to erupt. Then Gentleman Cecil Carter, a leading athlete in the Spartan Field Club, stepped to the dais and pledged the full support of his club to St. C., breaking the stalemate and putting pressure on Alpha to fall in line, which it soon did.[58]

This had to be worrisome news to Bob Douglas. If he were forced to stick to the amateur code, his beloved Spartan Braves would lose their way. How could he ask Strangler Forbes to bypass professional baseball in the summer so he could remain eligible for amateur basketball in the winter? It wasn't going to happen, not for Forbes and not for any of his other players. And if it wasn't going to happen, how was he going to put a quality team on the floor that could compete with Loendi or the top white teams?

Besides, assuming St. C. succeeded, one could argue that its back-to-the-basics crusade helped accelerate professionalism, not stop it. The crusade already had branded all-stars Fat Jenkins, George Fiall, and Johnny Capers as professionals, and many more top players eventually would land on the blacklist. They had to play somewhere. If St. C.

wouldn't take them, Will Madden and others of his ilk surely would. Madden, the pariah whom the amateur clubs had worked so hard to banish, once again would have the best team in Harlem. And then what?

Despite his objections should the reforms triumph, Douglas also had to feel obligated to follow them word for word. Amateurism was the world that he knew best, and it had treated him and the Spartan Field Club well over the last few years. Why wouldn't he support a system that had crowned him king during the 1919–20 season?

Not ready to make a decision, Douglas nevertheless got yanked into the fray when former St. C. star George Fiall told the *New York Age* that he planned to continue his basketball career as a Spartan Brave.[59] Douglas, who always had room on his team for a talented player, had to be salivating at the thought of adding Fiall in time for the first Loendi showdown, widely viewed as the game of the year in Harlem. As Douglas remembered, Fiall was the guy who single-handedly lifted St. C. over the Spartans in their first matchup a year ago. With Fiall wearing a green-and-gold Spartan uniform, he would run Loendi ragged and help elevate the Spartans to their first black world title.

But if Douglas dared to sign Fiall, now branded a professional, he risked serious repercussions. Not only would St. C. cry foul about Douglas's snatching its former star, the club would demonize him as the latest purveyor of professionalism. Given Madden's free-fall into basketball purgatory, it was a role that Douglas probably wasn't ready to assume.

Still, Fiall was Fiall, and the fans knew it. "When the Spartan Field Club was visited by our representative, every member ceased what he was doing at the mere mentioning of Fial's [*sic*] name by the reporter," wrote the *New York Age*. "Some were shooting pool, others were writing or playing checkers, and still others were idly lounging around in a state of relaxation after their day's work. . . . All were plainly jubilant at the prospect of acquiring such a valuable addition to the club's basket ball team."[60]

Douglas came to his senses. He couldn't sign Fiall. Claiming he didn't want to anger St. C. and that introducing Fiall would poison his team chemistry, Douglas passed on one of the top offensive weapons in the black game. "I don't want to have any ill feeling between my club and the St. Christopher people," he told the *New York Age*. "There will very likely be some ill feeling if we accept him even though any other club could do so and not have one word said."[61] It was the safe choice for Douglas to keep the peace, but nonetheless he was gambling that his strong but erratic Spartans could beat the Loendi juggernaut.

The gamble set the stage for one of the most famous games in the history of black basketball.

On January 7, 1921, Posey brought his men to Manhattan Casino to face the Spartans. Rumor had it Loendi had not lost to a black team in more than three years, and a scan of the Pittsburgh roster told why. Posey had been traveling with an all-star cast of players that included some of the great names of the day: Greasy Betts, Pappy Ricks, Specs Moton, U. S. Young, Legs Sessoms, and, until his untimely death in 1920 from pneumonia, former Howard star George Gilmore. And there was Posey himself, the now forty-year-old veteran and dean of black basketball. The respected Frank Young of the *Chicago Defender* wrote, "Posey is without a doubt the headiest, smartest, and best man for that position in the game."[62] But if there was one black team that might give Loendi fits, it was the Spartan Braves on a night when their motion offense clicked.

Oddly, no full newspaper accounts remain of the game. According to legend, Loendi clung to a one-point lead over the Spartans late in the game. That's when Posey, a pathological competitor who knew how Harlem teams tended to cheat in the final seconds, reverted to Plan B. Designated timekeepers for each team kept time on their pocket watches. Posey ordered his Loendi clock keeper to snatch the watch out of the hand of his Spartan counterpart and yell "Time" with about thirty seconds left in the game. He did, and in a flashback to the first St. C.– Howard championship game of 1914, hell broke loose in Manhattan Casino. After minutes of tempestuous debate, the referee bellowed the fateful words "No contest," meaning the Spartans and Loendi would have to replay the game. Cumberland Posey had struck again with as brazen a stunt as had ever been seen in black basketball and one that would live with him for the rest of his life.

That was as close as Douglas came to defeating Loendi that season. In round two, played in early February in Pittsburgh, Loendi whipped the Spartans 46-29 in a showdown that had little of the drama of the first game. "It was experience versus youth," wrote the *Baltimore Afro-American,* a statement that must have stung Douglas because his team was one of the most experienced in black basketball.[63] Then, on March 7, when the clubs resumed their hostilities in New York, the Spartans managed to stay close until the final whistle but finally fell a second straight time, 30-25.

The two losses disappointed the competitive Douglas. He had a tremendous team, nobody doubted that. In fact, with St. C. boycotting his club over its bitter loss the season before, the Spartans did indeed repeat as the 1920–21 black champions of New York and probably ranked as the second-best team in all of black basketball. But Douglas had to see that his unit was no match for the Loendi Machine in a two- or three-game series. And as a coach who was driven to win, Douglas didn't like finishing second to Cum Posey.

In late January 1921, the Triple Alliance and the other local black athletic clubs agreed in principle to form the Metropolitan Basketball Association, or MBA.[64] By March 31, association members passed a constitution, and the new rabidly amateur basketball league was born with Spartan, St. C., Alpha, Titan Athletic Club, Borough Athletic Club, Brooklyn Athletic Club, and possibly four others.[65] Written into the reforms was a rule stipulating that a panel established by the MBA must issue cards certifying the amateur status of each basketball player before the start of the season. If a player didn't have a card, he could not under any circumstances play in the MBA.

Despite these ominous developments, Douglas saw signs that St. C.'s resolve had weakened. After the demolition of the Red and Black Machine, St. C. discovered that none of its rivals was willing to tamper with the rosters. Faced with its weakest team in years and its toughest schedule yet with trips to Chicago and Pittsburgh, St. C. retreated from its hard line against professionalism and reinstated most of its regulars in early January.[66]

The athletic council claimed that it had no choice in the matter, and the reassembled Red and Black Machine rattled through a decent, though subpar, season. But if Douglas believed retreat meant surrender, he was mistaken. As the *Baltimore Afro-American* predicted after the season: "Quite a rumpus is promised for the fall when many basketball stars will be guilty of playing professional [base]ball in and around New York. The Metropolitan Basketball Association is compiling data that will be of much interest to the followers of the Big City."[67]

By the start of the 1921–22 season, the St. C.–led MBA had cleared more than 130 players as amateurs, but it still withheld judgment on at least two cagers.[68] One was Strangler Forbes of the Spartan Braves. According to the league, Forbes had tried out for several local professional baseball teams during the off-season. Though the twenty-nine-year-old Forbes reportedly did not play a game for a professional team that summer, he nevertheless might have violated amateur rules. The MBA's final decision was due in a few weeks.

In the meantime, Douglas went about business as usual. On November 8, 1921, his Spartan Braves tipped off the season in Manhattan Casino against the Dunbar Physical Culture Club of Orange, New Jersey. The Braves, featuring their veteran lineup plus a major new addition in former Loendi center Legs Sessoms, demolished Dunbar 46-17.

But in a sign of things to come, when Douglas signaled Forbes into the contest the Dunbar coach leapt off the bench, protesting that Forbes, whose status as an amateur still hung in the balance, was a professional. With the game already won, Douglas took the high road and inserted Head Ache Band Capers instead. But as the outburst had shown, the Forbes matter wasn't going to disappear.

On December 12, 1921, the MBA voted 5-3 to declare Forbes a professional, thereby barring him from further action in amateur circles.[69] Douglas didn't follow the logic. Forbes was an athlete for all seasons—football in the fall, basketball in the winter, and baseball in the spring and summer. No one disputed that Forbes had played professional baseball in the teens, first with the Philadelphia Giants in 1913 and later with New York's Lincoln Giants for $110 per month. But he hadn't played pro baseball for a few seasons, and according to the MBA, he had never played professional basketball.

Douglas now found himself in the same situation as a year ago when George Fiall wanted to sign with the Spartans. He could again keep the peace by bidding farewell to his top defender. Or he could ignore the MBA and keep Forbes in his club. Maybe St. C., given the prominent political position of the Spartan Field Club in holding together the MBA, would rather keep the peace this time around.

If not, according to Douglas's worst-case scenario, the MBA would label his team as professional, meaning member clubs would be under order to boycott Spartan. But Douglas had begun to act as though being the outlaw wasn't such a dreadful fate after all. In some ways, he already fit the profile of the renegade professional promoter. He had taken the irreverent step that season of hosting Sunday afternoon games and dances, a move that had the local ministers seeing signs of the apocalypse.[70]

If Douglas could weather the "thou shalt nots" of the clergy, he surely could withstand the fire and brimstone of St. C. and the MBA. Besides, in the short term, Spartan would hardly feel the brunt of the boycott, with big-time matchups already booked against Loendi; the Chicago Defender Athletic Club, with its former Olympic long jumper Sol

Butler; and the Puritans of Orange, New Jersey, featuring former Loendi sharpshooter Pappy Ricks and former St. C. star Fat Jenkins.

On New Year's Day 1922, in what the *New York Age* called the declaration of a "basketball war," a defiant Douglas ordered Forbes into a game against the Borough Athletic Club of Brooklyn, a fellow member of the MBA.[71] But Douglas wasn't the only spiteful soul. The Borough coach, who must have heaved a sigh of relief as he watched the Strangler saunter to the scorer's table, also defied the MBA by playing forward Leon Monde, who had been declared a professional because he had tried out for several pro baseball teams. Rumor had it that Alpha, too, had slipped a professional into one of its games, and suddenly the MBA found itself wrestling a bear of a question: Could the association bid farewell to three of the top five basketball teams in New York and still survive?

For St. C., which had booked more out-of-town teams in recent years, the answer was yes. But for the smaller MBA clubs that lacked the storied reputation and financial wherewithal of St. C., the answer wasn't so clear. Boycotting Spartan, Alpha, and Borough, all big draws, was a losing financial proposition that would hurt teams more than it would help. What's more, by voting with St. C., some clubs also had to worry about aligning their futures with a rival that, because it had its own gym and long-standing basketball program, would always be better trained and, in the words of Will Madden, always hold the whip hand of power over them on and off the court.

Whether St. C. could twist enough arms or muster enough sympathy to oust the rule-breaking clubs and keep the MBA and its amateur ideals intact was open to debate. But due to a technicality, St. C. would never have to put its strength to the test. According to a clause in the MBA bylaws, teams must be granted a ten-day grace period before their expulsion from the league.[72] This meant that association officials had to wait until their next scheduled meeting on January 24, more than three weeks after the incidents, to mete out justice.

As many of the MBA members would claim, a lot had changed during those three weeks to merit keeping Spartan and Alpha in the league. The clubs had admitted their guilt, and neither had repeated the offense. With St. C. satisfied that justice had been served, the MBA voted to keep the two clubs in the fold. For Borough, which hadn't been nearly as contrite, its fate was expulsion for the remainder of the season.[73]

It wasn't a happy ending for Douglas. The decision to play Forbes on New Year's night had sparked a raging debate at the Spartan Field Club between Douglas and those who believed he had gone too far to prove his point. Though Douglas remained defiant to St. C., he probably hadn't intended to raise the wrath of a club that he had poured his heart into for more than fifteen years. He now faced two choices: stay with the Spartans, amateur rules and all, or shove off on his own. As appealing as the latter choice sounded in some ways, Douglas couldn't afford to leave his home base in the middle of the season. Spartan, with a good but hardly world-champion reputation, didn't merit the kind of advance money needed to keep his players happy and the bills paid. Nor did his team have a fixed home court.

Once more, Douglas made peace with the amateur game. But the timing couldn't have been worse. After the Borough contest in early January, Douglas and his Spartan Braves had trekked to Pittsburgh hoping to snap the "Loendi curse" that many said Cum Posey had cast on opposing teams. Spartan once again had no antidote for Posey, and the Pittsburghers slithered to an easy 29-16 victory. On January 19, with the MBA ax still dangling over Douglas's neck, the Spartans tried again to turn the tables on Loendi in the more friendly confines of Manhattan Casino. In what many called the game of the year in Harlem, the Spartans lost a 30-26 heartbreaker.

Leading all the way until the closing minutes, the Spartans fell victim once again to George Fiall, the former St. C. star who now played for Loendi and who would have been playing for Spartan had it not been for the MBA. The wiry Fiall laced two backbreaking baskets in a row down the stretch to pull Loendi even with Spartan, setting up Posey for a game-winning bomb from beyond the free-throw line. All the while, Forbes and Sessoms, also considered a possible pro because of his past ties to Loendi, watched from the bench. Douglas had no choice. He couldn't substitute them into the game.

Afterward, still playing it conservatively, Douglas dismissed the popular Strangler Forbes from the team, then stewed about Legs Sessoms's future as a Spartan Brave. But before Douglas made up his mind, the New York police arrested Sessoms for allegedly having two wives, kicking up another cloud of scandal over the Spartan Field Club.

Though Sessoms would return and finish the season with the Spartans, the off-court distractions had killed the team's focus. On February 3, the Spartans faced the Chicago Defender Athletic Club, which ranked a close second to Loendi as the best team in the Midwest. Phil Jones, general manager of the Defenders, had bragged for months that his club, led by its terrible twosome of Sol Butler and Virgil Bluitt, could handle the eastern champions with no problem, a slap at Douglas that should have had Slocum and his fellow Spartans ready to strafe the Chicagoans with set shots when the two teams met.

But the Spartans, managing just four points in the second half, were the ones running for cover that night in Manhattan Casino. Playing before a surprisingly sparse crowd, a sign that Douglas's slumping team was fast falling out of favor with the public, the Chicago Defenders machine-gunned the Spartans 31-9, thanks in part to the defense of Butler and Bluitt. So complete had the Chicago massacre been, the *New York Age* sniped, "the champion Spartan Braves appeared to be anything but a championship team."[74]

If Smiling Bob looked forlorn after the Defender debacle, he had every reason to scowl three weeks later when the Alpha Big Five dumped the Spartans 36-27 to capture the 1922 eastern championship. This time, there were no boycotts or split decisions to taint the title. Alpha, built around its young forward Vanderveer (whose first name is absent from newspaper accounts), won it outright with wins over St. C., Spartan, and the other top MBA clubs. For Alpha, the original Harlem athletic club that had fallen on hard times immediately after the war, the championship trophy couldn't have shone brighter.

Douglas tried to regroup during the off-season, but his troops already were scattering. Rumor had it Sessoms was headed back to Pittsburgh to play for Cum Posey. Hilton Slocum, now under investigation by the MBA for wrongdoing, was said to be shopping his wares elsewhere. Head Ache Band Capers, the instigator of the famous technical foul in the Spartan–St. C. championship game of 1920, was departing for, of all teams, St. Christopher.

But if there was one thing that Harlem had learned, it was never to underestimate Smiling Bob Douglas. Basketball men had howled in the early teens when Douglas, the know-nothing kid from St. Kitts, and his Spartan neophytes clanged passes off each other. Ten years later, Douglas owned two eastern championships, and his peers hailed him as one of the black game's greatest minds.

For Douglas to rebuild his team and unleash his true genius as a coach and promoter, he would need to break free of the MBA. Always short of cash and now short of talent, he knew the odds were stacked against him. But if he could catch a break, as he had shown in the teens, Douglas had more than enough smarts to seize the opportunity and chase another title.

Jay Bee's Night on the Town

March 10, 1922. As Jay Bee whisked toward Murray's Casino on this drizzly evening, he spied the ticket line snaking onto the sidewalk of 9th and U Streets. Scores of intrepid souls huddled in their hats and over-coats, trying to stay dry long enough to score the remaining tickets to tonight's ball game. But Jay Bee wasn't about to join those shivering at the end of the line. He breezed past the hats and umbrellas, squeaked upstairs to the front entrance, and rolled out his press credentials with the self-importance of a cop flashing his badge.

"Hey, where's your ticket for the basketball game?" asked the usher.

"I don't need a ticket. I'm J. B. Davidson. You know, Jay Bee of the *Washington Tribune*. I'm covering tonight's ball game for the newspaper."

The usher nodded, apparently unaware that Jay Bee was actually the *Tribune*'s theater critic, and motioned for him to proceed into the splashy red, yellow, and green ballroom with the gleaming floor. For local basketball teams, the shine and glitz of the brand-new Murray's Casino was a welcome relief from fusty old True Reformer's Hall. Though seating was limited in the casino and the ceiling prohibitively low for basketball, the fifty-dollar-per-night rental fee bought them a fifty-four-by-ninety-foot dance floor, the largest on U Street, and mod-ern electric fans to keep the hall ventilated during games and the live music afterward, which on this night would be provided by a local kid by the name of Duke Ellington.

Jay Bee, a bespectacled middle-aged man who looked like a cross be-tween a banker and a mortician in his tight, dark suit and with a fresh shine shimmering on his shoes, waded through the crowd toward the long table at courtside that passed for press row. Five familiar faces al-ready were stationed there, and Jay Bee rattled off the standard litany of heys and hellos as he angled his rear end into his tiny seat.

A few feet away, eight or nine basketball players limbered up, each bearing a large embroidered "A" across the front of his cotton jersey. The "A" stood for Alco, a local black athletic club that had been field-ing basketball teams since the war. Few in the crowd knew what "Alco" meant. Jay Bee guessed, tongue in cheek, that it might have been either "Alco-rub or Alcohol."[75]

The Alcoes featured the talented threesome of center Dickie Graves, forward Buck Carroll, and a hot-shooting player named Kenner. Having won the wartime 12th Street YMCA league during its final season in 1920, and having never lost to a local team since, Alco had spent the past two years promoting itself as the reigning black champion of the District of Columbia, an assertion that many local fans labeled as balderdash.

According to the anti-Alco contingent, the true champion of U Street was the team loosening up this evening at the other end of the floor, the Carlisle Big Five. Still coached by the "West Indian Wonder," Ardneze Dash, Carlisle had solidified its once chaotic lineup with a regular tandem of wee Benny Hill, the one-man scoring machine; regulars Turner, Taylor, Barber, and Robinson (whose first names were never mentioned in newspapers); and the lanky newcomer Pinion Cornish, who had replaced center Ralph Tibbs, the fickle player-for-hire who died the previous November from the flu.

Solidifying the lineup had not brought much success, though. Opening the season with exhibition victories at home over the local Settlers and the Springfield, Massachusetts, Collegiates, Carlisle faced its moment of truth in New York on New Year's Day 1922 against the mighty Spartan Braves. If Carlisle could best the top court combo in Harlem— a second time, as some said—Dash and his men would be a hot ticket both on U Street and in Harlem, meaning games, travel money, and acclaim would float their way.

But Hill and his teammates couldn't find the hoop in Manhattan Casino, and the Spartans rolled to an embarrassingly easy 44-22 triumph. Three weeks later, with Hill absent, Carlisle stumbled on the road again against highly regarded Hampton Institute 29-19. Just like that, the once impressive Carlisles were merely ordinary.

Off the court, Carlisle got little help from its new, fast-talking, twenty-three-year-old manager, Ewell Conway. Nicknamed "Soup," Conway operated a graphic design shop with Duke Ellington on T Street, near the Howard Theater, where they churned out promotional posters for movies, concerts, and basketball games. Though Conway was nifty with a paintbrush, he hadn't quite mastered the fine art of arranging basketball games, probably in large part because he didn't spread around enough money to ensure a profit for visiting teams. According to Conway, he had come close to luring the Spartan Braves, Boston Tigers, and Chicago Defenders to U Street, all of which would have been sell-out attractions. Instead, Ardneze Dash and his crew spent most of January idle.

In the meantime, Alco had struggled through front-office woes of its own. The team had a new booking agent named Robert Williams who, despite claiming to be a mover and shaker, soon showed that he would have been lucky to schedule a game against the local Moose lodge. By January, Williams had failed to book a single big-name attraction, despite Alco's preseason promise to its fans to transform itself from a small-time YMCA club into "one of the best teams in the country."[76]

By mid-January 1922, accustomed to a full winter slate of basketball during most of the past fifteen years, H. Scott of the *Washington Tribune* finally sang the blues. Writing under the headline "What's Wrong with Basket Ball in the District?," Scott urged Carlisle or Alco to finish the season with "some big circuit stuff," meaning flash some money and bring the best teams from New York, Pittsburgh, or Chicago to town.[77]

Conway's answer was to book the less expensive Holy Name Guild, an up-and-coming but inexperienced local black quintet, in Murray's Casino. Though the game attracted a "record" crowd, Carlisle recorded a zero for effort. "The Carlisles machine was clearly out of condition and only in the latter part of the game did it show any of the old time championship form," wrote the *Washington Tribune.*[78] Featuring three of the best young players in the city in Earl Frazier and the Davis brothers, Ed and Everett, all of whom would later join Carlisle, the Guild left Murray's Casino with a surprising 22-21 win and a legitimate claim to the 1922 city championship.

Conway and his Carlisles had dribbled themselves into a trap. The only way out was either to seek revenge against the Holy Name Guild or to throttle once and for all their old arch rivals from the local wartime YMCA league, the Alco Athletic Club. Conway, who had been hounding Alco for a game all season, opted for the latter. And so the stage was set for the championship rumble in Murray's Casino.

As Conway once quipped, Carlisle and Alco got along "about as good as a dog and a cat."[79] So it came as no surprise on this drizzly evening in March that when the diminutive referee Benjamin Washington, clad in his standard-issue suit and bow tie, tossed the basketball into the air to start the game, the cats started chasing the dogs. Or as Jay Bee mused from courtside, all hell broke loose.

"The game had all of the ear-marks of a genuine football game," he wrote. "There were center rushes, forward passes, off-tackles, end-runs and plays that savored of a footballish nature. Padded floors would have been a welcome addition. 'Twas hard to distinguish between [the] referee's whistle and the shrill screams of the enthusiastic flaps"—by which he meant the irreverent young ladies in the stands.[80]

Between the fumbles and forward passes, Alco managed on offense to swing the ball into the hot hands of Buck Carroll, its long-distance bomber, who singed the nets for fifteen points. Though Carlisle's star forward Benny Hill tried to answer Carroll, he could break through the airtight Alco defense for only seven points. When Benjamin Washington waved the game to an end, Alco had claimed a 25-19 win and sole possession of the 1922 city title.

By the time the stands finally cleared and Duke Ellington and his band started blowing their horns to kick off the postgame dance, a weary Jay Bee already had trudged home, feeling richer for his experience. "The game was a thriller from start to finish," he said afterward, joking again about the rough play: "Had the laps of some of the flaps been baskets, we would have been counting goals until now."[81]

Carlisle, however, had little to show on the positive side of the ledger for its night's work—or for its season's work, for that matter. Like the young Duke Ellington now motioning on the bandstand, the Carlisle players had begun the season with the look of stardom twinkling in their eyes. Conway had vowed to give U Street "the best that can be had" in basketball, but he and his team had hit all the wrong notes. If the Carlisles were to succeed, they would need to prove to the public that they were a team worth watching.

The Professionals Arrive

In the fall of 1922, Bob Douglas landed his big break. It came from a gabby, college-educated Irishman from Brooklyn named Jess McMahon, who swooped down over the off-season and, bucking tradition, organized Harlem's first big-time black professional basketball team, the Commonwealth Big Five. McMahon's stay in the game would last exactly two seasons, or just long enough to upstage the MBA and position professional basketball as the dominant game in town. More important, his departure would leave the door open for Douglas to step forward, snap up the remaining Commonwealth players, and anoint himself the new king of black professional basketball in New York.

McMahon's name had been synonymous with professional sports for more than two decades. Many remembered his ownership of the original Lincoln Giants, one of the most beloved black pro baseball teams in New York during the early teens. By the early 1920s, with a longstanding ban on boxing in New York recently lifted, McMahon moved full time to shilling Saturday-night boxing shows at his newly refurbished Commonwealth Casino, located on 135th Street in Harlem.[82]

Unlike most boxing promoters in New York City at the time, McMahon and his brother/partner Rod openly booked black fighters for their racially mixed cards, earning them bottomless praise in black newspapers. Jess, an incorrigible opportunist who had absolutely no civil-rights agenda, maintained in his cranky Brooklyn staccato that it was good business sense for an old sport like him to cater to black fighters in a black neighborhood.

It was this good business sense that attracted Jess and his brother to basketball. Uneasy that their Commonwealth Casino stood empty between boxing shows, earning them no money, the two promoters decided to scout around for other attractions.

By mid-1922, having committed to hosting weekly wrestling and roller skating shows, they had another idea: Why not start their own basketball team? The McMahons had seen firsthand while barking for customers on Saturday nights just how wildly popular basketball was in Harlem during the winter. At the same time, master New York promoter Tex Rickard recently had attracted huge crowds to watch his white New York Whirlwinds, a sign that professional basketball could be profitable.

The brothers knew that Strangler Forbes, once a shortstop on the McMahons' Lincoln Giants, and other top basketball players banned by the MBA were searching for a professional team. Harlem knew these players, Harlem loved them, and Harlem would support them—especially, as the McMahons calculated, if their team played on Sundays, as the old Lincoln Giants once had done, when businesses were closed and many Harlemites climbed the walls from boredom.

By early November 1922, having promised Harlem the moon, the McMahons rolled out the stars. They had hired defensive ace Forbes as the team's player/coach and surrounded him with a partial who's who of black basketball.

There was sure-shot Fat Jenkins and his springy-legged brother Harold; the human greyhound George Fiall; the steady Hop Hubbard, formerly with the Forty Club of Chicago; Specs Moton, a regular in seasons past with Loendi; the hot-tempered Leon Monde, an athletic marvel from Borough Athletic Club who was now banned by the MBA; and former Spartan center Hilton Slocum, who had run afoul of the MBA during the off-season.

Just like that, after years of fanatical infighting aimed at exorcising professional basketball from Harlem, the ghost of Will Madden was poised to wreak havoc on the amateur game. This time, St. C. mounted no counterattack. Unlike with the ugly demise of Little Napoleon, who was so hated and undercapitalized that the top amateur clubs could simply freeze him out of Harlem basketball, St. C. had no means to banish the McMahon brothers. The white promoters had capital, a stable of stars courtesy of the MBA, and connections with several of the top white teams in New York. These connections had the brothers poised to open Harlem to mixed-race professional games, including a promised showdown against the white world-champion Original Celtics that had Harlemites downright giddy.

Bob Douglas, meanwhile, had a few showdowns of his own in mind, although nothing as grand as a date with the Original Celtics. The Spartans, sorely missing Slocum, Forbes, Capers, and Sessoms, lacked the muscle to tangle with Commonwealth. But Douglas's team still could tackle its traditional rivals, St. C. and Alpha, and that gave Douglas an idea. As the new kid on the block, the Commonwealth Big Five would be vulnerable; and if his and the other longtime clubs could sell their fans on supporting the tried-and-true rivalries of amateur basketball, all three teams might have an easier go competing against the McMahons.

It seemed like a straightforward idea, yet when Douglas made overtures to schedule the games, St. C. and Alpha gasped at the very idea. To these two, once bitter rivals and now thick as thieves, Douglas was an infidel who couldn't be trusted to abide by the amateur rules or uphold the association's ban on Cum Posey. A loss to the Spartans would only help thrust Douglas back into the spotlight and sink them into an even deeper hole with the public. It was a chance they didn't want to take.

The situation came to a head on Thanksgiving night when St. C., under order by the MBA games committee to have its junior team square off against the Spartan juniors, backed out at the last minute, sending Douglas, the promoter of the event, scrambling to find a replacement. Douglas was livid. In an indignant letter to the *Amsterdam News*, he denounced the petty jealousy aimed at the Spartans and the cancellation that put him "in the role of hoodwinking the public" with a bait-and-switch preliminary game.[83]

Douglas's outburst fueled speculation that the Spartans had withdrawn from the MBA. While he denied it, Douglas fed the rumor mill when he agreed to match his team against a recently formed black professional team called the New York Defenders in the preliminary game before the Commonwealth Big Five main feature on New Year's Day, a clear breach of amateur rules. The MBA, which probably would have thrown the book at Douglas the year before, no longer seemed to care about the company he kept. Like in a marriage gone bad, both sides sensed that they needed to walk away from the other and get on with their lives.

But would Douglas walk away alone? Or would the Spartan Field Club join him in leaving the association? If the Spartans walked, MBA officials would have to contend with an angry throng of critics who claimed the association and its unyielding philosophy had poisoned the once harmonious amateur game. In recent weeks, several smaller MBA clubs had jumped the association for the brighter lights of the professional game, and if Spartan, one of New York's most influential black athletic clubs, also left, many believed the MBA would unravel. As Romeo Dougherty later explained, fans would never believe that the MBA "is working for the best interests of all concerned when they fail to see Alpha, Spartan, and St. Christopher engaged in friendly contests."[84]

The answer came on the night after Christmas. In a polite, three-paragraph letter, club secretary Edgar Mercer informed the MBA that Douglas's Spartan Braves had voted to leave the association and finish the season as an independent team. Though the low-profile Spartan juniors remained under the MBA umbrella, Mercer's letter left little doubt that the members of the Spartan Field Club now backed Douglas and accepted his decision to leave the MBA and, in essence, yank them out of the association, too.[85]

The MBA downplayed the departure, clinging to the belief that it would survive because of its positive moral influence in the community. Romeo Dougherty wondered: Who would watch a fading amateur association that had handed its best players to the pros in favor of fielding what in years past would have passed for untested junior teams? He warned: "In basketball . . . the crowd will go to see the professional games because the men are well up in the game and there's no thought of any crowd cheering for 'the game's sake.' They are with the proficient players and this thing of trying to tell us about a National Game and having us believe that it comes from a true love of the sport is all bosh."[86]

How right Dougherty was. While attendance plummeted at the amateur games, the lines in front of the McMahon brothers' casino grew longer by the week. "Now it is considered 'the thing' to see Georgia [sic] Fiall, 'Fat' Jenkins, Hilton Slocum, 'Hop' Hubbard, Leon Monde, and 'Strangler' Forbes appearing against the best," wrote the Amsterdam News.[87] With this star-studded lineup, many predicted the Commonwealth Big Five had the talent to wrest the black championship from Cum Posey with one hand and grab the white world championship from the Original Celtics with the other.

At first, few could quarrel with the predictions. Though the Commonwealths dropped a couple of games on the road, including an embarrassing loss to the black Vandal Big Five of Atlantic City, Harlem's darlings were nearly invincible on their home floor. How invincible, though, is hard to tell. Too many of the games wound predictably down to the wire, an old ploy in which the better team would keep the score close to hold the interest of the fans. Blowouts as a rule were considered bad for business.

Newspaper accounts suggest Commonwealth, while clearly one of the top black teams in America, probably packed more punch on paper than in person. Part of the problem might have been poor conditioning in these days when work schedules often interfered with practices. Some of it was personnel. Strangler Forbes, the team's player/coach who was nearing the end of his career, showed that he had lost a step, and impatient fans fumed at his tired substitution patterns that always seemed to leave him rooted on the floor in the fourth quarter at the expense of the quicker, more entertaining Leon Monde.

On December 10, the discontent erupted into open rebellion when, according to the New York Age, the Commonwealth crowd "was yelling"[88] from the opening whistle of a victory over the white Professional Collegians for the Strangler to park himself on the bench. Seven days later, the fans declared war. During a much ballyhooed rematch against the white Perth Amboy Five, the only team to defeat the Commonwealths on their home floor, fans heckled the stubborn Forbes for refusing to

pull himself from the lineup and helping the New Jersey state champions slip past Commonwealth for a 29-24 victory.

Sensitive to the boos, the McMahon brothers dismissed Forbes as
coach after the debacle and replaced him with popular Commonwealth
star Fat Jenkins. Business was business. The Strangler would squeeze
out a few more cameo performances with Commonwealth, then retire
for good at the end of the season, closing a basketball career that, perhaps more than any other of his era, could never escape controversy.

Despite the midseason shake-up, Commonwealth kept the victories
coming. On January 14, the McMahons' men schooled the Bronx Collegians for a third time that season 51-24 behind the whirlwind play of
Jenkins. A week later, Fat swished a last-second runner to lift his club
to a dramatic 26-24 overtime victory over the Italian Catholic Five, one
of the better teams in New York City with a lineup that oddly enough
featured three Cohens, a Lindbloom, and a McKew.

While the crowd filed out of the Commonwealth Casino after the
win, a short, well-dressed white man could be seen weaving his way toward an exit. He was Jim Furey, manager of the New York–based Original Celtics, the defending champions of the Eastern League, the top
professional circuit in America. Always searching for new kingdoms to
conquer, Furey had exchanged handshakes with the McMahons that
night for his Original Celtics and the Commonwealth Big Five to tus-
sle in Harlem on March 4, marking the first game ever between a top
black and a top white team.

The handshake had been an expensive one. Though no records remain of the financial arrangements, the McMahons probably had
greased Furey's palm with a generous cash advance, which they clearly
hoped to recoup at the box office. Tickets sold for $4.10 each, a more
than 350 percent markup from the standard 55 cents to attend other
Commonwealth games, or roughly the cost of a ticket to hear the New
York Philharmonic.

The McMahons also agreed to two questionable concessions that all
but negated the Commonwealths' home-court advantage. First, the referee for the evening would be the veteran Chick Meehan, who called
most of the games for the Original Celtics at Madison Square Garden,
the team's home court. Second, Meehan would call the first half under
the one-dribble-and-shoot AAU rules, which the Commonwealths had
used all season, but the second and deciding half would be played under
the anything-goes professional rules that the Original Celtics used.

Still, many Harlemites couldn't contain their glee that finally the best in something that the white sports world had to offer had agreed to face a top black team. Ever since white America snatched back the heavyweight crown from Jack Johnson, black folks had been waiting for the day when black athletes would have a chance to compete against whites again at the highest levels of sport.

"The McMahon Brothers will repair with a heavy committee of leading [black] citizens before [New York City] Mayor Hylan to ask that a legal holiday be declared if the Commonwealth Five defeat the Original Celtics," joked Romeo Dougherty.[89]

When the big night rolled around, Will Madden could be seen in the stands eyeing the largest turnout ever for a basketball game in Harlem, and no doubt daydreaming about what might have been for his defunct Incorporators. By 10 P.M., the crowd erupted, and out lumbered a line of large white men clad in lucky shamrock green: Nat Holman, Horse Haggerty, Johnny Beckman, Pete Barry, and Chris Leonard.

"For fully 10 minutes the cheering could be heard for blocks," wrote the *Chicago Defender* of the pregame warm-ups, which had many Commonwealth fans gaping at the girth of the broad-shouldered white champions. "The Commonwealths shaped up like babies in comparison to their white brothers, which caused much comment among the fans. Many were of the opinion that the white boys would make a runaway of the game."[90]

A runaway it wasn't. For most of three quarters, the smaller Commonwealths tested the Celtics. Fiall hit a few clutch shots, and Fat Jenkins hoisted a few more to pull the Big Five to within a point, 24-23. The veteran Celtics, however, were unfazed. In this day of no shot clocks to hasten the action, the white champions kept lofting the ball to center Horse Haggerty, who wheeled and dealed until one of his teammates—usually Holman or Beckman—broke free and he could whip him a pass for an easy basket. By the fourth quarter, the flawless, machinelike execution of the white champions had ground down the less experienced Commonwealths, and the Original Celtics cruised to a 41-29 victory.

Though the Commonwealth players were disappointed with the outcome, many fans were upbeat about the evening. "The Celtics found themselves in one of their hardest games when they played the McMahon players and they so confessed after the final whistle blew," wrote Romeo Dougherty,[91] echoing the opinions of other black sportswriters.

As historic as the game was, it also marked the beginning of the end for the popular Commonwealth Big Five. The man who would bury them already was well known to Jenkins, Fiall, and the others. In fact, he had attended the Commonwealth-Celtic game, dissecting the Big Five's on-court tendencies with the cold, calculating eye of a paid assassin. His name was Cum Posey.

Posey originally had been standoffish, condescending even, in his negotiations with the McMahons to bring his Loendi ball club to New York. But his caution turned to defiant anger during the Commonwealth-Celtic game. With the mighty Posey seated at a courtside press table in full view of thousands of fans, the announcer introduced the Commonwealths to the roaring crowd as "the colored champions of the world," a slap in the face to the five-time defending black champion Loendi club.

"Posey's face turned an ashen hue," commented someone sitting nearby.[92] Although the temperamental star forward never explained his sudden change of heart, he hastily inked a two-game contract and duel for the 1923 black professional basketball championship.

The declaration of war called for game one to be played in Pittsburgh on March 16, followed two nights later by a rematch in the Commonwealth Casino. It also called for the black professional championship series to be contested under amateur rules, one of Posey's pet demands in past negotiations with the McMahons. As crazy as it sounds today, it was quintessential Posey. Why meet the Commonwealths on even terms if he could negotiate an advantage? In this case, the one-dribble-and-shoot amateur rules would slow down the game—and more important, the speedy Fat Jenkins—placing an emphasis on a more sedate pass-and-shoot game, a style of play that better suited Loendi.

Why the McMahons caved in to Posey remains a mystery. Yet many basketball fans believed that if the Big Five arrived in Pittsburgh with its "A" game in tow, the club had a legitimate shot at beating Posey's powerhouse. Fiall and Jenkins had dominated the opposition all season long, and the older Loendi guards Greasy Betts and U. S. Young would need to play the games of their lives to stop them. Commonwealth center Hilton Slocum also seemed capable of holding his own against the taller Legs Sessoms, and while the young Loendi bank-shot artist Pappy Ricks still had his best years ahead of him, Posey had reached his early forties, when the wear and tear of a long career often became painfully obvious.

Despite all the heartfelt pleas for victory, the Commonwealths choked in the infamous City of Smoke. The amateur rules might have had something to do with the New Yorkers' funk, but the *Amsterdam News*'s Dougherty suspected that the Commonwealths had yet to recover from the disappointment of the Celtic loss. In any case, Jenkins and crew couldn't have chosen a worse time to wallow in past misfortunes. Loendi, riding the hot hands of Sessoms and Ricks, showed no mercy as it rolled to a 51-27 victory to claim the opening game of the 1923 black championship series.

In Harlem, a season of high hopes spiraled into despair. Another winter, another basketball title for Pittsburgh. Still, fifteen hundred diehard fans filled the Casino for game two in the hope that Commonwealth would somehow find the magic to cast a spell on Posey and his team. In the first half, the post-Celtic slump continued. "The Commonwealths displayed about as poor a brand of basket ball as has been seen at the Casino this season," wrote the *Chicago Defender*.[93] "They were slow and didn't seem to be able to get out of their own way."

Having buried themselves in a 23-8 hole at halftime, the Commonwealths retreated to their locker room prepared to face the inevitable when play resumed. Original Celtics manager Jim Furey, who sat in the house that night and whose team would play Loendi in a few weeks, had seen enough. He reportedly marched to the Big Five locker room and snapped off the reasons that the team could come back and beat Loendi. Furey's advice invigorated the Commonwealth cagers, and according to the *Chicago Defender*, "the second half found the Commonwealths fighting for all they were worth."[94] Fiall knocked down three or four hoops in a row, and to the delight of the crowd, the home team drew within striking distance. Would this be the Commonwealths' night after all?

But Posey and his pugs had been through the drill many times before. Long, tall Legs Sessoms, who Dougherty later described as playing "like a house afire," answered by scorching the nets for two baskets, followed by a ringer from Posey and a greaseball from Greasy Betts. With the lanky Sessoms winning all the after-basket jump balls, Loendi controlled the basketball, the clock, and the crowd.

Commonwealth had no answers to stop the juggernaut. Adding insult to injury, Posey's men went into a stall in the closing minutes, tossing the ball to and fro in an infuriating game of keep-away. Despite the boos raining down onto the court, Loendi closed out its 43-33 victory and claimed its sixth straight black world basketball title, a string then unequaled.

Posey might have won the title again, but Harlem didn't have to like it. "Revelling in her pound of flesh, Pittsburgh wins both games," groused a headline in the *Amsterdam News*.[95]

But Dougherty, an outspoken foe of everything Posey, soon reveled in a little gristle of his own. John Roan of Xenia, Ohio, had tapped out a letter to the *Amsterdam News* claiming that because his local black American Legion team had defeated Loendi earlier in the season, the black title rightfully belonged in the Buckeye State.[96] Dougherty championed the idea, writing that the Legion club had beat Loendi fair and square. The *Chicago Defender* seconded the notion, noting that the Legion boys were a worthy all-star contingent of Chicago and Cincinnati cagers, including Olympic athlete Sol Butler, that should not be overlooked.

Posey steamed in silence, knowing that none of these barbs would matter if his team could defeat the Original Celtics in an upcoming showdown. But it was not to be. The Celtics routed Loendi 48-27. As a *Pittsburgh Courier* headline summed up the passing skills of the white champions: "Bewildering play of Celtics too much for Loendi quintet."[97] This game, like the Commonwealth-Celtic contest before it, was proof that despite the many fine teams in the black game, none could match the offensive prowess of the top white teams.

Back in Harlem, whether the black title belonged in Pittsburgh or Ohio was irrelevant to the Commonwealths. Despite the team's impressive 75-15 record, despite the big crowds, despite the victories over several good white teams, only one fact seemed to matter: Commonwealth had failed to defeat Loendi. In fact, the team closed out the season with an uninspired 35-21 loss at home to the Original Celtics in early May, as Fat Jenkins missed the game with a case of pneumonia.

With the loss, the first full year of professional basketball in Harlem came to an end. As the newspapers had predicted before the season, the amateur game was in a funk and showed no signs of snapping out of it. In the meantime, Bob Douglas seemed to be seriously toying with the idea of launching his own professional team. It was a crazy notion on every level. How could he possibly compete against the McMahon brothers? They had money, the best players, and connections to white teams throughout New York. But as anyone who had bumped up against Douglas's steady resolve knew, it was even more foolhardy to bet against him.

FOUR

The Rise of Professionalism

1923
1930

Opening Night at the Renaissance Casino

Harlem, January 8, 1923. With a tap and a swish of conductor E. Gilbert Anderson's baton, the Renaissance Theatre Orchestra roared off after another melody. Men in cummerbunds and women in spangled gowns shimmered to the dance floor, where they shook their hips and surrendered their souls to the sweet sensation of the Shimmy, the Black Bottom, and other popular, devil-may-care jazz dances of the 1920s. And why not? They were making history. Tonight, Harlem had thrown open the doors to what was hailed as one of the finest black-owned ballrooms ever built in America.

While the band played on, several well-wishers gathered round to shake the hand of William Roach, the father and founding manager of the Renaissance Casino.

A native of the tiny Caribbean island of Montserrat, Roach had come to the United States several years earlier, flat broke and fueled only by his desire to succeed in America. In June 1918, after working odd jobs, he launched a housecleaning service in Manhattan. The business boomed, and four months later Roach laid his mop aside, hoping to prosper as president and general manager of a new cooperative real-estate venture, the Sarco Realty and Holding Company.

Though he had every reason to fail in the high-stakes, cut-throat world of real estate, Roach proved to be a shrewd businessman. By 1921,

Sarco reportedly boasted nearly fourteen hundred stockholders and numbered among its assets at least four fashionable Harlem apartment houses, including the Renaissance Apartment on Seventh Avenue.[1]

Harlem—the nation's "Black Mecca"—was evolving into a bustling, after-hours jazz theme park, and Roach smelled money. In 1921, he opened a movie house called the Renaissance Theatre at 137th Street and 7th Avenue, a stone's throw from the Renaissance Apartment. Roach and his investors banked on the idea that the 950-seat first-run theater would wow Harlem with its elegant interior and jazzy house orchestra that, according to the *New York Age*, rivaled "the first class Broadway Theatres."[2]

Wow the theater did, and Roach soon sank more of Sarco's profits into his next and even more grandiose project: the Renaissance Casino Building, a two-story red-brick structure at the corner of 138th Street and 7th Avenue. The bottom floor would house the only black-owned department store in the city, and above it Roach promised the grandest race-friendly casino and ballroom in Harlem.

After months of costly construction delays, Roach kept his promise. With a motion-picture camera rolling in the background to record the moment, he threw open the doors to his gleaming ballroom for a gala that included a beauty pageant, music, dancing, plenty of toasts, and handshakes all around. As the black intellectual W. E. B. Du Bois would remind cynics in speeches later that winter, when black people put their minds and their wallets to a task, the results could be spectacular.[3]

Spectacular did not necessarily mean highly lucrative. Roach knew that in the coming months his plush casino would face stiff competition from other ballrooms, theaters, and nightclubs. No longer was it enough in Harlem to hire a polite society orchestra to attract a crowd. These were the roaring, anything-goes twenties, when the self-proclaimed dukes and divas of rhythm hi-de-hi-de-hoed Harlem off each night to a lush life of jazz and cocktails. How could Roach and his polite Renaissance Theatre Orchestra survive against the show-stopping antics of Billy Higgins, Flo Mills, Bessie Smith, Duke Ellington, and the other jazz and blues superstars then making the rounds at other Harlem night spots? It wasn't going to be easy.

Roach also had to remember where he conducted his business. In the great melting pot of Harlem, clannish southern blacks and native black New Yorkers often balked at throwing their support behind businesses run by their island brothers.

Just ask Arthur Hart, a Jamaican immigrant and the keeper of the five-and-dime store on the first floor of the Renaissance Casino Building. As Roach made the final preparations to open his Renaissance ballroom in January 1923, Hart announced that the bank had foreclosed on his store, a failure that some contended owed not to the shortcomings of Hart, but to the reluctance of the black American majority to support a Jamaican establishment.[4]

To avoid the same fate as Hart, Roach would need a gimmick, a one-of-a-kind attraction that would have New Yorkers lining up in the snow for a chance to see the show. Though Roach didn't know it as he stood there shaking hands on opening night, his red-hot attraction would not ride roughshod over a piano keyboard or breathe fire into a saxophone. It would be a one-of-a-kind basketball team headed by a fellow West Indian immigrant named Bob Douglas.

Smiling Bob Douglas Turns Pro

As the 1923–24 season approached, Bob Douglas knew that he had reached a crossroads. Should he retire as a basketball promoter after almost twenty years of toiling in the amateur game? Or should he take a chance and plug his entrepreneurial hopes into Harlem's now dominant professional basketball circuit? He would be taking a huge risk competing against the wealthier McMahon brothers, with whom, as the *Amsterdam News* noted, players knew "their money is assured each and every week."[5]

With encouragement from his many friends at the Spartan Field Club, Douglas reached a decision. He would follow in the footsteps of Major Hart and Will Anthony Madden as a professional promoter. God help him, he would go toe-to-toe with Jess McMahon, Jim Furey, Cum Posey, and the other double-talking mavericks of the money game.

When Douglas announced his decision in October 1923, he no longer worried about dodging the MBA. St. Christopher, Alpha, and their amateur partners had scrapped the ill-fated association, relinquishing control of New York black basketball to McMahon and the professional game.

"The MBA is dead, indeed it should have died a-borning," wrote the *Pittsburgh Courier's* W. Rollo Wilson in a good-riddance eulogy decrying the "buck-passing" and "double-crossing" that plagued amateur black basketball in New York from the late teens to the early 1920s. "It was actuated and motivated by ambition, selfishness and greed. When it failed to uphold its own rules when star players were the guilty ones the death knell was sounded."[6]

While Douglas was innocent of any charges of selfishness and greed, he was guilty of ambition. It was his willingness to field a lineup of tainted amateurs and his deep-seated desire to best Cum Posey that had worn out his welcome in the MBA. And it was the force of this ambition that ultimately estranged Douglas's Spartan Field Club from the MBA, poking a hole in the association's delicately spun political fabric.

The irony was that by outlasting the MBA, Douglas now carried on its legacy. At age forty-two, Smiling Bob was the lone surviving New York old-timer in the modern professional game, a suddenly nostalgic figure whom fans revered as having lived and breathed the glory days of the amateur game.

Even the *Courier's* Wilson, a critic of everything Gotham, tipped his hat to Douglas. In the fall of 1923, Wilson dubbed him "Harlem's Roderick Dhu," referring to the legendary founder of an ancient Scottish clan. It was a suggestion that Smiling Bob reigned supreme as the founding clansman of New York's black amateur game[7]—an assertion that no doubt rankled many at the clubhouses of Alpha, St. Christopher, and Smart Set, where New York's black game originated.

Douglas had no time to waste contemplating his place in basketball history. With the 1923–24 season just weeks away, he still had no home court where his new set-shot-shooting clan could protect its honor. Manhattan Casino, once the Madison Square Garden of the black game, had fallen on hard times since Prohibition and the shutdown of its once lucrative bar. Management had jacked up the rent on the place, all but pricing it out of the basketball market. In protest, St. C. had played all its home games at the nearby New Star Casino for the past two seasons. Though no longer a force in big-time basketball, St. C. and its influential sponsor, St. Philip's Church, would have no part of Douglas's whisking its Red and Black Machine off its home floor. The same went for Jess McMahon and his Commonwealth Casino.

The obvious solution was William Roach and his beautiful Renaissance Casino. Douglas knew the ballroom well, having played at least one game there in 1923 against the New York Defenders. He also might have known that Roach was not keen about continuously opening the doors of his pristine palace to the so-called "Gallery Gods," the scruffy, leather-lunged pranksters who staked out the cheap upper-balcony seats at basketball games and rained down a torrent of salty catcalls that made the higher class folks in the lower balcony squirm with embarrassment. Roach feared that if, as sometimes happened, a fight broke out on the court, the Gallery Gods would trash the ornate interior of his casino, stiffing him with an unwanted repair bill.

In October 1923, Douglas made his pitch to Roach about hoisting a pair of basketball goals onto his eighty-nine-by-one-hundred-foot dance floor and bouncing out a few warm-up games before the late-night dancing commenced. As Douglas later recounted, Roach waved him off. "I asked him about having a team there and he said, 'Definitely not. You guys will play rough basketball and those rough crowds will break up my place.'"[8]

Douglas countered that the real issue was a chance for Roach to make money. As Douglas saw it, he was the one who arranged games and paid the teams, so Roach had nothing to lose with the arrangement. In fact, he had a lot to gain. By hosting an early-evening basketball game at no cost to himself, Roach stood to fill his casino with paying customers for the featured late-night dancing, assuring him that he would amass enough cash from the large basketball crowd to pay the band and even walk away at the end of the night with a little extra in his hand. At the very least, Douglas said, his professional team would bring loads of good publicity to the new Renaissance Casino, just as his amateur squads had done once for the fledgling Spartan Field Club.

Roach eventually caved in to the idea.[9] But Douglas consented to two key demands. First, Roach would receive a comfortable percentage of the gate, though the exact cut remains unknown. Second, for the sake of publicity, the team would have to be named after the Renaissance Casino, a demand that Douglas honored by calling his club the Renaissance Big Five, or Big R Five for short.

With his home court now settled, Douglas entered a field already populated by many talented black professional and semipro ball clubs. Some of the names still stir the imagination: Philadelphia Flashes, Memphis Comets, Grand Central Red Caps, Hell Fighters, Philadelphia Panthers, Vandals of Atlantic City, Baltimore Athenians, Harrisburg Scholastics, Cleveland Acmes, Carlisle Big Five, and Peerless Big Five.

However, the 1923–24 championship race boiled down to the same two high-powered teams: McMahon's Commonwealth Big Five and Posey's Loendi. From all indications, this once contentious-but-civil rivalry had turned downright ugly. In August 1923, Jess McMahon declared that he was "determined to have the best basketball team in the country next season."[10] McMahon, the wealthiest promoter in black basketball, said he already had lured Loendi star Legs Sessoms into the Commonwealth camp for the upcoming season, and negotiations were under way to sign Loendi's Pappy Ricks.

The likely losses of Sessoms and Ricks, the catalysts of Loendi's victories over Commonwealth, had to have been painful for Posey. But his ego must really have taken a hit when Will Accoe of the *New York News* crowned the Commonwealth Big Five the de facto world champions for the upcoming season. That pronouncement came in the wake of a Romeo Dougherty broadside in the *Amsterdam News* bearing the headline "Once Famous Pittsburgh Basketball Team All Shot to Pieces, Says Report" and a similarly worded blurb in the *Baltimore Afro-American*.[11]

Posey scoffed at the preseason smear campaign. "Despite rumors, hopes and fears, Loendi will be on the court this basketball season," he announced in a letter to Dougherty. "Each season Loendi is threatened by opposing all-star organizations, but the only result is 'a new star uncovered by Loendi.'" Posey assured Dougherty that Loendi already had several new stars waiting in the wings to join the club's "three undisputed All-American men"—Pimp Young, Greasy Betts, and himself—and that a seventh straight world title for Loendi was not out of the question.[12]

With all the preseason posturing, something had to give. That something was the Commonwealth Big Five. On October 14, 1923, the Big Five—clad in shiny new silk uniforms and hamstrung by the same old glaring weaknesses of unrealistic fan expectations, poor team chemistry, and greed—opened its second season at home against the white Ascension Aces.

The greed factor flared on opening night with none other than the "New Jersey Kangaroo" himself, Pappy Ricks. After agreeing to play for the Commonwealths, Ricks backed out of his commitment during training camp when Posey promised to sweeten the pot to keep his star in Pittsburgh. The McMahon brothers, not to be outbid, countered with another offer, putting Ricks in the middle of a tug-of-war that he hoped to tweak to his own financial advantage. But Ricks soon misjudged his strength at the bargaining table when he balked on signing a contract with the McMahons, then loped into the Commonwealth Casino a few nights later carrying his equipment bag to face the Ascension Aces. The McMahons, angry and feeling used, told Ricks no thanks and "advised him to continue on his way to the City of Smoke."[13]

With Ricks out of the mix, Commonwealth fans pinned their championship hopes on the celebrated newcomer Legs Sessoms. But when the former Loendi star struggled in the first few games to adjust to his new teammates, the impatient Gallery Gods attacked him with a vengeance. By early December 1923, Sessoms thought he had endured enough of their wrath. He and teammate Specs Moton broke their contracts and headed back to Pittsburgh.

Left behind was a Commonwealth contingent comprised of an odd assortment of something old, something new. The old were the stalwarts from the previous season—Fat Jenkins, George Fiall, and Hop Hubbard. The new were rookie players Stretch Grant, a tall New Yorker fresh out of high school; Six Garcia, a former St. C. junior team member who got his nickname because "he couldn't score seven"; and Roy Noel, who had jumped center for Cincinnati's Peerless Big Five in seasons past.

With so many newcomers on the court zigging instead of zagging, Commonwealth struggled to find its rhythm. Though the team ground out wins in most of its early-season games, the Big Five hardly looked like the unbeatable machine that Jess McMahon had advertised in August—and people started talking.

"'The New York basketball champions,' Commonwealth Five, do not look so good to us, brothers," wrote Wilson of the *Pittsburgh Courier.* "It seems that Jenkins and Fiall must carry five men's burden. That is too much for a pair of giants and those boys are almost midgets in size, you must remember. That lineup can't stand the gaff, folks."[14]

Nor did it as the season progressed. In February, Commonwealth faced the Original Celtics for the third time in two seasons. With a victory over the mighty Irishmen, Fat Jenkins and his mates stood to redeem themselves from the tarnish of their lackluster season. But redemption was not to be. Nat Holman, Horse Haggerty, and their fellow shamrocks once again painted the Commonwealth Casino emerald green, skipping to an easy 40-28 victory before two thousand mostly disgruntled fans.[15] The *New York Age* downplayed the drubbing, but the loss must have stung the McMahon brothers, especially since Loendi had battled the Original Celtics down to the wire that same week before falling 42-39.[16]

With Loendi's superior performances against the Original Celtics and other big-ticket teams, Posey's club seemed ready to claim the 1924 title as the best black team in America. By March, though Loendi had dropped a game to the black Vandals of Atlantic City, not even Romeo Dougherty, the editorial thorn in Posey's side, could quarrel with Loendi's runaway championship credentials. As the *Washington Tribune* wrote after watching Posey's juggernaut earlier in the season, "It looks like another Loendi year."[17]

Had Commonwealth lived up to its championship billing, Bob Douglas might have lost his shirt in his first season of professional basketball. As Dougherty had warned before the season, Harlem basketball fans already had hopped aboard the Commonwealth bandwagon, and it was unlikely that "another big colored team" would rally any support.[18]

But with Commonwealth in a state of unrest, Douglas showed once again that he was a promoter extraordinaire. He scheduled the Big R Five's home games on Saturday nights, or twenty-four hours before the Commonwealth Big Five contests, which allowed him to hold the first basketball shootout and dance of the week. He also had the leg up on the Grand Central Red Caps and his other lesser known rivals by booking his team's games in the most stylish hall in Harlem.

That's not to say the Renaissance Casino was an ideal venue for basketball. With fewer seats than Manhattan or Commonwealth Casinos, the Renaissance Casino also generated less cash. This meant that Douglas couldn't survive for a few weeks feeding off the fat of a lucrative matchup, especially with Roach skimming a percentage of the night's proceeds off the top. Douglas had to pack the house every week to meet his payroll—or else hear the threats of Roach, his players, and opposing teams. As Dougherty predicted, "Two [financial] failures at the Renaissance and the team will go to pieces."[19]

As Douglas prepared for his Big R Five's debut in the Renaissance Casino on November 2, 1923, he pulled out all the stops.[20] He booked the white Collegiate All-Stars for the contest, probably knowing, as Dougherty wrote, that interracial contests drew well in Harlem and cost less to book than a top black team like Loendi. More important, Douglas milked his popular new image as the grand master of Harlem basketball. Newspaper advertisements touted none of the court magicians who would be in uniform on opening night, stating instead that the Big R Five was "under the personal management of 'Smilin' Bob' Douglas."[21]

Douglas's strategy of self-promotion worked. The Big R Five not only defeated the Collegiate All-Stars 28-22 before a large opening crowd, it earned the vows of delighted fans to mark next week's game on their calendars. "Every indication points to a much larger house next Saturday night as the thrill of a contest, added to good dance music, will attract even more when those who were present go out and tell of the evening's enjoyment," wrote Dougherty, who admittedly had a soft spot for Douglas.[22]

By focusing attention on himself, Douglas also eased some of the pressure on his team, which was probably a good thing. Though he had hoped to retain his old Spartan club name in the pros, Renaissance proved a better fit for his fledgling five. Most of the players were castoffs—or in modern parlance, free agents—hoping for a rebirth of their past glory on the court.

No one hoped for a second chance more than the thirty-two-year-old team captain, Strangler Forbes, who had been ousted as the leader of the Commonwealths and booed into semiretirement during the 1922–23 season. Joining him on the Renaissance roster were Kid Slocum, the Commonwealth ace who came running to Forbes and Douglas when Jess McMahon signed center Legs Sessoms during the off-season; the hot-tempered young forward Leon Monde, whom Commonwealth had released the previous year for berating referees during games, which the McMahon brothers feared was bad for business; and Hooks Wallace, the former Spartan veteran who had faded into the twilight of his career.

By midseason, Douglas's band of free agents enjoyed their own renaissance on the basketball court. Forbes bounced back to earn cheers for his hard-nosed play. The same went for Slocum, Monde, and early-season acquisitions Harold Mayer, a former St. C. junior team stalwart and defensive specialist cut from the same cloth as Strangler Forbes; Tucker Waddell, once a star forward on Alpha; and center Hy Monte.

With a catchy lineup, capacity crowds, and contented Gallery Gods, Douglas thought his team was ready to shoot for the greatest challenge of its maiden season. He signed on for a grand finale championship series of Harlem, pitting his Big R Five against the Commonwealths, with the first game scheduled for late February in the Renaissance Casino.

In game one, Douglas and his men found themselves overwhelmed by the suddenly hot-shooting Commonwealth Big Five. Stretch Grant mocked the Rens with fifteen points as Commonwealth copped a 38-35 victory.[23] Two weeks later at the Commonwealth Casino, it was Jenkins's turn to make faces at the Rens. Fat knocked home fourteen points in leading his club to a decisive 31-21 victory and a quick and easy sweep of the series.[24]

Harlem newspapers carry no mention of how the McMahons reacted to wearing their new crown. But as the months passed, it seemed to be with a shrug. Defeating Douglas and his first-year team had never been on their preseason agenda. Rather, the McMahons had staked their basketball future on dethroning Loendi and the Original Celtics, and their team had bombed on both counts. Even more troubling, the Commonwealth Big Five rarely sold out its Sunday-night home games, despite battling some of New York's top white teams and even slashing its ticket price from seventy-five to fifty cents at midseason.

Ever mindful of the bottom line, the McMahons had to wonder whether their third season would be even more of a financial bust. Jess McMahon didn't stick around to find out. Just as quickly as he had formed his all-star quintet two years before, he disbanded the Commonwealths and returned full time to shilling his Saturday-night boxing shows, still a popular attraction in Harlem.

By the mid-1920s, Jess would close the Commonwealth Sports Club and move to midtown, where he served as matchmaker for the legendary Madison Square Garden boxing promoter Tex Rickard. In the 1930s, McMahon switched to professional wrestling, and he sold the thrills and spills of body slams and sleeper holds for the next twenty years. When he died suddenly in November 1954, his son Vince McMahon continued in the wrestling business. Vince Sr. eventually passed the baton to his son, Vince Jr., who today reigns as the czar of the multibillion-dollar World Wrestling Entertainment empire.

With the McMahon name today synonymous with pay-per-view wrestling, almost forgotten is the fact that Jess, the patriarch of the family, brought down amateur basketball in Harlem. As Will Anthony Madden stated, the seeds of professionalism in Harlem had been sown long before McMahon's arrival; and the professional game likely would have taken root with or without him. But McMahon was the man who accelerated the process, and without him, black professional basketball might have taken several more years to develop properly in Harlem.

Here's to You, Wendell Phillips

April 21, 1924. One by one, the tall young men cast a glance through the doorway into the Oval Office. There he was, President Calvin Coolidge himself, as dignified as a banker in a dark suit and tie, managing the country's business like his personal stock portfolio.

It was a glimpse of power that few ordinary black teenagers ever got to experience in these separate and unequal times. But these were no

ordinary black teens being escorted through the White House by prominent Illinois congressman Morton Hull. These were the members of
the Wendell Phillips High School basketball team, runners-up for the
1924 Chicago city title. They were in town to tour the White House,
stroll the National Mall, and, in about eight hours, battle Washington's
Armstrong Tech for the first national championship of black high school
basketball.[25]

Unlike today, neither team had ended the season atop a national poll
or tournament to earn the right to compete in the championship game.
The *Chicago Defender* simply had requested a game in Washington on
behalf of the Phillips team, and that was enough. A national championship game it would be.

Nevertheless, few could have quarreled with the selection of Phillips.
As Calvin Coolidge and his staff saw firsthand, all its players except one
stood more than six feet tall, a collective height that was unheard of in
the five-foot-something world of 1920s prep basketball. Leading the
charge for Phillips was six-foot-four All-Chicago center Reuben Spears
and six-foot-two fellow Goliaths Dennis Simpson and Lester Johnson,
all of whom could dribble, pass, shoot, and rebound with dexterity.

Playing in the unsegregated Chicago public school league, these giants from the South Side had bested a who's who of white teams during
the regular season only to fall in the city title game to Crane Tech, led
by a black all-city cager of its own. They rebounded from this bitter defeat to trample Kansas City's Lincoln High School for the mythical black
title of the Midwest. And now they planned to return home as national
champions, too.

If any black high school team in America could give Phillips a run for
its money, it was Armstrong Tech. Armstrong was engineered with the
pep and precision of a Stutz Bearcat racer. Led by seniors Harry "Soup"
Turner and Sam Lacy, Armstrong ran a fast-breaking offense and alter-
nated between man-to-man and zone defenses, both of which were innovations rarely seen in the 1920s. With its progressive approach to the
game, the Orange and Blue had raced to back-to-back 19-4 seasons and
two straight black city championships. Numbered among the victims was
every top black high school quintet from Baltimore to Bordentown, New
Jersey, and several college and club teams to boot, including an improbable win over U Street's championship semipro team, the Alco Big Five.

Though Armstrong's tallest player stood just a shade under six feet,
roughly five inches shorter than Spears, most folks on U Street swore

that size didn't matter. Armstrong still had plenty of speed to burn, and with a few steals here and a few baskets there, David would slay Goliath. It was money in the bank, they said. So much so, in fact, that the local oddsmakers had Armstrong penciled in as the favorite to cop the national championship.

As the big night neared, most fans had never witnessed a basketball promotion like this one, both in scale and in substance. Local promoters James Fletcher and Victor Daly paid a bundle to rent Convention Hall, then the grandest public hall in Washington. And they spared no expense to import Harlem's world-famous, thirty-member Clef Club Orchestra.

With this mix of first-class entertainment and championship basketball, the night couldn't go wrong. By seven P.M. the crowd began arriving, and the people just kept coming and coming. Young and old; male and female; some well dressed, some hardly dressed. All told, according to the *Washington Herald,* more than four thousand fans filled Convention Hall, by far the largest crowd ever to witness a black basketball game in Washington.[26]

At precisely 10:20 P.M., the Clef Club Orchestra having finished its first set, referee Ed Henderson motioned the contenders to center court for his pregame instructions. A moment later, Armstrong's five-foot-ten Soup Turner shook hands with Reuben Spears, Henderson tossed the ball into the air, and Convention Hall erupted.

"Deafening applause greeted the start of play," wrote the *Chicago Defender* in a rare play-by-play account of the big game. "Spears took the tip-off and knocked it to Wright. The ball was worked down towards the basket which Armstrong defended. For a full minute and a half Phillips kept the ball there.

"[Chicago's] Eaves missed a close shot at the basket and hurt his hand when he fell against the post [backboard support]. Ball still in Armstrong's territory, Spears took the ball away from a Washington player only to lose it himself. Turner brought Armstrong's followers to their feet by dribbling all the way down the court only to miss a try. The ball went out of bounds."

Before the crowd could catch its breath, however, Goliath roared. "On the toss-in Johnson bluffed a short pass, then heaved the ball over the heads of Armstrong's players the entire length of the floor to Spears, who had got clear 10 feet from the basket. It was an easy shot for the Chicago player and the play stunned the Armstrong followers."

When Phillips wheeled back on offense, Spears showed again why he was the most dominant player on the floor. "Eaves tossed in to Spears, who, in turn instead of making a shot, forced Armstrong to make a quick play on him, and Spears made a quick pass to Simpson, and in the ball went without touching the rim."

By the start of the fourth quarter, Goliath held a 12-6 advantage. It still was a surmountable lead, but as the *Washington Herald* wrote, the Armstrong players "seemed over anxious in their shooting" and showed no signs of being able to stop the Chicagoans.[27]

"The Phillips players . . . frustrated us during the game by keeping the ball in the air and out of our reach," remembered Armstrong's Sam Lacy nearly seventy years later.[28]

Orchestrating the aerial attack was Spears, who had played most of the game with a nasty gash over his eye from catching a stray knee during a pileup. Bloody and battered, Spears rattled home another basket to start the fourth quarter, then won the ensuing center jump. As the *Defender* noted, Phillips immediately snapped off "some clever passing" until the ball squirted out of bounds beneath the Phillips basket. "Wright tossed it in to Simpson, the Chicago boys keeping the ball and Johnson seeing Spears loose, again pulled another length of the floor pass to Spears and a basket resulted. Phillips 16, Armstrong 6," wrote the *Defender.*

Just when its hopes of victory looked bleakest, Armstrong's Neagie Ellis answered with a basket to trim the score to 16-8. Seconds later, Ellis canned another shot to cut the margin to 16-10. Convention Hall rang with cheers. Had the oddsmakers been correct all along? Would Washington speed prove mightier than Chicago height?

Not with big Reuben Spears jumping center after Ellis's basket. Spears easily tipped the basketball to a teammate, who heaved it ahead until Dennis Simpson held it and the hearts of thousands of Washingtonians in his hands.

"Twenty seconds left," wrote the *Defender.* "Phillips passed it away in some clever passing stunts." Ten seconds. Referee Henderson eyed the clock, then issued the final shrill blast of his tin whistle. The game was over, and Chicago had claimed the nation's first black high school basketball championship 17-10.[29]

Within minutes, a Western Union telegram sailed into the offices of the *Chicago Defender* bearing the good news. Shoulders were slapped, hands were shaken, and glasses were raised. And the celebration didn't stop that night. Two days later, when the team members arrived at

Chicago's Dearborn Station holding the silver championship trophy like it was made of gold, a small army of revelers awaited them.

As drums beat and horns wailed, Spears and company marched off the train in triumph and headed for a line of waiting taxicabs. The taxis lurched forward in a slow, hand-waving, hat-tipping procession back to the South Side, where "a rousing reception" awaited the champions.[30]

It was a fitting final tribute to one of the great black high school teams of the 1920s. But for seniors Spears, Simpson, and Johnson, their basketball careers would continue for at least four more years. They had decided before the Washington trip to attend Howard University in the fall, a decision that had many in Convention Hall thinking that Phillips's performance had been a preview of wonderful things to come for Howard's team, which had fallen on hard times during the early 1920s. The dream was that Spears, Simpson, and Johnson would ring in the opening of Howard's new gymnasium with a series of championships that would restore the Bisons to their past glory on the hardwood.

It was a dream that would never come true.

The Saga of Reuben Spears

Reuben Spears today probably wouldn't garner a single vote on anybody's list of all-time great high school players. In fact, most voters wouldn't know his name or recognize where he played high school ball. But in 1924, Spears was a force to be reckoned with in any prep gym or recreation hall in America. He towered over his peers, overpowered them with his size, dazzled them with his athletic ability, and above all, showed them that he understood how to play the game at both ends of the floor.

Had Spears graduated from high school a half century later, major college scouts might have camped on his front stoop just to say good morning to him. But in 1924, Spears, an All-Chicago center and arguably the best black high school basketball player in America, probably couldn't have gotten five minutes alone with any major college basketball coach in the country to plead for a scholarship. As sad as it seems today, integration still was out of the question in the all-white world of major college basketball.

For Spears, an idealistic teenager with his life still ahead of him, this had to be a bitter pill. He had spent his entire high school career without incident battling for rebounds against white kids named Carney and Calahan. Just ten sweaty guys in sneakers trying to slide a slippery leather ball through a shiny iron ring. No more, no less. Then, as college approached, the rules changed. His skin color suddenly defined him, excluding him from the same opportunities that loomed so readily for lesser white players.

It was as though Spears had been "shut out of their world by a vast veil," as W. E. B. Du Bois once described the division between black and white society.[31] Spears could watch his former white gym mates from afar, praise them, curse them, even sit in the old-time college field houses and cheer them. But an insidious force prevented him from descending the bleachers and joining the fray.

So in 1924, the high school player of the year in black America had three options to continue his basketball career. One, he could suit up at night for the talented Wabash Avenue YMCA team, which he had helped to the 1922 and 1923 state titles. Two, he could hitch his star and wallet to one of the traveling black semipro teams then making the rounds. It was an option that he already knew well, having filled in for a few games with the barnstorming Chicago Defenders during high school. Or three, Spears could attend Howard University, thanks probably to the influence of his high school coach Albert Johnson, an alumnus of Howard. Since black colleges lacked the funds to scout prospects, Howard relied on loyal alumni like Johnson to recommend promising out-of-town prospects for partial scholarships.

Spears opted for Howard and a college education, and by the fall of 1924 he had begun attending classes at Howard.[32] He was joined on campus by his former high school teammates Dennis Simpson, Lester Johnson, and another Chicagoan named Phillips. These four tall, strapping freshman were quickly dubbed by their fraternity brothers the "Four Horsemen," the popular nickname for the fabled Notre Dame backfield of 1924.[33] Just as surely as had Notre Dame's Four Horsemen ridden roughshod over college football that season, these four freshman phenoms would dominate Howard's interfraternity basketball league, then a wildly popular campus pastime.

As promised, Spears and his teammates wreaked havoc on the league that winter. But surprisingly, the Four Horsemen chose not to join the Howard Big Five in 1925, and instead formed their own semiprofessional team, the Chicago Dribblers. Why Howard would recruit Spears and his buddies then allow them to barnstorm through hill and dale is a mystery.

The *Washington Tribune* noted that the Dribblers had scheduled games as far north as Bridgeport, Connecticut,[34] and by season's end, the newspaper wrote that Spears's club had given "the fans plenty of high class action for their money" and was one of the more popular teams on U Street.[35]

With such high praise, Spears might have forsaken college for the juicier and more immediate spoils of professional basketball. But by late 1925, with his partial scholarship still to honor, Spears traded in his barnstorming ways—or at least promised to curb them for a few months—to play center on Howard's 1925–26 varsity basketball team.

In exchange, Spears earned the dubious honor of joining a storied college quintet that for several seasons had teetered on the brink of disaster. The club's first near death experience had occurred in January 1922 when the Howard Athletic Board abruptly suspended its once great basketball program until further notice. The official reason was the school's lack of a gymnasium. As the argument went, how could Howard produce a top-flight basketball team if it had nowhere on campus to practice?

But Howard had managed just fine without a gymnasium in the years when Hudson Oliver, Ed Gray, and George Gilmore toyed with the opposition. And maybe that was the point. Since Gilmore's departure in 1916, Howard had fared poorly against most college teams. Rather than admit parity, the Howard Athletic Board packed up its basketball and went home—proud, prissy, and proposing to build a gymnasium of its own.

In January 1924, with plans for the gymnasium solidified, the athletic board had restarted the basketball program, fully expecting a return to greatness. But black college basketball had evolved since the glory days of the Howard Big Five. There were more teams, more players, more rules, more regulations, and far more reasons to bicker over right and wrong. Though the Bisons would finish their first season with a respectable 4-2 record, prompting the *Washington Tribune* to write that Howard "will again be . . . classed among the best teams of the race," their young coach John Burr soon would discover that the politics of sports often was more important than what happened on the playing floor.[36]

Trouble arrived on December 12, 1924, when, depending on the source, Howard either withdrew or was tossed from the Colored Intercollegiate Athletic Association in a dispute over the eligibility of a Bison football player. Ten years earlier, the Howard-CIAA tiff would not have made much of a splash. Skeptics would have shrugged off the new association as just another pie-in-the-sky idea that was fifteen years ahead of its time.

But in the 1920s, as black collegiate sports had taken root and strong rivalries had blossomed socially and at the box office, Howard's withdrawal was viewed as cataclysmic. Letters and editorials flooded black newspapers, some pointing fingers, others pitching self-doubt. Would a viable black version of the Ivy League or Big Ten ever reach fruition? Or would politics and the pathology of competition poison the process?

No textbook in the world could have prepared Burr, a college-educated physical education teacher, for the zaniness of the 1925 season. With just two weeks before the start of his team's twelve-game season, Hampton, Lincoln, and his other CIAA opponents canceled their contracts with Howard. As the *Washington Tribune* reported, they had no choice. The CIAA had blackballed Howard, prohibiting its member schools from playing the Bisons under the threat of expulsion.[37] To top everything off, Spears, Simpson, and Johnson had decided to sit out the season in favor of starting their own semipro team.

Burr, a polite, twenty-five-year-old New Englander, managed to salvage the season by booking mostly road games against Wilberforce, Storer, Morgan, and West Virginia State Colleges, all of which were still unattached to a league.[38]

Lincoln, meanwhile, walked out on the CIAA to continue its lucrative annual football game against Howard, then considered the Rose Bowl of black college football. More important, Howard's new gymnasium would open in late February 1926, meaning Burr's team would finally have a home of its own.

Into this mess stepped Reuben Spears in the fall of 1925. The uncertainty surrounding the season must have left him at least a tad frustrated; but Reuben had played on winning court combinations all his life, and there was no reason to believe that he couldn't win at hard-luck Howard, too. Coach Burr had assembled one of the school's finer quintets with Spears at center, team captain Bill Lawton and the steady Louis Coates at forward, and a tenacious trio of guards in Dennis Simpson, Archie Berry, and Lester Johnson. Though there was no league title to chase that year, Burr had to believe that with Spears working his magic on rival centers, the Howard Big Five had a chance to dominate black college basketball in 1926 and for years to come.

On December 11, the Reuben Spears era at Howard debuted on the road against the semipro Baltimore Athenians in the crowded New Albert Auditorium. In these days of low-scoring games, Spears dropped home seven points for his new team, tying him for the high-scoring honors, but the Athenians roared back from a one-point deficit in the final thirty seconds to nip Howard 27-24. A few nights later, back on the road in the Waltz Dream Auditorium, Spears scored just four points but Howard still took the measure of the previously unbeaten, semipro Philadelphia Flashes 25-24.

After Howard rang in the new year by uncorking on Storer College 44-12, Burr's next challenge was to defeat the much improved Morgan Bears twice in a row. If his players could subdue their neighbors from Baltimore—a big if—Howard still would have to contend with Wilberforce and Morehouse, the other powerhouse college teams. But with a little luck and consistently dominating performances from Spears, Howard could finish the season undefeated against its college rivals, a big step toward reestablishing its dominance of the sport.

On January 13, Burr and his Bisons traveled to Baltimore to tame the Bears. Once the laughingstock of black collegiate sports, Morgan now was numbered among its small athletic empires, thanks to the infectious, rah-rah personality of its young athletic director, James Law. So serious had Law been about transforming the college into a football and basketball powerhouse that, according to the *Philadelphia Tribune,* a Morgan coed who once openly rooted against the Bears was forced to apologize publicly to the coach, the team, her dean, and the entire student body.[39]

In 1926, Morgan had built its team around Ed "Lanky" Jones, a brilliant six-foot-two freshman center. Jones, a native of New Orleans who migrated to East Orange, New Jersey, as a teenager, was a two-time all-state selection in high school. But like Spears, Jones found no takers at the white colleges. Off to Morgan he went, where his long arms, uncanny sense of timing, and nonstop energy already had given slower opposing centers fits.

According to the *Baltimore Afro-American,* nobody had beaten Morgan all season, and on this night, Howard wasn't up to the task either, falling 25-18. For Spears, the loss must have hurt. Basketball had been so easy for him growing up; he had always been the tallest, the strongest, and the most skilled kid scrapping on the court. But against the frenetic Jones, Reuben had landed in foul trouble early and finished the game without tallying a single point.[40]

On January 23, Lanky and the Bears loped into Lincoln Colonnade on U Street for game two against Howard. For Burr and his players, a win would mean Howard was back in the quest to become the best college team of the 1925 season; a loss meant they were out of the running, a scenario that few could have imagined when the Four Horsemen rode proudly into Washington two years earlier.

Remembering his star center's early foul trouble in Baltimore several days earlier, Burr benched Spears to start the game, a questionable move that had predictably disastrous results. Without Spears tugging on his jersey, Lanky drained the opening shot of the game and, according to the *Washington Tribune*, "then made another field goal from a difficult angle" before Burr motioned down the bench for reinforcements.[41]

Into the game trotted Howard's three remaining Four Horsemen—Spears, Simpson, and Johnson. With Spears and the rough-and-tumble Simpson leading the charge, Howard kicked and clawed its way back into the game by halftime to trail 18-13. Then Lanky stole the stage. Cradling the oversized basketball between his wrist and forearm, Lanky snaked his arm through the air as though he were waving a brown derby in a vaudeville show.

The once hostile crowd roared in delight at this flashy stunt. "He is the only basketball player in colored basketball that can handle a ball with one hand," wrote the *Baltimore Afro-American* of Lanky's trademark move, which he used to dazzle the crowd, unnerve his defenders, and flip the ball to open cutters. "In the words of a Howard player, 'how can we beat them when he can handle a ball like that?'"[42]

They couldn't. Morgan cruised in the second half to a 32-23 win. Spears finished with eight hard-fought points, but as the *Philadelphia Tribune* wrote, Jones "outplayed Spears" and "was easy the star of the game."[43] Five games into its season, Howard's national championship hopes had been dashed.

By April, Dean Mohr, the coach at Wilberforce College who published an annual college All-American team, named Lanky Jones first-team All-American at center. The Morgan club clearly was the team of the year in 1926, having hammered all comers except, oddly enough, lowly Lincoln University.

Spears got the nod for second-team All-American center, having averaged just over five points per game, tops in the Howard club.[44] But he suffered in comparison to Jones.

"Jones is in perpetual motion while on the floor, and is one of the few players that can stand the terrific 40 minutes grind without showing signs of fatigue," wrote the *Baltimore Afro-American*. "He has all of the requisites of a natural player: height, speed, stamina, and what is known as a 'basketball eye' [an intuitive sense for the game]."[45]

As the *Washington Tribune* wrote, "Spears is outshone by his rival Jones because the Lanky Oriole is without reasonable doubt the best pivot man in present day basketball. This, of course though, does not mean that Spears is not a great center—he is."[46]

Indeed, Spears remained a coveted commodity for a variety of black teams. He had continued to star in fraternity basketball circles, and he also commanded the close attention of professional teams.

Though Spears might have been hard-pressed to earn a spot on the Renaissance Big Five or Cum Posey's veteran club team, he easily could have joined other semipro combinations in Washington, Baltimore, Philadelphia, and Chicago. In fact, several of his former high school teammates would soon barnstorm through Wisconsin, and a former Howard player had just signed to play with a new Chicago-based club called the Harlem Globetrotters. The Globetrotters planned to tour the back roads of Illinois that winter in a Model T Ford driven by their gabby, five-foot-something white owner Abe Saperstein, and Saperstein was always looking for top young talent like Reuben to ride along with them.[47]

Though professional basketball and its promise of a regular paycheck remained a temptation, Spears stuck to his decision to pursue his college education—and, in the winter, keep up with the likes of Lanky Jones.

On December 10, 1926, Howard again opened its season in New Albert Auditorium against the semipro Baltimore Athenians. This time, riding its solid defense and fourteen easy points from Spears, the new team captain, Howard dominated the game from start to finish and cruised to a 31-24 victory. For the next month, the newspapers mentioned nothing about Howard's travels. Any games that the team might have played in December were merely a prelude to the Bisons' big home opener and grudge match against Morgan, now coached by Charles Drew, a young Washingtonian who would later win international fame off the court for revolutionizing the science of blood banking.

It took less than a minute for Morgan to score; the *Washington Tribune* wrote, "Jones broke away and caged a neat one-hand shot over Captain Spears's head." After Morgan guard Cutie Brown sank one of his long heaves, Spears gathered himself and went to work. He caged two

field goals in succession to knot the score at four, and for the next fifteen minutes, both teams grabbed and grimaced until the referee whistled the first half to a close with the scoreboard showing thirteen apiece.

To start the second half, the ref decided to clean up the game,
whistling Brown and his Morgan teammates again and again for rough
play. But Howard, flat from intermission, shanked its free throws, hit-
ting just two of ten in the third period.

Meanwhile, the crafty Jones continued to outbattle Spears for jump
balls, tapping the orb to Morgan forwards Mars Hill and Pinkey Clark,
who sliced to the basket to create a 20-15 advantage for the Bears. Running these and other plays wasn't always easy in a hostile gymnasium,
though. "On several occasions Morgan players were held in the crowd
while the game was in progress," wrote the *Washington Tribune*.
"Wheatley and Jones were actually held by their arms and were prevented from participation while their teammates battled against the
local odds."[48]

In the end, the Morgan players battled the local odds—and fans—
well enough to claim their third straight victory over Howard, 24-19.
Though Spears held his nemesis to only four points while scoring six
points himself, Jones nevertheless catalyzed the win in the second half
with his well-timed taps and leadership, leaving Reuben once again
standing in his shadow. As even the partisan *Washington Tribune* joked
afterward, "Headed by Lanky Jones—who, by the way, can do as much
with a basketball as Dr. Smith can do with indigestion—the 1926 collegiate champs showed that they have lost none of their old-time skill."[49]

In February, Howard traveled to Baltimore for another crack at Morgan. Sensing a classic confrontation was in store, eager Baltimoreans
mobbed New Albert Auditorium before the game, a scene that Hall of
Fame sportswriter Sam Lacy, then a cub reporter, captured:

> After a severe mauling [from the crowd] we finally succeeded in
> being shoved in one direction we want to go. Women are crowding
> the box office like it is a bargain counter, and after securing our
> pasteboards [tickets] we are pushed one way and then another until
> at last some kind hearted person gives us, collectively, a gentle nudge
> which carries us to the stair way leading to the playing court. . . . On
> the steps we are hard pressed to keep from being run over as every-
> body is rushing head over heels with the single determination of get-
> ting himself or herself that which has been minus since long before
> 8 o'clock—a seat.[50]

For those who finagled seats, the first half was as torrid as any game ever seen in the hall. "Both teams were playing real basketball but were somewhat handicapped by the tremendous crowd that swarmed the playing court," wrote Lacy. "The lightning-like passing by both teams brought great uproars from the fans. Coach Burr's men were checking on the defense [alternating between zone and man-to-man to confuse Morgan]. . . . Captain Lanky Jones for Morgan realizing the situation, called time out and talked some things over with his team. From this point on Morgan was master of the situation."[51]

Master of the situation and the game. Morgan rolled on to its fourth straight victory over Howard, 27-13. Spears, suffering through another horrible performance against Jones, failed to score a single point, while nonstop Lanky laced nine points, logged another solid floor game, and aroused the now standard postgame encomiums.

However, when Spears strolled out of New Albert Auditorium later that evening toting his equipment bag, he had plenty to think about besides Lanky Jones. His old friend and Howard teammate Dennis Simpson had dropped out of school before the Morgan game to play pro ball with the Baltimore Athenians, whose ambitious manager reportedly also planned to sign the popular Olympic long-jump champion DeHart Hubbard and Wilberforce's court sensation Wu Fang Ward. In short, the Athenians planned to go big-time on the barnstorming circuit, and with his own offer from the team on the table, this was Spears's chance to make some dough.[52]

Spears had heard all the grandiose, run-don't-walk promises before. Still, he clearly was tempted by the offer. Playing for the Athenians meant he could forget about exams for a few months, travel the country, and fatten his wallet. Burr would be there waiting to take him back for the 1928 season, just as he had been waiting after his stint with the play-for-pay Chicago Dribblers. Who else did Burr have to play center?

Though Hubbard and Ward would decide not to play with the Athenians, Spears already had made up his mind. He quit the Howard Big Five in midseason, dropped out of college, and became the newest member of the Baltimore Athenians.

It was a decision that would become his curse.

On March 13, in Spears's second game with the team, the Athenians lost in Atlantic City to the black Buccaneer Five. Spears scored eight points. As was often the case in the no-frills world of pro basketball, Spears and his teammates had orders to pile into the big sedan that was

waiting outside the arena after the game and journey back to Baltimore
to save on hotel costs.

While the players settled in for the four-hour ride home, their driver,
Erwin Hokerman, pulled the sedan onto White Horse Pike, just outside
Atlantic City, and headed west toward Philadelphia. A steady rain pat-
tered against the windshield, and thick fog clouded Hokerman's vision.
It was a horrible night to be on the road, and maybe that's why Hokerman didn't see the large panel truck stopped in the roadway directly
ahead. Though Hokerman pumped the brakes at the last second, the
sedan plowed into the back of the truck. A few seconds later, a third car
that had been behind Hokerman barreled into the wreckage.

Miraculously, nobody but Spears was injured seriously. The impact
of both crashes had twisted him around, snapping a bone in his leg and
probably causing a compound fracture of his right ankle. A motorist who
happened upon the scene drove Spears about ten miles to Atlantic City
Hospital, where doctors immediately admitted him for treatment.

No records exist today on whether Spears, as a young black man, received adequate care at the hospital. From all indications, he didn't.
Within two weeks of his hospital stay, Spears contracted scarlet fever
in the wound near his ankle, a possible sign that the doctors had practiced poor hygiene. With the discovery of penicillin still decades away,
a deadly bacterium ravaged his body unchecked. In late April, doctors
wheeled the former Howard star into the operating room, his mother
standing heartbroken outside, and amputated his right foot to remove
the source of the infection. "Doctors have every hope that the removal
of the foot will be all that is necessary and that a speedy recovery is
sure," wrote the *Chicago Defender*.[53]

Spears eventually returned to Chicago and his mother's home on
Calumet Avenue, frail and broken, with his promising basketball career
finished, his partial scholarship withdrawn, and his hope of obtaining a
college degree evaporated.

Why Not Fat Jenkins?

In the early 1920s, the Commonwealths' Fat Jenkins was a nightmare
for most opposing teams to defend. At five-foot-seven and built like a
fireplug, the twenty-six-year-old left-hander possessed the brute
strength to break free from the grab-and-hold defenders of his day and
the pure speed to blow by them. Once in the clear, Fat tortured de-

fenses. Having learned the game from Jeff Wetzler, a former college player who had coached the St. C. Red and Black Machine during the teens, Fat could pivot, pass, and shoot with the best—white or black.

So when the McMahon brothers opted out of professional basketball at the end of the 1924 season, why didn't either Jim Furey or his brother Tom, the brains behind the Original Celtics, pick up the telephone and make an offer to Jenkins?

As the owners of an independent, family-run team, the Fureys had no mandatory league color lines to stop them. Nor were they unaware of Jenkins's prowess. Having sat courtside at Commonwealth Casino on several occasions, the Fureys certainly had noticed Jenkins tie defenders in knots, and they easily could have imagined that the fleet-footed Jenkins would be unstoppable slashing to the hoop in a Celtics uniform behind the broad hind haunches of the 240-pound Horse Haggerty.

The easy answer is the Fureys weren't desperate to sign Jenkins. The Original Celtics already were loaded with talented veterans, and as owners of the best and probably highest paid team in America, the Fureys could afford to be choosy.

But by all indications, Jenkins would have been a nifty, low-cost addition to the Original Celtics, and so the question remains: Why would the Furey brothers want to be choosy about signing Jenkins? Were they simply old-fashioned racists who didn't want to suffer the indignity of seeing a black man on their team? It's unlikely. The Fureys never drew the color line to avoid playing Loendi or Commonwealth. Neither did they seem particularly threatened by the entry of black teams into the professional game. It was Jim Furey who once roared into the Commonwealth locker room to deliver a "beat Loendi" halftime speech, an indication that he viewed Jenkins and company as peers.

The better answer is the Fureys were businessmen, not social reformers. As the owners of a proud Irish-American basketball team, they had to field a squad that looked at least a wee bit Irish. Though the Fureys could get away with slapping a shamrock on the chest of a white Jewish player such as Nat Holman, they would have faced a tough sell putting the dark-skinned Jenkins into a green-and-white uniform.

The Fureys also would have had trouble convincing their fans that integrating the team was the right thing to do. In New York, as in the northern cities and towns where the Original Celtics barnstormed, most whites had been exposed to a lifetime of talk about the necessity of keeping their black neighbors segregated, respectful, and under control.

As the black writer Charles Johnson described life in the "liberal" North in 1925:

A Negro worker may not be a street or subway conductor because of the possibility of public objection to contact but he may be a ticket chopper [puncher]. He may not be a money changer in a subway station because honesty is required yet he may be entrusted, as a messenger, with thousands of dollars daily. He may not sell goods over the counter but he may deliver the goods after they have been sold. He may be a porter in charge of a sleeping car without a conductor, but never a conductor; he may be a policeman but not a fireman; a linotyper, but not a motion picture operator; a glass annealer, but not a glass blower; a deck hand, but not a sailor.[54]

A black professional basketball player, but not an Original Celtic. The Fureys could play against black pro teams without fights breaking out in the stands. In fact, white fans expected the Original Celtics, as the best white pro team in the country, to humble the best black teams—otherwise, interracial games never would have been staged. But that was different from signing Jenkins and appearing to champion integration. Some in the crowd wouldn't have liked having the issue foisted upon them, and the Fureys and their players wouldn't have liked the extra tension on the road. To keep up appearances, the Fureys played it safe when the Commonwealth Big Five folded and passed on Jenkins.

The Die Is Cast

Jim Furey's loss was Bob Douglas's gain. In early October 1924, Douglas secured commitments from Jenkins and former Commonwealth star George Fiall, the so-called "Heavenly Twins."[55] They joined a solid supporting cast in center Kid Slocum, the team captain and playmaker, and the high-energy guard tandem of Six Garcia and Harold Mayer.

For Douglas, life couldn't have been sweeter. His second-year team was as fast as lightning, the McMahons were out of business, and Harlem was his for the taking on Saturday nights. His only threat at the box office came from a team managed by former track star Roy Morse and bearing the borrowed name of the defunct Commonwealth Big Five. But Morse's team never caught on and would be gone by the end of February, an example of how fast teams came and went in the topsy-turvy world of black professional basketball.

Douglas got down to business. By January 1925, he had his club playing three and sometimes four nights a week, a radical departure from
the days when his amateur Spartan teams dribbled out ten to fifteen
games a year. The more games played, the more money Douglas and
his men stood to pocket. But there also may have been a more calculated reason. By booking a slew of weak black and white teams, inter-
spersed with a tough game here and there, Douglas and his Rens could
pad their record. More wins meant more fans, more hoopla, more
shoot-for-the-moon promotions, and more reason to close out the season with a bang.

Shoot for the moon the Rens would. In early March, with the club
sporting a heady 60-8 record and young star Pappy Ricks now also in
the lineup, Douglas announced to his growing legion of fans that the
Kingston Colonials and the Original Celtics, two of the top white teams
in basketball, were coming to Harlem. Two games, two bangs, two more
reasons to hop aboard the Renaissance bandwagon.

In Harlem, the mood was upbeat but noticeably different from that
surrounding the big interracial showdowns of the past. Gone were the
adolescent swoons and self-doubt that had prevailed when the Original Celtics invaded the Commonwealth Sports Club two years earlier
riding the emerald-green haunches of Horse Haggerty. For the first
time, local fans seemed sure their boys could best any team that dared
to enter Renaissance Casino. It wasn't overconfidence; it was pride.
Pride in the Renaissance's then undefeated home record during the
1924–25 season. Pride in Jenkins, Fiall, Slocum, and others groomed in
the local amateur clubs who had "made good" as professionals. And
pride in Bob Douglas, who in the spirit of the Harlem Renaissance had
cultivated one small slice of Harlem life and elevated it to "world-class"
entertainment.

On March 10, when the Kingston Colonials straggled onto the
makeshift court for their pregame tosses, most Harlemites probably believed the Renaissance Big Five would prevail. But they knew it wasn't
going to be easy. Kingston had won the world basketball championship
two years before by beating the Original Celtics two out of three games,
a feat no other team could claim. To make matters worse, Kingston
coach Pop Morgenweck had brought a secret weapon with him to
Harlem. He was Benny Borgmann, a former Colonial and one of the
most feared set shooters in the game. Benny had been handcuffed by
the Rens' defensive ace Harold Mayer in two previous matchups, and

tonight, with Kingston's bulky front line pitching elbows for him, Borgmann no doubt intended to teach Mayer a lesson.

But before Borgmann and his brutes knew what hit them, the shorter and speedier Renaissance Big Five had ducked and jabbed to a 24-14 half-time lead. Outside on Seventh Avenue, word spread that the Douglas boys had the Kingston Colonials on the ropes, and the streets emptied into Renaissance Casino, where the turnstile hoppers squirmed and squeezed into stairwells, atop radiators, anywhere, just to be able to say the next day that they had shared in the euphoria of the final twenty minutes.

Kingston, however, was far from finished. The Colonials slowed the pace of the game to start the second half, settled into their ball-control offense, and sank a shot. Then another. And another. Twelve excruciating minutes later, Morgenweck's club had ground out a 12-2 run, tying the score at twenty-six and sending a nervous rumble rippling through the house. Had Morgenweck and his boys been faking it? Had they let the Rens race ahead to keep the sold-out crowd interested, planning all along to breeze to victory in the final few minutes?

"Then like a bolt of lightning from a clear sky came the New Jersey Kangaroo, Pappy Ricks," wrote the *Amsterdam News.* "With unerring aim, Ricks measured his basket and sent the sphere whizzing through the basket without touching the rim. It was one of those long shots that would bring to life most anybody and the Kangaroo doubled the trick before the people had time to subside with their screams and whoops."

Pappy had spoken, and Morgenweck had no answer. When referee Jack Murray tooted the game to a halt, Ricks had scored thirteen points, Mayer had shut down Borgmann, and the Rens had outlasted the Colonials 39-31 for their greatest victory ever. "Pandemonium broke loose," wrote the *Amsterdam News,* and more than one fan no doubt let the wishful words ring out: "Bring on the Original Celtics."[56]

Kid Slocum and his Renaissance men believed they could compete against the white world champions. "That loss at Manhattan Casino carried no sting as the Douglas men looked upon the contest in the nature of a test of their ability and Captain Slocum and his men left the court that night satisfied they had at last arrived in the sacred circles of big time basketball," wrote the *Amsterdam News.*[57]

On March 22, their fans got their wish. They got the Original Celtics.

For the first twenty minutes, the Rens had two thousand true believers balancing on the edges of their seats as they answered the world champions bucket for bucket. "I thought the rafters would come down and the walls burst through with the noise and enthusiasm that was displayed," wrote Will Anthony Madden of the crowd's reaction when the Rens scored.[58] Pappy Ricks ended the first half with a then eye-popping seventeen points, most off of quick feeds from Fat Jenkins.

With the pro-Renaissance crowd hollering for more, the veteran Celtics shook off the cobwebs and trotted out for the second half ready to defend their Irish honor. The Celtics switched Dutch Dehnert, one of their crafty, barrel-chested veterans, onto Ricks, and the Renaissance's young star disappeared for the rest of the game. As the Rens discovered, the Celtics knew all the spins, all the angles, all the shots—and the balls just kept falling and falling for a 49-38 victory.

"To the real student of basketball, it could be seen that the famous Celtic team was playing under wraps," wrote Madden, who watched the game perched atop a radiator in the sold-out hall. "They scored when they pleased and they missed when they pleased, and they loosened up when they pleased. . . . Personally, I believe that the Celtics purposely missed their last try for a foul goal to prevent the score from reaching 50 points, which would look too overwhelmingly in print . . . the Celtics have so much weight and strength and such a wealth of basketball brains that they could have doubled the score against Renaissance if they had so desired."[59]

Though many dismissed Madden's remarks as the green-eyed musings of a basketball promoter scorned, he probably spoke the truth. Douglas built the Renaissance Big Five in the image of the black game that he knew so well. His players were short, relatively lightweight, and fast.[60] They were sprinters, not bruisers.

But as Douglas had seen firsthand, the Celtics and the other top white teams relied far more on height and brawn than black teams did. And with no shot clock ticking in the background to speed up the action, these bigger, slower teams settled into ball-control offenses, in which speed was a luxury, not a necessity.

"The five-man offense is based primarily on individual ability to handle and pass a basketball and on the necessity of keeping the ball and the entire team in motion until the opportunity presents itself for a quick break to the basket by one of the players," explained Nat Holman in a 1930s textbook that described the general principles underlying the Celtics' ball-control offense.[61]

What made world champions of Holman and the Celtics was their ability to improvise on their set ball-control offense with unexpected cuts to the basket and pinpoint passes that opposing defenses were powerless to stop. "They pass the ball without looking where it is going, as they know one of their mates will be there to receive it," wrote the *Washington Herald* after watching the Celtics play cat and mouse with the white Washington Yankees. "They dart here, there, and everywhere in cutting around the pack to win a position to toss."[62]

Or as U. S. Young, the longtime guard on Cum Posey's Pittsburgh teams, put it: "When you read an account that says 'The Celtics scored at will' that statement is literally true. Until I watched and studied them at play, I never realized that it was possible to play the game as they play it."[63]

To compete against the Original Celtics, the Renaissance needed desperately to give Slocum, the team's only six-footer, a hand in the middle against the brawny Dehnert and six-foot-five Joe Lapchick. In some ways, this was the easy part of the equation. Douglas now could leverage his team's tip-top reputation to sign a promising big man and develop him. In fact, in the fall of 1925, Douglas would add Stretch Saunders, the tall center for the Atlantic City YMCA, the only black team to upset the Rens during their second season.

The harder part of the equation would be ramping up the team's execution on the court. On defense, just playing the Celtics on a more regular basis would go a long way toward learning how to stop them, especially with Mayer, a defensive Johnny-on-the-spot, in the lineup. Not only had Mayer shut down Benny Borgmann for three straight games, he also had stymied Nat Holman, a key cog in the Celtic attack.

On offense, the Rens needed desperately to refine their passing attack. They needed to pull together and play as five men moving and thinking as one. They needed the same intuitive oneness, the same five-part harmony that the Celtics had. If the Rens could rise to the occasion, the Celtics would have to defend the Rens for forty minutes straight, a strain for a veteran and often road-weary team.

According to legend, after Bob Douglas signed the contract for his first game against the Celtics in 1925, he declared, "Well, the die has been cast."[64] Put another way, the Renaissance Big Five now had the time and opportunity to take the measure of the Celtics. Assuming a solid big man could be found to win center jumps, the Rens faced a historic opportunity to meld the superior team speed of the black game with the sophisticated ball-control tactics of the white game. If these two different styles meshed, the Rens' offense would run as seamlessly as that of the top teams in the white game. At the same time, they would have a competitive edge over the Celtics in being a step or two faster in executing their offense.

Harlem's Team

For Romeo Dougherty, the dapper young dean of the nation's black sportswriters, the Renaissance Big Five transcended mere set shots. The Rens were Harlem's team, the good guys with the Gothic "R" stitched across their chests, who in just two seasons had upstaged Cum Posey and returned the black championship of the world to Harlem.

Though the Rens and Posey's Loendi had never met due to scheduling difficulties, Dougherty wrote in his newspaper columns that only a fool would dispute the Rens' claim to the black championship. They boasted three of the premier offensive weapons in the black game in Jenkins, Fiall, and Ricks, and Dougherty crowed that Douglas's club had toppled more top white teams than any other black quintet in history. And the latter point mattered. After a dozen years of watching the latest black court sensations fall like gnats against the bigger, taller, slower white teams, Dougherty finally could point to a Harlem outfit with the speed and skill to defeat the likes of the Kingston Colonials and other ranking members of New York's all-white Metropolitan Basketball League, one of the top professional circuits in America.

For Dougherty, simply competing wasn't enough. As a black man and a West Indian immigrant who had spent too many years bedeviled by the injustice of a racist society, Dougherty wanted it all. He wanted the black champions to beat the white champion Original Celtics and prove that given an equal opportunity, black athletes could defeat the best in the white world. Jack Johnson had proven it with his fists. DeHart Hubbard had proven it recently in the long-jump pit. And, God willing, the Renaissance Big Five soon would prove it on the basketball court.

When the new season tipped off in October 1925, Dougherty seemed upbeat, almost cocky, about the prospects for the Rens. "I have no fear in predicting that the biggest season since they started will be the reward of the Renaissance Five," he wrote after Douglas's team christened its new campaign by thumping the white Perth Amboy Five on the road and the white Bronx Stars at home.[65]

But as the weeks passed, Dougherty sensed a disillusioning trend. Though his beloved Rens had an unblemished record through Novem-

ber at the Renaissance Casino, the team seemed to lack a killer instinct
on the road. As coaches today would say, the Rens couldn't "close out"
opposing teams in the final minutes. Granted, white referees were
known to whistle the Rens for phantom infractions late in close games.
But the Rens had to know that they couldn't play it close on the road
and allow the referees to steal games from them. They had to take care
of business: wow the crowd early in the game, hold down the score to
keep the fans interested, then close out their opponents midway
through the second half. That's what champions did.

The bottom line was the Rens had botched three close outs already
during the young season. Their latest collapse had come at the hands of
the Original Celtics in Orange, New Jersey, 31-29, and Dougherty
groused afterward like a man betrayed: "Now let me tell some of you
fellows why you can't make the grade when the occasion calls for that
extra spurt which these white boys put forth in beating you.

"First, you can't play the cabarets from midnight until the early morning hours and maintain the form necessary to reach championship
form," he wrote. "Secondly, it is impossible to succumb to the bland-
ishments of the female of the species and at the same time take your
work seriously. In the third place the morale of the team is not there
when you fail to make practice and get to your destinations, when playing out-of-town teams, on time."[66]

Still, Dougherty believed that if these young nighthawks would
rededicate themselves, they would enjoy a moment of glory to last a
lifetime.

Dougherty also believed that Jenkins and his teammates owed it to
their manager to beat the Celtics. In Dougherty's weekly columns, the
name Bob Douglas now carried all the weight and wonder of a folk hero.

Of Douglas and his three assistants—Reginald King, Joe Sibley, and
Edgar Mercer—Dougherty wrote, "They have been staging Saturday
night dances at the Renaissance successfully and could have 'carried on'
without a basketball team. But they refused to do so. Instead they kept
going something that brought extra dollars into the pockets of more than
a score of their own people all season. They have furnished amusement
and thrills in a clean and healthy manner for thousands of white and colored enthusiasts."[67]

Dougherty also knew that the amusement and thrills came at a financial risk to Douglas. The Renaissance Casino held only about fifteen
hundred people, meaning Douglas had to sell out every game to meet

his payroll. Plus, the waxy dance floor/basketball court wasn't exactly Madison Square Garden. Nor, for that matter, was it even the Commonwealth Casino.

"The basketball court at the Renaissance Casino is far less desirable than the one at the Commonwealth," wrote William Clark, sports editor of the *New York Age*. "It is much shorter, the ceiling is low and the lighting is bad for basketball."

But as Clark had seen firsthand, Douglas was still going strong, still puffing his victory cigars, still planning bigger and better coming attractions. How did he keep the fans hustling back for more when Jess McMahon had failed with far greater financial resources? Clark claimed the Rens' success had little to do with basketball. Rather, it was a case of Douglas's simply knowing how to connect with his audience.

"Instead of giving two basketball games, as was done in the past, only one game is played and that is made a secondary matter," Clark wrote. "Cabaret entertainment is of prime importance at these games. Good orchestral music, an occasional song, Charleston contests and uncensored dancing are the features."[68]

What Clark failed to mention was the Rens also exuded an air of invincibility that the Commonwealths had sorely lacked. It wasn't just smoke and mirrors; the Rens' invincibility was a matter of style and panache.

While the streets of Harlem had grown clogged during the 1920s with bootleggers, numbers runners, and low-society coots and criminals, the Renaissance Big Five represented class. It was a black team that was earning the respect of the larger, dominant white world, the same brand of respect and admiration that Alaine Locke and his fellow artists spoke of receiving with the "world-class" art of the Harlem Renaissance.

But whereas Locke and the others charmed with their unfamiliar primal images, provocative rhythms, and down-home chatter, the Rens wowed whites with their own popular pastime. That was the beauty of it. White fans weren't "slummin' it" when they hopped the A train to Harlem to catch a Rens game. They were feasting on some of the best basketball that fifty cents could buy anywhere in the great city of New York. For many who made the journey to "the 130s," the numbered streets of Harlem, watching black men openly compete and outperform whites must have given them pause. It must have forced many to confront a lifetime of lies and street-corner assumptions about a "weak and inferior" race.

"I doubt much whether the mere acquisition of hundreds of degrees or academic honors have influenced the mass mind of America as much as the soul appeal made in a thrilling run for a touchdown by a colored athlete, a jump by Gourdain [sic] or Hubbard or the heart touching strains of [singer] Roland Hayes," wrote Ed Henderson in 1927. "Fairness creeps out of the soul in the athletic world to a larger extent than anywhere else."[69]

That's why Romeo Dougherty fixated on his beloved Renaissance Big Five. It also was why Dougherty couldn't wait for his favorite team's scheduled rematch with the Original Celtics during the Christmas holidays. As Dougherty believed, the Rens were overdue.

It Happened One Night in 1925

The contest was played on December 20, 1925. Flip through just about any history of basketball, and there will be no mention of the game. No grainy photographs, no historic box score, no postgame reflections of the combatants. This treasure of basketball history has been buried for nearly eighty years, overlooked and forgotten.

Yet enough of a record remains in surviving newspapers of the era to revisit that rainy Sunday night. Temperatures were hovering in the low forties. Along Lenox Avenue, the brownstones were trimmed in the reds and greens of the Christmas season. A hard turn onto West 137th Street, then a block further up, and there in lights pulsed the words "Renaissance Casino." On the sidewalk, more people were moshed together than the eye could see.

"A milling throng of almost four thousand fans tried to jam their way into the Casino," wrote Dougherty of the crowd, which likely included several Celtic fans. "[A]fter about three thousand had been admitted the doors were barred and the unlucky ones forced to wait outside to get the news of one of the most historic battles in basketball ever."[70]

Inside the casino, the Harlem faithful rah, rah, rahed through the pregame cheers while the cynics—and there were many in attendance—must have had a good chuckle at ambitious Bob Douglas. Here he was venturing outside his league yet again.

The Celtics barely had worked up a sweat in sweeping their six prior engagements in Harlem, including two ho-hum victories over the Rens. Did Douglas really think his team could beat the white champions of the world? If Celtic owner Jim Furey had passed out calling cards before the game, they might have read: "Original Celtics. Highest paid basketball team in America. Defending champions of the world. Claimants of a 20-1 season record. Holders of a fifteen-game win streak."[71]

Bob Douglas had faith in his team. His Rens had nearly snapped the Celtics' winning streak three weeks earlier in New Jersey, and since then, his players had practiced harder than ever in hopes of finally turning the tables on the Celtics. It was the kind of after-hours commitment that Douglas and Dougherty had been hoping for from day one and the kind of attention to detail that they seemed to believe would make the team unbeatable.

Like most coaches before a big game, Douglas agonized over the unknown. He hoped, of course, that his players would make him proud, but there were many what-ifs. What if the Original Celtics were on top of their game? What if the Rens, despite the extra practice, caved in to the pressure of defeating the white champions?

That would mark three straight blowouts at home against the Celtics. His fans were growing more impatient with every season, and Douglas had to know that the boo-birds would be out in force, delivering their told-you-so tales about the rise and fall of the "invincible," "world-class" basketball team from Harlem that never was. These thumbs-down opinions could hurt attendance at the Renaissance Casino, erode his already thin bottom line, and imperil the future of the team.

Given the gravity of the moment, the usually calm and cagey Douglas couldn't stop fidgeting as he awaited the entrance of his players.

"With Manager 'Bob' Douglas sitting on the sidelines biting an unlit cigar to pieces the colored players took the court . . . confident of victory and proving that their strict attention to the demands of the game during the past few weeks had left them resolved to put forth the greatest effort of their career and bring victory, thereby staving off the censure, which was slowly but surely cropping up among those who have faithfully supported the team," wrote Dougherty.[72]

Douglas and the Ren faithful must have groaned in unison when the Celtics grabbed the opening tap, raced downcourt, and dropped home the game's first two points. A 2-0 deficit surely hadn't been in the game plan; but before Douglas could mangle another Havana to protest his team's sloppy defense, the Rens answered with a score of their own. Then came a second and a third ringer from the Rens, and just like that, a battle was on.

As the two teams grappled on the tiny wooden floor, the game might have seemed like a replay of their last clash in Harlem nine months earlier, when, according to Will Madden, the Celtics feigned a tough-fought first half to keep the crowd happy.[73] Yet on this evening, the Celtic players seemed sluggish. They kept slipping on the freshly waxed floor, or so they claimed, while the more sure-footed Rens wheeled and dealed on offense. Cutters broke free, passes arrived on time, shots rattled through the hoop. Never had the Rens' passing game looked sharper against such top-flight competition, and the finest white basketball players in the world had to resort to grabbing jerseys and other means of foul play just to keep pace.

After twenty minutes of razzle-dazzle, the Rens held only a 20-15 lead at halftime. The Celtics could close a five-point deficit in a heartbeat, and as both teams arrived at center court to shake hands and tip off the second stanza, many in the crowd had to wonder whether the white champions, per usual, would taste victory in the final twenty minutes.

But all the Celtics would taste in the second half was their own tough luck. With their tall center Joe Lapchick out of the lineup for the evening with a bum knee, the Celtics failed to win the after-basket jump balls, meaning the champs also failed to control the basketball and dictate the tempo of the game.[74] Instead, the ball belonged to the smaller, zippier Rens, and more often than not, it landed in the hands of the zippiest Ren of all, Fat Jenkins.

"Jenkins gets away from a standing start at full speed," marveled the white *New York Daily Mirror.* "Once under way, he leaves a trail of scorched boards behind him."[75] The reporter noted: "Harlem folk have a saying, 'Any time you want to find the ball, find Fat Jenkins.' Jenkins proved that saying to be a well founded truth last night. The Celtics could do nothing with this great little star of roly-poly build."[76]

As the final seconds ticked down on the game, Harlem rose as one—young and old, native and foreign born. Their Rens were about to defeat the greatest legends of the white game 37-30, and how sweet it was. How sweet that the Ren players, through growl and grit, had willed themselves into one of the finest teams going in professional basketball.

Wrote Dougherty: "At last! After more than five years of trying, the colored people of America are today rejoicing in another championship."[77]

In truth, the win did not entitle the Rens to the world championship. But it did boost their credibility among fans and their fellow professional teams. To prove their superiority, the Rens had to win their six-game season series with the Original Celtics. The Ren-Celtic series was now tied at one game apiece, with four more to play. But it was a huge first win for Douglas, his team, and their loyal but persnickety fans.

Outside this small circle, the game received remarkably little attention either as an athletic contest or as a civil-rights watershed. Most white newspapers carried no mention of this sudden setback for white sportsdom, and those that did, such as the *New York Daily Mirror,* shrugged off the bad news with a better-luck-next-time tone. Even stranger, none of the nation's black newspapers ran banner headlines celebrating the moment. Few black newspapers even ran accounts of the upset.

Does this collective shrug mean the victory wasn't historic after all?

One could argue the point, but in the end, the arguments don't hold water. There is no reason to assume, based on a scan of the newspapers, that nobody heard a peep about the Celtics' unsuccessful outing in Harlem. After all, a couple thousand fans had sat in the Renaissance Casino and cheered themselves hoarse at the outcome. And even as far back as the 1920s, New Yorkers loved their basketball and their Original Celtics, the kings of American hoops, the New York Yankees in sneakers and cotton undershirts. On those rare occasions when the invincible Irishmen from Manhattan's West Side lost a game, especially to a "Negro team," thousands of basketball-happy New Yorkers eventually heard about it.

Moreover, because no championship had been on the line in Harlem, white fans also had no reason to react to the final score with race-based hatred. They could safely chalk up the upset to beginner's luck or, more likely, to a slew of other excuses common to 1920s basketball. At the top of the list would have been the slippery basketball court and Jim Furey's red-faced claim that Chris Huiswood, a longtime black referee who was on Bob Douglas's payroll, had stolen the game from the Celtics with his one-sided calls—a claim that, interestingly, the white *New York Daily Mirror* rejected.

Black newspapers gave the game little attention because pro basketball was not a big-money national pastime in the 1920s. There was no coast-to-coast league, and many black newspapers of the time, among them the *New York Age,* dismissed professional basketball as a bastardization of the highbrow amateur game that dominated the teens. They were loathe to highlight the Rens in their pages.

It is important to remember, too, that the Rens had yet to travel further south than Philadelphia. Without television, most fans outside of Harlem had never seen the Renaissance Big Five. They might have heard of Harlem's wonder team, but they had no way of knowing how wonderful it was.

Finally, because intercity rivalries had been so vital to the development of the black game, some cities simply couldn't bear to give credit to a New York team. Take Pittsburgh and Cum Posey. Though the *Pittsburgh Courier* ran a team photo of the Rens following their victory over the Celtics, the basketball-happy newspaper carried no mention of the upset. Why? "Leondi or Loendi are still the champions and recognized as such in every city in the country," Posey wrote after the Ren-Celtic game, noting his team's recent name switch. "Even New York knows Loendi are received as colored champions and until a team beats them in a two game series, they will continue to be champs."[78] Putting personal prejudice aside, Posey, Dougherty, Douglas, and black sports fans could agree that beating the Celtics was a significant and symbolic step forward for the race in its quest for equality on and off the court.

To sense just how significant and symbolic, one must understand the times. During the first two decades of the twentieth century, when many color lines had been relaxed, many white kids on the playground would have known and admired the names of black athletes Sam Langford, Joe Gans, Joe Walcott, George Dixon, Fritz Pollard, Howard Drew, Major Taylor. And they would have recognized—and probably loathed—the name of the controversial black world heavyweight champion Jack Johnson, who had kayoed the myth of white physical superiority in 1910 and earned the wrath of millions for his rakish embrace of fast cars, late nights, and white women.

But jump ahead to the post–Jack Johnson 1920s, and basketball guides show that all the top teams were a collection of white faces. The same went for major league baseball, college football with a few exceptions, and, to a larger degree than ever, professional boxing. Just a decade earlier, there had been a growing sense of hope that barriers were falling for black athletes. What had happened?

"How long is this state of affairs going to continue to exist?" asked the *New York Age*'s Ted Hooks in 1920, issuing an early plea for black players to integrate major league baseball, which was entering its third decade of holding the color line. "Are our ball players—despite the active part they took in the war for Democracy, despite their gentlemanly behavior on the diamond and in civil life—to be forever confronted with this unsurmountable color barrier? Is there no conscience in the white solons' hearts? Will there never be any way out for the Negro?"[79]

When the discussion turned to professional boxing, the indignation of black sportswriters turned to indigestion. In boxing, unlike baseball, the race had already enjoyed the rise of Johnson and other black world champions Gans, Walcott, and Dixon. Most black sportswriters couldn't stomach the fact that the white men who ruled the sport had retreated behind the color line to stay on the right side of post-Johnson state laws banning mixed-race boxing and to protect their business interests from controversy.

Even as New York and other northern states eased their restrictions on mixed-race bouts during the early 1920s, all attempts to land a title fight for Harry Wills, the unfortunate heir to Johnson's heavyweight legacy, ended in bureaucratic sabotage. It seemed that a black man would never again get a chance to rule the heavyweight division. Maybe something could be arranged in the lower weight, lower profile divisions; but in the heavyweight division, where master promoter Tex Rickard had captured the nation's wonder and wallets with his million-dollar, rags-to-riches pug Jack Dempsey, there was too much money to lose.

The *Baltimore Afro-American* mocked Rickard and his Barnum-and-Bailey commercialization of the sport:

But nowadays it's different
They have drawn the color line
And instead of the old time masters
The pugs have sawdust in their spine

Yet the fans spend oodles of dollars
And whoop in sheer delight
While a "hope" and "has been" tap each other
And call the thing a fight.[80]

By the time the Rens beat the Original Celtics for the first time, most black sports fans were disillusioned by this revisionist, multimillion-dollar revival of white athletic superiority. In those rare instances when black athletes were allowed to prove themselves in the white world, millions of black folks certainly made note of it.

"The victory of the Renaissance of New York over the Original Celtics (white) last week, who are the world champions, places the New

York club at the top of the basketball world," noted the sports editor of the *Baltimore Afro-American.*[81]

"We have had a Drew, a Gourdin and a Hubbard who could beat the world in the sprints and jumps," wrote Ed Henderson, who had predicted this day nearly twenty years earlier when he began teaching physical education in Washington's black schools. "We have had others towering in other fields in their time and today we have a basketball team that has pulled down the world champions, the Celtics. We congratulate the boys of the Renaissance five for their splendid victory."[82]

In the case of Dougherty, the victory opened the door to push once again for racial equality in America. "Championships in those lines of sports where the color line is drawn remain with the whites, because they deny the colored brother a chance to compete with them, but once they let down the bars they prove the fallacy of their claims of superiority which only the white race enjoys," he wrote. "All Negroes have asked is a fair chance, and when given that chance they have more than made good. A consultation of records in sports where the colored brother has taken part will prove this claim to the satisfaction of anyone. Well, it happened [again] at the Renaissance Casino last Sunday night."[83]

In late January the Rens bungled their return match against the Celtics 35-26, playing before a racially mixed crowd in Orange, New Jersey. Dougherty, who continued to claim that the Rens were the new world champions, might have had to issue a retraction had the Rens a few night later, again in Orange, not claimed their second win and first road victory over the Celtics 32-28.

Deadlocked at two victories apiece in their season series, the teams returned their hostilities to Harlem in mid-February for a game that was touted like a heavyweight championship fight. So anticipated was the matchup, Bob Douglas moved it to Harlem's cavernous 369th Regiment Armory, where an estimated crowd of ten thousand paid to watch the fireworks.

Or, more like it, to watch the fizzle. With the tall Joe Lapchick once again in the lineup to control center jumps, the Celtics blasted the Rens 46-21 to claim a 3-2 advantage in their season series. "We stood no chance at the armory on Monday night," wrote Dougherty. "Brawn topped by a scientific knowledge of the game mixed with the desperate effort which can be put forward when their backs are against the wall brought the Celtics the victory they felt, even when losing to Renaissance in previous games, belonged to them."[84]

However, the Rens got the last laugh. In the waning weeks of the season, they scraped out a 32-20 victory to deadlock the season series at three games apiece.

Black and white had ended the season as equals.

Washington and New York

Even with the success of the Renaissance Big Five, white professional basketball teams showed no rush to integrate their rosters. The opposite was true. Late in 1925, about a month before the Rens first beat the Celtics, a group of ambitious white promoters launched the first attempt at a national pro league, called the American Basketball League or ABL. Accepting new or existing teams as far west as Chicago and as far south as Washington, which then passed for national in scope, the ABL followed the lead of major league baseball. The nation's basketball league would be all white and proud of it.

In Harlem, Bob Douglas never blasted the color line in print to force his Rens into the big leagues. As Romeo Dougherty later noted, Douglas was the "last one to engage in battle, whether mental or physical, [but] you'll find him very much there when the occasion warrants it."[85]

During the 1925–26 season, with business booming and his team in demand, Douglas could afford to be cagey and wait to see if the league survived. After all, the Original Celtics had balked at joining the ABL. Without the Celtics in the fold in its first year, the league faced a huge credibility problem at the box office. Fans would wonder how the ABL could be a true major league without the premier team in basketball as one of its members.

Still, the new league raised questions. What if the ABL succeeded in monopolizing the pro game, a prospect that received a boost when the Original Celtics finally joined the circuit in December 1926? Would the league one day freeze out the Rens from playing exhibition games against the Celtics or its other members? And what if the pro champion was crowned each season during the ABL playoffs, already dubbed "the World Series of basketball"? Would the Rens, like the great Kansas City Monarchs of Negro League baseball fame, never get their rightful shot at the world title? Worse, what if the color line loosened, as it had in boxing, and the ABL stole Douglas's players and put him out of business?

The Renaissance Big Five tipped off its fourth season in October 1926 without even a hint of uncertainty about the future. Vernon Andrade, the popular Panamanian king of swing, cranked up his orchestra about an hour before the game, setting the mood for the Rens to shake and shimmy past the overmatched white Catskills Five 37-23.

Douglas had reconfigured the seating in Renaissance Casino to improve the sight lines for his fifteen hundred customers, a constant gripe in seasons past. He also ordered that the front doors be opened earlier on Sunday nights to allow the action to start at 9:30 sharp, meaning the games always ended early enough to leave a few hours for dancing.[86] Douglas even kept "several hostesses on hand to dance with any stranger without charge to the patron."[87]

Featuring a familiar sextet of Slocum, Jenkins, Ricks, Mayer, Fiall, and Saunders—plus newcomer Eyre Saitch, one of the top-rated black tennis players in America—the Rens bested most of the finest teams in New York and a few just passing through. Among the fatalities in 1927 were the Hebrew Giants, the Visitation Triangles, the Boston Whirlwinds (featuring Flash Crotty and Snappy O'Connell), and even a few ABL clubs, a sign that the color line was still a work in progress.

"We are playing big time basketball, and the harder the teams the better we like it," said Douglas. "Give the fans a run for their money, whether you are on the winning or the losing end, and they will be satisfied."[88]

Douglas also finagled two home games against the Original Celtics. Though luck and the long arms of Celtic center Joe Lapchick were against the Rens, each clash seesawed in classic fashion to the closing seconds, when the more veteran team hit the clutch shots to claim victory. According to the admittedly biased Romeo Dougherty, the Rens were quicker and faster than the Celtics, played just as tenaciously on defense, and nearly matched the white champions in their ability to pass the basketball. Where the Rens still fell short was in size, big-game experience, and free-throw shooting. The Celtic sharpshooters rarely missed at the line.[89]

"There are only two big sporting classics staged among colored people during the year, one the football game between Lincoln and Howard Universities and the other the basketball game between the Renaissance and the Celtics," crowed Dougherty.[90]

Though Dougherty's statement was a stretch—what about the more widely followed championships of the Negro baseball leagues?—it did hold a grain of truth. The Rens were the only black titleholders in all of team sports that went toe-to-toe each season against a white champion. Baseball was segregated, ice hockey was for whites only, football offered nothing comparable, and soccer was even less organized than basketball. As the Rens continued to challenge and occasionally beat the Celtics, these legendary battles slowly but surely became a matter of common knowledge outside Harlem. The Rens had arrived as the objects of national black pride and a conspicuous measure of the physical progress of a race once considered by whites to be too frail for athletics.

The rise of the Rens still irked some of the more curmudgeonly in the crowd. Cum Posey claimed that an old acquaintance who had watched the Rens confided to him that "the Renaissance club of today is no stronger than the old St. Christopher or Commonwealth clubs, and would be easy meat for a fast-moving good shooting team."[91] Another outspoken critic was William Clark of the *New York Age*, who grumped again about the taint of professionalism on the formerly amateur game of basketball: "As much as we like Jenkins and Slocum and Fiall, they cannot get any publicity for their time in The Age until the games the Renaissance Five play appear to be real sport competition instead of an exciting show."[92]

But for most sports fans in black America, Douglas's Renaissance Big Five scored rave reviews. John Howe of the *Philadelphia Tribune* called the Rens "the greatest machine in the history of colored court teams" after watching the New Yorkers battle four times that season.[93] Even the old spoilsport Cum Posey grudgingly admitted that the Rens were "the best colored team in America."[94]

As one measure of their growing reputation, the Rens were suddenly in greater demand in black America. As the 1926–27 season wound to its conclusion, the black Philadelphia Giants brought the Rens to the City of Brotherly Love with tremendous fanfare. In March 1927, the *Chicago Defender* featured a photo of the "Pride of New York" and noted that "a movement is on foot to bring [the] easterners to Chicago next season."[95]

One town that was no longer a necessary stop for Douglas on the black basketball circuit was Washington. Twenty years earlier, New York and Washington had been the cradles of the black game, equals in every way. Each city had traveled the same bumpy road through amateurism. When the game turned professional, the best play-for-pay quintets on U Street could not compete with the Renaissance Big Five.

What had happened?

The answer boils down to one word: opportunity. New York had always had the better infrastructure to develop pro basketball. Although many Harlemites considered the Renaissance Casino too small and unprofitable by New York standards, it still had a standing-room-only capacity of three thousand fans. On U Street, Murray's Casino maxed out at about seven hundred people, and the Lincoln Colonnade stuffed in about fifteen hundred fans.

U Street also offered a far shorter menu of competitive teams to build interest in the pro game. The constants were the Carlisle Big Five, Alco, and to a lesser extent, the Community Yellow Jackets, a former YMCA team that won the city's black title in 1927. A few other solid teams burst onto the scene, such as Reuben Spears's Chicago Dribblers in 1925, but they lasted only a season or two at most, hardly long enough to build popular and lucrative rivalries.

That meant U Street had to subsist on a spare diet of Carlisle-Alco games—spare because these rivals could put aside their competitive differences long enough to meet only two or three times per season. It also meant that between their big games, Carlisle and Alco either had to tease their fans with humdrum local attractions or import their thrills. Given the hefty advance money that top out-of-town teams demanded and the small capacity of Murray's Casino, local promoters more often than not didn't have a prayer of breaking even. If promoters boosted admission prices to help cover expenses, the fans invariably squawked.

Finances were less austere in Harlem. In the rare instance when an attraction bombed at the box office—for example, the Rens–Morgan College game in Renaissance Casino during the 1926–27 season drew a disappointing three hundred fans—Douglas could absorb the blow more easily than most black promoters. As an insider at Renaissance Casino,[96] which hosted a range of events other than basketball, Douglas in some ways played with house money to book his attractions. Not so for the U Street promoters. Carlisle manager Ewell Conway operated a modest sign-painting business. Henry Hill, who replaced the cash-strapped William Carter as manager of the Alcoes in late 1925, ran a local barber shop.

To cut corners, the Carlisles and the Alcoes sometimes booked makeshift fraternity teams or fly-by-night attractions that wheeled in and out of town faster than a traveling medicine show. For promoters, booking these games was a gamble because they never knew exactly how weak the competition would be, or whether the outfits even would show.

"For a long time the basketball populace of Washington has been fooled," wrote Sam Lacy of the *Washington Tribune*. "The people have grown tired of it. The cash customer is [sore] at being considered by local promoters, as being 'blind as the proverbial bat.' The folks who lay down their quarters and halves are gradually decreasing in numbers, and it's because of the fact that they are refusing to pay for what they feel they won't see."[97]

Meanwhile, Harlem benefited from its proximity to some of the best white basketball in America. Although race was always a front-and-center issue in 1920s America, it was less so in a large cosmopolitan melting pot like New York. As black writer James Weldon Johnson noted, "New York, more than any other American city, maintains a matter-of-fact, a taken-for-granted attitude towards her Negro citizens. Less there than anywhere else in the country are Negroes regarded as occupying a position of wardship; more nearly do they stand upon footing of common and equal citizenship."[98]

Thus, Douglas had the opportunity to book the finest white clubs and push the development of his team. The Rens leveraged this opportunity to meld the speed of the black game with the advanced floor game of the top white clubs, a critical ingredient in the team's success. In addition, Douglas shrewdly used the white teams to build a loyal fan base. By consistently slaying the best in the white world, Douglas enticed fans to pack his casino, and the word soon spread that the Rens were the finest black team in America. Had Douglas scheduled black teams only, he would have been beholden to the whims and fancies of Cum Posey and his champion Loendi club. As Jess McMahon and so many others had discovered over the years, Posey didn't play nice, which would have complicated Douglas's climb to the top.

But in Washington there was little melding of the white and black game. The nation's capital had never produced a white team comparable to the Original Celtics. The Celtics once spanked the white District champion Yankees 44-12, and according to one newspaper, the margin "could have been much larger" had the Celtics not stalled and purposely missed shots to keep the score remotely respectable.[99]

To start the 1924–25 season, however, the situation changed dramatically. The local Palace Laundry Big Five, the city's ten-month-old experiment with big-time pro basketball, joined the ABL and upgraded its roster with more name players from other cities, including former Celtic center Horse Haggerty. Unlike Bob Douglas, U Street had nothing to lose with the arrival of the ABL. In fact, local black teams had cause to celebrate. Carlisle and Alco, like the Rens three seasons earlier, now had in theory a chance to book exhibition games against the Palace Laundry Big Five, learn a few tricks from a sophisticated white team, and leverage the opportunity to learn from the masters into a popular winter attraction.

Enter Jim Crow. The management of the Palace Laundry had no interest in booking "Negro teams"—not the Carlisles, not the Alcoes, not the up-and-coming Community Yellow Jackets.

It's not that interracial games were unheard of in the District. Conway and his Carlisles sometimes booked middle-of-the-road white teams into Murray's Casino.[100] So did the Alcoes. In his later years, sportswriter Sam Lacy remembered fondly when in the 1920s his Community Yellow Jackets faced the Epiphany Roses, the white amateur champions of the District. No police officers stormed the court, and no screaming newspaper headlines decrying the mixing of the races ran the morning after.

Yet Lacy never saw the Palace Laundry Big Five play a game.[101] He wasn't welcome there. The team, like the ABL, had a whites-only policy. George Preston Marshall, the twenty-nine-year-old white manager of the Palace Laundry Big Five, was at liberty to choose his clientele, and he didn't choose to sell tickets to blacks. Legalized discrimination had been the prevailing policy in the nation's capital since 1913, when the owner of the posh Belasco Theater, as Ed Henderson once remembered, "won a court decision giving him the right to exclude whomever he chose, and you could hear the doors slamming all over town."[102]

Marshall's door-slamming was motivated if not by racism then surely by concern for turning a profit. As the white *Washington Herald* described the scene, the Palace Laundry's weekly Sunday night home game "is becoming a habit. This is especially true of many fair [female] basketball fans who are regular patrons of the games. . . . There is something doing every minute. . . . During the intermission breathing spell; there is more music. Following the big game the floor is cleared for dancing."[103]

Reading between the lines, if Marshall wanted to market his games as fashionable Sunday-night soirees featuring pretty young flappers flouncing around in the stands and on the dance floor, he couldn't permit African Americans to crash the gate. The white gentry wouldn't stand for it.

For black players, the lack of opportunity also was a factor in the development of their individual court skills during the 1920s and 1930s. In New York, though neighborhoods often were rigidly segregated, the public schools were integrated. This meant young black players could glean the best of both basketball worlds, white and black, and make their games more complete.

William "Pop" Gates, who joined the Rens in the late 1930s, started playing basketball as a youngster at the segregated Harlem YMCA. In high school he continued to play for the YMCA on the side while he refined his talent under the tutelage of one of New York's most respected white coaches.

"We had no problem playing with each other or against each other," recalled Gates, who, contrary to the modern stereotype, said he rarely battled on Harlem's playground courts. "I developed my style of play directly from coach Bill Spiegel at Benjamin Franklin High School. He was a coach who taught you basic fundamentals."[104]

The same could be said of other top black players in New York. George Gregory, the first black college All-American player at Columbia University in 1930, also learned to play basketball at the Harlem YMCA. But he prepped at DeWitt Clinton High School with teammates named Cohen, Bernstein, Lind, and Cleck. Lanky Jones, the star center at Morgan College, honed his skills in high school on an integrated team in New Jersey. Even Fat Jenkins, though he chose not to play basketball at his integrated high school, learned the game from a respected white coach at St. Christopher.

That's why, though rarely mentioned in most books on basketball history, the top Harlem players from the 1920s and 1930s were the antithesis of today's free-lancing playground legends. Jenkins, Fiall, Slocum, and others were fast, athletic, and capable of showboating when the need arose. But they all played steady, fundamentally sound team ball in which smarts, not flash, won games.

"Making stupid passes was a no-no, not only with the Renaissance, but for all of the old-time teams, white or black," said Gates of his Renaissance days. "We knew that as long as you had possession of the ball, the other team can't score. We knew that as long as you've got the ball and take proper shots, you'll win. It was that old saying in basketball: 'Possession is eight-tenths of the game.'"[105]

This fundamental mastery of team basketball—combined with speed, talent, and experience—set the Rens apart from other black

teams in the late 1920s and 1930s. Bob Douglas seconded this point before his death in 1979. "Abe Saperstein [owner of the Harlem Globe-
trotters] died a millionaire because he gave the white people what they
wanted," he said. "When I go, it will be without a dime in my pocket,
but with a clear conscience. I would have never burlesqued basketball.
I love it too much for that."[106]

In Washington, by contrast, both the neighborhoods and the public
schools were segregated. While a black school system had been an advantage when Ed Henderson introduced basketball at the turn of the
century, providing the ready-made infrastructure to develop the game,
segregation had become something of a liability by the 1920s. It wasn't
that Henderson and his colleagues were poor coaches. The 1924 Armstrong Tech "Wonder Team" ran an innovative fast break and shifted defenses on the fly from zone to man-to-man. But whereas New York players like Pop Gates had the chance to take the best from both worlds and
grow as players, Washington players were locked into separate worlds.

Black players responded to the limits of segregation by experiment-
ing with new styles and methods that diverted from the more rigid, scientific approach of whites. This freedom to experiment became vital
to the growth of the black game in the 1930s, when center jumps after
each made basket were abolished and the faster, more wide-open modern game took root. Black basketballers had more freedom than their
white counterparts to free-lance and, like jazz musicians, invent or hone
popular innovations such as Hank Luisetti's one-handed heaves in the
1930s, the precursor of the modern jump shot. That's not to say there
weren't authoritarian black coaches ready to crack down on unorthodox
play. But the training of coaches was more uneven in black high schools
and colleges, so conformity was less often the rule.

"Black players had skills that they developed themselves, basically,"
said Willie Wynne, the first black player at Boys High School in Brooklyn during the 1930s, who later starred at Howard University. "Some
of them had good coaches who had been to white institutions and were
in touch with the strengths and weaknesses of the white game. But black
players didn't always get the best coaching, and a lot of them were developed on the scene at black colleges [where, without any previous experience, they tried out for the team].

"You see, you learn from other people by playing with those who have
skills," Wynne continued. "Like you saw it in Luisetti. You didn't see
black ballplayers use the same type of skills that Luisetti did, but when

you went to the white sector, you didn't see many white boys who could throw the one-handed shot either. They didn't have that skill. . . . It was something that was passed from player to player, rather than coach to coach."[107]

NBA great Julius Erving made this point more eloquently in the 1980s. "Basketball was—and is—a very simple game. But what the black athlete did was to enhance the game with an expression all his own, taking the basics to another dimension. Soon the white player began to emulate these thoughts and moves and eventually the game became what it is today—a stage where a unique combination of the team concept and individual expression are presented in pure form."[108]

But opportunity was a fickle concept in America during the early 1900s. Though one can point confidently to grass-roots differences as influencing the distinct evolutions of the black game in New York and Washington, these factors tell only one side of the story. The other side of the story is, once their high school days had passed, black athletes in New York and Washington shared the same frustrating lack of opportunity to continue playing basketball.

In the profit-happy world of white pro basketball, their skin color stigmatized blacks as unmarketable commodities. Most promoters were convinced the sight of blacks and whites playing together would drive away fans.

Neither were black players being readily embraced by coaches at white colleges. There were exceptions, such as Columbia University stars John Johnson and George Gregory. But scores of black high schoolers never got a chance. In 1938, Pop Gates led Franklin High School to the championship of New York City, for which he received all-city recognition. If it had happened today, the scholarship offers would have piled up in his mailbox. But Gates didn't receive a single scholarship offer to a white college. It was the same old tale, one that Chicago's Reuben Spears in 1924 and countless others since would have recognized.

"We didn't have any dreams of playing on major professional basketball teams like kids do today," said Gates. "Our thought was to play with the best high school, YMCA, or group team in our area. At that time, it was very hard to go to college because major colleges throughout the country weren't accepting blacks.

"After high school, we thought about playing with the Renaissance," he continued. "But they only carried eight men. Or I thought about playing with one of the better neighborhood teams. . . . Nobody was thinking about money at that time. It was just about being able to play and the ability to play."[109]

Gates got lucky when he landed one of eight spots with the Rens in 1939. But dozens of talented but less polished Harlem players had little chance of making a living on the hardwood. Neither could they sell their services to black semipro teams in other cities, where the court combinations were generally low paying, cash strapped, and incapable of paying to relocate players. As hard as it is to fathom today, when so many black teenagers dream of signing fat NBA contracts, basketball was a lousy career choice in New York, Washington, and every other burg in black America.

That's why the success of the Renaissance Big Five was so vital to black basketball. The Rens kept alive the hope and winning legacy of twenty years of black basketball on the East Coast. There was no other team to do it. Cum Posey's Loendi had lost its high standing by the mid-1920s, and the Harlem Globetrotters were still just another unproven gleam in Abe Saperstein's eye.

It was the Rens who, as America's premier black team, were there to challenge by example the wisdom of the ABL's color line. And it was the Rens who kept black America excited about basketball during the 1920s and 1930s.

Amateurism Revisited

By mid-November 1927, several black newspapers had confirmed the rumors. The Eastern League of Associated Basketball Clubs, the on-again, off-again revival of black amateur basketball on the East Coast, would tip off its maiden season on Thanksgiving night. The association had assembled seven reputedly amateur clubs for its first year, including most notably Harlem's St. Christopher Red and Black Machine, the Vandals of Atlantic City, and U Street's own Carlisle Field Club.

Amateur basketball was back in the headlines. Led by commissioner Andrew F. Jackson, the men behind the Eastern League vowed to restore sobriety to a game they believed had grown drunken and lawless through four seasons of professionalism. "That the forming of the organization is for the good of the sport can not be denied," declared the leaders of the league. "The public, after all, must be served."[110]

Following the announcement, many old-time basketball fans stepped forward to pledge support for the league and its bid to organize a permanent home for the amateur game. The enthusiasm peaked a few weeks later when the Eastern League reached a tentative agreement with a new amateur association in the Midwest, led by the beloved long-jump champion DeHart Hubbard, to play a postseason world series of black amateur basketball. It was rumored the leagues would merge into the first national black amateur basketball association, a network that would overshadow the disorganized professional game.[111]

"This league is in the future going to be a powerful body from present indications . . . and if they do not deviate from their present policy to keep the players strictly within the simon pure class they will reach the pinnacle of the basketball ladder," wrote John Howe, sports editor of the *Philadelphia Tribune*.[112]

Then, as so often happened to the best laid plans of black amateur basketball, the high hopes landed with a thud. By early winter, the Eastern League began to buckle brick by brick, assumption by assumption—starting with its definition of amateurism.

For many old-timers and potential Eastern League fans, the term "amateur" meant a trip down memory lane to the Golden Age in the teens when athleticism, high culture, and gentility ruled the weekends. As the *Pittsburgh Courier*'s W. Rollo Wilson mused:

> But when all is said and done, what the fans want is the good, old days when intercity competition was at its best. They want the days when they red-inked the calendar for the Monticello-Alpha, Hampton-St. C., Howard-Alpha and Alpha–St. C. games weeks in advance. They want the days when the visiting teams were entertained by the various clubs and organizations of the cities, when Alpha held open house on 131st street and the Loendi club was thrown open for the New Yorkers. Then the GAME was only one of a series of social events of the week-end.[113]

For some, amateurism also meant a finishing school for the physical and social cultivation of young black men, a cherished social ideal that had to be protected from the corrupting influence of professionals. It was class conscious, altruistic, and dogmatic. Still others viewed amateurism much like it is today, as the happy, come-what-may custodian of school and neighborhood athletics. Participation, not winning, was the standard.

The Eastern League sidestepped these popular notions. Its organizers weren't visionaries like the amateur men of old; they were frustrated

fans who reacted against the shady promotions of the professionals—
Renaissance Big Five possibly withstanding—which they viewed as destroying the sport and its popularity in black neighborhoods. Their duty
was first and foremost to restore fair play on the basketball court. And
therein lay the problem. By simply imposing a rule book on the game,
they failed to grab the public's fancy.

Nowhere was this flaw more apparent than with the great symbol of
the amateur era, the St. Christopher Red and Black Machine. Though
the longtime St. C. figures Reverend Shelton Bishop and former star
Charlie Bradford still roamed the sidelines, few other visible links to the
dignified past remained. Gone were Fat Jenkins, George Fiall, Paul
Robeson, and all the big names of the glory years. In their wake loped
a gaggle of young, unproven cagers, most of whom would have lan-
guished on the Machine's junior team in years past, so dramatic had the
drop in talent been at St. Christopher.

Gone, too, were the classic teams that gave the bygone amateur era
its luster. Alpha had met its omega, Spartan had lost its battle, and the
Smart Set Grave Diggers had given up the ghost years ago. Hampton,
Lincoln, and Howard were now college teams first. Loendi, though
hardly amateur, was tottering on its last legs.

Taking their places were six relatively obscure, middle-of-the-road
teams. There were the Vandals of Atlantic City; the Newark, New Jersey, Buccaneers; the Capitol Club of Asbury Park, New Jersey; Brooklyn's Vanguard Postal; the Monumental Elks of Baltimore; and Washington's Carlisle Field Club. Of these six names, only the Vandals and
Carlisle likely would have elicited a nod of recognition from the Harlem
basketball faithful.

Harlemites also would have needed to keep an eraser handy to track
the Eastern League entrants. Originally, the league had announced the
Alcoes as its Washington entry; a few days later, it was the Carlisles instead. A week into the season, the Monumental Elks dropped out and
were replaced by the Tuxedo Tigers, a more seasoned team based in Orange, New Jersey. This left the league in charge of four New York–area
teams and two out-of-town quintets, meaning its vow to foster the good
old days of intercity competition had been scaled back only one game
into the season.

With all these structural flaws, the Eastern League appeared to be
one jolt away from implosion. That jolt came soon enough from none
other than Ewell Conway, the U Street sign painter, small-time pro-

moter, and manager of the Carlisle Big Five. Then in his fifth season with Carlisle—better known on U Street as "Conway's Checks," a wry commentary on the team's snazzy new checkerboard uniforms—Conway had gone on record long ago as supporting a regional or national amateur league.

But Conway's support smacked of hypocrisy. His Carlisle Big Five was a semipro, not amateur, team. He not only paid his players, he masterminded the types of fast-and-loose promotions that the Eastern League vowed to abolish: overhyping mediocre opponents, raiding players from other teams, promoting bogus championship games.

Conway's sudden embrace of amateurism was probably born out of necessity. Ever since Carlisle lost the District championship to Alco in 1923, its fortunes had been as volatile as the New York Stock Exchange. In 1925, after two disappointing seasons, Carlisle regained the District's black title behind its trio of stars, the aging Benny Hill and the Mutt-and-Jeff tandem of Eddie and Everett Davis. The next season, heartbreak returned. Though Conway and his assistant manager Matt Taylor vowed to "spare neither effort nor expense in producing another championship quintet," the Purple and White of Alco grabbed two out of three games from Conway's Checks to reclaim the city crown.[114]

For Conway, it was the same old problems—no generous owner to pay the bills, subpar facilities for first-rate promotions, meager local competition, a skimpy season schedule, and fickle, footloose players.

The Eastern League seemed to offer Conway a way out of his predicament. The league format, in theory, imposed structure—a full schedule, a championship race, a shared set of rules—and offered the status of belonging to an up-and-coming association. There was also the chance to compete in Harlem and, if all went well, boost his club's reputation on U Street as the slayer of New York's finest amateur teams.

Conway's Checks, however, arrived for play in the Eastern League a mere shadow of their old selves. Two of Carlisle's best players—long-armed center Slim Henderson and fleet-footed forward Eddie Davis—had left for college. The team's weaknesses became clear on December 23, when St. Christopher walloped Carlisle 46-24 in Harlem.[115]

The real drama began after the game. According to league resolution 13, all team managers had until the start of their second game to submit their full and final rosters to headquarters, which in Conway's case meant fewer than five days.[116] This mandate, a cornerstone of the league, was an attempt to quash the popular practice of "wildcatting," or adding players from game to game, often by outbidding other teams for their services.

"In some cities there were three or four teams and the habit of borrowing players for particular games became disgusting," declared a league press release. "The result was it became impossible for visiting teams to get a square deal. The commissioners of the league have each players' list and each team member has a membership card."[117]

Though the clock was ticking, Conway chose not to hand over his list of players, giving him more flexibility to tweak his lineup from game to game as need be. This bold move immediately prompted controversy. Manager Trueheart of the visiting Vandals demanded that alleged wildcatters Slim Henderson and Eddie Davis be barred from the contest. Conway countered that although Henderson and Davis were members of the Virginia Seminary Institute's basketball team and were home from school on Christmas break, both still maintained active memberships at the Carlisle Field Club.

"A. F. Jackson, president of the association, was present and the situation cleared up with dispatch," wrote the *Pittsburgh Courier*.[118] Henderson and Davis would play. But the questions persisted after Carlisle, riding the two men's dominant performances, victimized the Vandals 43-20.

"The Eastern League . . . was formed for the purpose of doing away with 'wild-cat' tactics on the part of players," wrote the *Washington Tribune*'s Sam Lacy. "I'll 'blow a blatter' the league will soon insert a clause for the purpose of stopping the 'wild-cat' methods of team managers who in their desire to win use players home on vacation from school that their team might cope with the superior basketball displayed by their opponents."[119]

Just like that, Jackson's integrity and the credibility of his month-old league were on the line. Was Jackson truly an amateur man? Or was he willing to bend the rules like the oily men in the pro game?

With pressure mounting to rein in Conway, Jackson and his fellow commissioners finally put down their foot in late January. In a harsh and ill-timed decision, they canceled the Vanguard Postal–Carlisle game minutes before tip-off and declared that Conway must forfeit both of his team's previous victories. The Eastern League leaders maintained that their decision had nothing to do with the eligibility of Henderson and Davis. Rather, it was based on Conway's failure to submit a final roster to the league.[120]

Conway immediately tried to sabotage the league. He refused to send his team to Atlantic City for its scheduled rematch against the Vandals, fanning rumors that Carlisle had withdrawn from the league. Conway, claiming he had received a frantic letter from the league to reconsider, withheld the inevitable for a few days. Then on February 1 he made it official: Carlisle was through with the Eastern League.

League officials tried to explain away the bad news, claiming Conway had been in financial trouble anyway. "Although it is to be regretted that the Carlisles went out of the league; it must be remembered that no one team can make or break an organization that thrives on co-operation," wrote J. S. Caldwell, general manager of the Eastern League. "The rest of us are sticking for the 'good of the sport.'"[121]

But the league was broken. Though Caldwell asked for volunteers, no teams stepped forward to replace Carlisle. With intercity competition nearly dead, the league had mutated into an almost strictly New York–based outfit that, to bolster its fan base, sometimes played the preliminary games on Sunday nights before the Renaissance Big Five took the court in the main event. Such a bastardization of the amateur game would have incited a round of complaints about the taint of professionalism just six years earlier. In 1928, Bob Douglas's professional team represented a lifeline.

The Eastern League had a chance to save face in late March when, as previously agreed, its regular-season champion St. Christopher would battle DeHart Hubbard's Cincinnati Comets, the midwestern amateur league winners. This clash had all the hallmarks of a high-society event. There was tradition, popular public figures, high culture, intercity competition, a championship at stake, and plenty of dancing afterward.

But for reasons lost in time, the big, face-saving game never happened. Scheduled for March 28,[122] it appears to have been canceled at the last minute. Likewise, newspapers provide no details about the final moments of the Eastern League. Just as suddenly as it had appeared on the scene the previous Thanksgiving, the league vanished like a cat in the night. Amateurism had lost another of its nine lives.

True believers continued to insist that the amateur spirit would survive. Fueling their faith was the Original Collegians, an undefeated, three-year-old Harlem team composed mainly of high school players that won the Manhattan and New York state amateur championship in 1928.[123]

"We can never forget the glorious past, when the big three, Alpha, St. 'C,' and Spartan were the bulwark of the city's defense against such teams as Loendi, Hampton, Howard, etc.," wrote the *Amsterdam News.* "The sparkling playing, keen rivalry, organized cheering squads, and general good-fellowship will always live in our minds.

"If the Original Collegians can revive this spirit again," the newspaper continued, "basketball in New York City will be better off for it, for we want the vehicle by which our young players can be developed."[124]

But as a traveling, independent team without ready-made rivals, the Original Collegians proved to have a short life. Young players came and went, and the team faded from view, leaving the legacy of the amateur clubs again in the hands of Bob Douglas and his Renaissance Big Five.

After their falling-out with the Eastern League, Conway and his Checks rebounded to defeat the Columbia Lodge Elk Big Five, formerly Alco, and claim the 1928 District title. To cap the team's tumultuous season, the *Washington Tribune* reported, blows were exchanged in the dressing room after the game.[125] Some things never changed.

What did change, however, was Conway's finances. In October 1928, Abe Lichtman, the white owner of several local black theaters, agreed to sponsor Carlisle for the 1929 season. According to the agreement, Conway would remain manager of the team, with the help of J. Marcus E. Vance, better known for promoting local fraternity basketball games.[126]

Conway now had a benefactor for his team, a willing financier who was known around U Street for two very exploitable qualities: his generosity and his inability to say no.

But as Conway would soon discover, the money would arrive too little, too late to save his team.

In the End

In mid-January 1929, Conway received more good news. The Renaissance Big Five had agreed to play the Lichtman Carlisles at U Street's Lincoln Colonnade. Using Abe Lichtman's bankroll as his calling card, Conway already had upgraded his team's schedule with several white teams, and now he could add the Rens to his list of big promotions, something neither the Community Yellow Jackets nor the Elks could match.

The Rens "are the greatest drawing card today," Conway blustered in an advertisement for the game. "It has taken over four years of ceaseless effort to bring this famed aggregation to Washington. . . . This may be your last chance to see this famous collection of colored court stars in action."[127]

Conway's battle with the truth might have mattered to a lesser opponent, but not to the Rens. Their world-beating reputation preceded
them, and U Street clearly relished the chance to pass judgment on
Harlem's wonder team, even though Conway had jacked up the price
of admission from fifty cents to a dollar. According to the *Washington
Tribune*, bets had begun to pile up days before the contest, with most
trying to hit the final margin of victory for the New Yorkers, not which
team would win.[128]

On January 23, U Street got its first real look at Harlem's court sen-
sations. The names of the players were familiar to basketball fans: Kid
Slocum, Fat Jenkins, George Fiall, Pappy Ricks, Eyre Saitch, Stretch
Saunders, Harold Mayer.[129]

Though Carlisle had a decent team this night, featuring diminutive
Ev Davis and steady Tim Braddick, the club had no prayer of stopping
the Renaissance machine. "The first eight minutes of the game kept the
hopes of local fans high as the visitors were held scoreless," wrote the
Washington Tribune, describing a common ploy of the dominant team
to keep the crowd interested. "The spell was broken, however, when
Jenkins dropped in a free shot from the foul line and the champions
began their wild onslaught."[130]

After their easy, workmanlike 69-35 victory, the Ren stars gathered
their belongings and prepared to shove off for another city. The inno-
cence of the amateur days was gone. The game had been one more
whistle-stop along the road for these seasoned veterans. In the next
week, the Rens would roll through Fort Wayne, Chicago, and Cleveland, marking their first midwestern road swing. Another game, another
crowd, another win.

It had been nearly ten years since that memorable night in Manhat-
tan Casino when Bob Douglas and his tardy timekeeper had robbed
Carlisle of victory. It had been five years since Douglas's first-year Big
R Five and Carlisle last met in Washington. Then, the futures of both
teams had been equally uncertain. Now, the Renaissance Big Five and
Carlisle were drifting toward two far different destinies.

Carlisle would run aground, probably within the next few months.
Though the details are unclear—the *Washington Tribune* briefly ceased
publication in the early 1930s—the likely culprit was the Wall Street
crash in November 1929. The lean years of the Depression left U
Street's semipro basketball teams strapped for cash and worthy opponents. The Community Yellow Jackets soon disbanded, the Alcoes/Elks

disappeared, and Abe Lichtman apparently ceased paying the bills for Conway and his Carlisles.

Interestingly, black club teams survived in other cities—probably because of larger facilities and more stable ownership. In Baltimore, the Athenians played on for a few more seasons. In Philadelphia, a competitive club team could always be found. And in Chicago, Abe Saperstein already had big plans for his Harlem Globetrotters.

For Douglas and the Renaissance Big Five, meanwhile, the waters would be choppy in 1929. On their first trip to the Midwest, the Rens went 0-3 against white combatants the Fort Wayne Hoosiers and the Chicago Bruins, both members of the American Basketball League.

"When they meet the best of the white teams, we look on them as our representatives and expect them to give the best in them to uphold our claim to the front rank," wrote a columnist for the *Amsterdam News*. "The management and players should know this and play by it in the future."[131]

Games against the top white teams kept coming. The ABL and its whites-only policy had turned out to be more of a nuisance than a menace. Douglas could still arrange exhibition games with any ABL team. As long as the ABL teams made money and remained viable, upper management didn't seem to care. They just didn't want any black players or teams in their league.

Though Douglas could have complained about his team's exclusion from the ABL, he clearly had little to gain in doing so. Not only would he have jeopardized his exhibition games against ABL clubs, he might also have destroyed his team. After all, when the Original Celtics won the 1927–28 ABL championship, the czars of the league busted up the team like a telephone monopoly, dispersing players to various franchises.[132] The fear was that the men in green were too dominant, hurt competition, and made the league look bad. If the Rens were truly a shade behind the Celtics in the late 1920s, how would the ABL czars have coped with an all-black team's outshining its other white member teams?

As good as the Ren Big Five was, the team showed in 1929 that it was still a couple of players shy of consistently dominating its opponents, especially on the road. With a chance to redeem themselves at the end of the season, the Rens lost a traveling seven-game series to the "reorganized" Celtics, featuring Nat Holman, Joe Lapchick, and the same cast of legendary characters. Game one of the series in Harlem's 71st Regiment Armory reportedly drew more than ten thousand fans, a huge crowd in those days.

The Rens also stumbled on the road against two African American teams, a sign of the improving black game. They had to claw back from an eleven-point deficit against Chicago's new Savoy Big Five. The original Savoy Big Five had changed its name in January 1927 to the Harlem Globetrotters, but this team was most likely not Saperstein's dynasty in the making.

The other thorn in the Rens' side was the Philadelphia Giants. This up-and-coming team consistently gave the Rens fits in 1928 and 1929 and even upset the New Yorkers twice.

But the hard times for the Rens in Philadelphia would bring them good times in the 1930s. No doubt at the behest of his players, Douglas signed two former Giants to his roster. One was the heady young Billy Yancey, whose mastery of the set shot is legendary.

"[Yancey was] the greatest outside shooter I ever saw," coaching legend John Wooden recalled. "I remember once before a game, he laid out nine spots on the floor, all from a distance of today's three point line, and he'd shoot from each spot. He'd hit from all nine spots, then turn around and hit nine more coming back the other way, all without a miss. . . . Yancey used a two-handed set shot and got that shot away very quickly. I don't think there's anybody in the game today who could shoot any better or more accurately."[133]

The second star was the broad-shouldered, six-foot-three Charles "Stretch" Cooper. Tagged with the nickname "Tarzan" as a Ren, Cooper was big enough to win jump balls, rebound, and take up space near the basket. He also was an excellent passer and playmaker, always in rhythm, always in sync with his teammates.

"Nicest guy in the world," recalled Pop Gates. "He played mostly out of the pivot. He knew when you were going, when to give the ball to you, and when not to. All of the fine little techniques of how to play the game, he knew."[134]

Though George Fiall died suddenly in 1931, the upgraded Rens proved nearly unbeatable during the 1930s. The team featured two tip-top scorers in Yancey and the bank-shooting Pappy Ricks, a savvy floor leader in Fat Jenkins, and a talented big man in Tarzan Cooper. Ricks, rumored to have a taste for alcohol, left the team in the mid-1930s and died shortly thereafter from cancer. Over the course of the decade, Douglas would add Zach Clayton, Puggy Bell, Wee Willie Smith, Johnny Isaacs, and Pop Gates to the fold, great players one and all.

With their star-studded cast, the Rens ruled like no black team before them. "Fat Jenkins was basically the one that played the style of play that we had," recalled Pop Gates. "Every man was moving. One of the main rules that we had was, wherever the ball was, you always had to come to the ball and meet it. You always had to play the angles on the floor.

"Nobody stood around watching the other guys play, like you see today," Gates continued. "While the players on one side of the floor worked the ball, the other two or three players who weren't in that particular set started moving and working to get free."[135]

According to Wee Willie Smith, the Rens also kept dribbling to a minimum. "The thing they stressed was not to miss a man," said the six-foot-five Smith, who joined the Rens in 1932, teaming with Cooper to dominate play inside. "And they said if you dribble the ball and the ball is on the floor and a man went to cut, you couldn't get it to him—so that was the theory of not dribbling. To get the ball off the backboard sometimes, you had to dribble. But most of the time, we would come up with the ball off the backboard and pass it to an outlet man, and we would keep the ball up off the floor, keep it moving all the time."[136]

The Rens survived the hard times of the Great Depression in part because Douglas purchased a team bus, affectionately known as the "Blue Goose" in later years. Having their own transportation meant the Rens were free to spend the bulk of their season on the road, allowing them to quit the tiny New York dance-hall scene and move their show into much larger, more financially attractive arenas throughout the East and Midwest. Barnstorming also meant the Rens could fit in two or even three "paydays" per day, depending upon the distance between games.

Douglas also signed his players to generous exclusive contracts, a move that cemented his lineup and bolstered its star-laden image. The highest paid Ren was team captain Fat Jenkins, who earned a reported ten thousand dollars a season, then one of the largest contracts in pro basketball. During this era of bread lines, soup kitchens, and rampant unemployment, Jenkins's salary earned him automatic star status in most white newspapers. So too did his nickname: "The colored Babe Ruth of basketball."

On the road, the Rens confronted the harsh realities of Jim Crow America. As Joe Lapchick's son Richard Lapchick noted, the Rens "usually had to sleep in their bus because they were denied hotels. They traveled by bus because many forms of public transportation wouldn't have them. They ate on the bus when restaurants refused to serve them."[137]

"We sometimes had over a thousand damn dollars in our pockets and we couldn't get a good goddamn meal," said Eyre Saitch. "Our per diem was $2.50 a day. Fats [sic] Jenkins was so tight that he'd save the tea balls and later ask for a cup of hot water."[138]

The Rens also kept close watch on the promoters. Eric Illidge, the team's no-nonsense, pistol-packing road secretary, counted the fans sitting in the stands before each game to ensure that the Rens would get their fair percentage of the evening's profits. "Eric would tell guys not to come out on the court until he had the money," said Wee Willie Smith. "It was the only way we could survive."[139]

Despite the negative aspects, the Rens' true legacy is that they rose above the racist times. As Illidge stated, "We would not let anyone deny us our right to make a living."[140] If a heckler got out of hand, Jenkins and crew didn't curse or cower. They would exchange a glance, and then, as Pop Gates recalled, a Ren would immediately position himself in front of the rowdy fan. When a pass whizzed in the player's direction, he would step aside at the last moment and watch the ball nearly behead the heckler. "After that, they got the message and kept quiet," laughed Gates.[141]

With the Original Celtics now in their twilight years, the Rens had their way with the top professional teams. Though it's impossible today to account for every game that the Rens played during the decade, their record was clearly formidable. According to the Naismith Basketball Hall of Fame, the Rens officially compiled a 2,588-539 record during their existence. Included in this total was an eighty-eight-game winning streak over eighty-six days during the 1932–33 season.

The Rens were one of the few black teams in America positioned to promote equality during these segregated times. In January 1935, for instance, they rolled into Anderson, Indiana, to face the white Kautsky Athletic Club, featuring John Wooden. It might have been just one more stop for the Rens, but it was one of the premier sporting events of the year in Anderson. "While the curtain raiser was in progress, O. H. Havens, an Anderson sportswriter, was spotted darting here and there, and I was successful in holding him long enough to get the dope on the game he was promoting," wrote the black *Indianapolis Recorder.* "I over heard the words give 'em the works, as he was conversing with the Renaissance players, and naturally that was all that could be expected of the team by the few thousand patrons who jammed the gym.

"Fans from Kokomo, Newcastle, Marion, Muncie, Carthage, Indianapolis, Richmond, and many other spots were seen passing through the turnstiles to get a glimpse of the 'World Champs,'" the writer continued of the game that drew "5,000 frenzied fans."[142]

After the Rens won 52-44, the town's two white newspapers raved about their performance. "Fans who saw the New York Renaissance world champion basketball team in action here Thursday night not only saw the hardwood game at perfection—from the professional standpoint—but also realized how unattainable perfect basketball is to any team which has been organized for only a comparatively short period of time," wrote one.

Said the other: "The opposition put up by the Kautsky team—representing as it does about the finest that Indiana can offer—was evidently not up to standard in the game, but judging from the number of times that the Eastern visitors deliberately avoided making baskets, the winning score could easily have been much higher."[143]

And so it went, night after night.

"For all the years that the team was in existence, we treated the fans to some of the classiest basketball in the world," said Douglas, noting that his club traveled about thirty-eight thousand miles per season, reaching as far west as Wyoming and as far south as New Orleans.[144]

The Rens also connected with African Americans wherever they played. "About 400 of the crowd, estimated . . . at 1,800, were colored fans and they had a big time when the Rens staged a spectacular exhibition of passing in the last half," wrote the *Evansville Courier.* "They fired the ball all around their end of the court for several minutes without losing it, and the colored fans were highly excited."[145]

It was a moment for fans to savor in Evansville, Indianapolis, Anderson, and the other black neighborhoods along the way. The Rens were *their* team. They inspired pride, passion, and a sense of hope for the future.

Most of these fans have now passed on, taking with them their personal tales of Fat Jenkins, Tarzan Cooper, Pappy Ricks, and the rest. All that remains are newspaper clippings and a few oral histories. But if the history of basketball is a continuum, the Rens serve as a vital bridge linking the early and modern eras. Their influence on the development of the game should always be remembered.

Epilogue

On March 20, 1939, the Renaissance defeated the white Oshkosh All-Stars 43-25 to win the first-ever world professional basketball tournament in Chicago. Though the Rens likely would have won other tournaments had they been held earlier in the decade, the 1939 title officially validated the New Yorkers as the world champions.

"That was a thrill that will live in my memories forever," Fat Jenkins later recalled. "For years we had been trying to gain recognition as the world's professional basketball champions, but it wasn't until the twilight of my career that we officially won that title."[1]

Following their 1939 championship season, however, the Rens began to decline. The following season, they lost to the Harlem Globetrotters 37-36 in the quarterfinals of the professional tournament. The Globetrotters would later win the tournament championship, supplanting the Rens as the dominant black professional team. In 1941, the white Detroit Eagles defeated the Rens 43-42 in the semifinals of the professional tournament, which the Eagles would later win.

A major reason for the Rens' decline was age. After enduring a decade of tens of thousands of miles and more than 130 games per season, some of the Rens had grown weary of the road. Jenkins, the team's captain and coach, was pushing forty years old, and the blazing speed that once left behind "scorched boards" had slowed to a stiff trot. Jenkins's advancing age was an issue because the center jump after each made basket had been eliminated in 1937. More than ever, basketball was a young man's game that required speed and quickness. Sensing that his body had endured enough punishment, Jenkins retired before the start of the 1939–40 season.

Without their captain and linchpin, the Rens' once solid lineup began to turn over. Tarzan Cooper and Wee Willie Smith, perhaps the two top big men in the pro game, both left the team soon thereafter. The aging Cooper retired briefly, and Smith abruptly signed with the rival Globetrotters in 1941.

Though Douglas had Pop Gates, Dolly King, Wilmeth Sidat-Singh, and several other talented young players waiting in the wings, the outbreak of World War II prevented this new version of the Rens from gelling into an experienced, world-beating team. Pop Gates explained, "You couldn't buy gasoline, and we traveled by bus. So we knew that Bob Douglas wouldn't be able to travel to make the money to pay our salaries. We didn't quit him or the team. If it wasn't for the war, we'd still be playing for Bob Douglas."[2]

Gates and most of the Rens started looking elsewhere for their money. One place they looked was the nation's capital, where sportswriter Sam Lacy had patched together a new black professional team by the start of the 1940–41 season. "I got the idea because there was nothing for blacks to do in the winter, particularly on Sundays," he recalled.[3] Lacy enlisted the help of two friends, Harold Jackson and Art Carter, and the Washington Bruins were born. At first, Lacy and crew coaxed Fat Jenkins out of retirement to coach the team. But Jenkins left the Bruins in a huff after a contract dispute, and Lacy opted to build his Sunday-afternoon entertainment around several local players and retired Ren Tarzan Cooper, who had begun working during the war at Washington's Navy Yard. Playing in Turner's Arena, a drafty garage-turned-gymnasium, the Bruins became a popular attraction in black Washington, though the team rarely held scheduled practice sessions and free-lanced without a set offense during each game.[4]

By the following season, Lacy had left for Chicago, where he helped lobby for Jackie Robinson's admission into the major leagues. Taking Lacy's place was none other than Ewell Conway, the former manager of the Carlisle Big Five. Conway asked Abe Lichtman, still the owner of a prosperous chain of local black theaters, to sponsor his new team. Though wise to Conway's street-hustling ways, Lichtman reluctantly agreed to foot the team's bills, and the Bruins were dubbed the "Lichtman Bears."

With more money to spend, Conway and crew reunited Tarzan Cooper with many of his Ren teammates, including Pop Gates, Johnny Isaacs, Dolly King, Puggy Bell, and, before his untimely death, Wilmeth Sidat-Singh. "The Bears were reminiscent of the 1935–1939 Renaissance teams," noted the *Washington Afro-American* of the team, which would play until the end of the war in 1945. "As a matter of actuality, there were times when the entire playing five was composed of former Rens."[5]

In 1943, the Washington Bears won the professional tournament in Chicago. With the win, black professional teams had claimed three out of the first four tournament titles.

Applauding the Bears' championship was Ed Henderson. Now in his late fifties—more than thirty years removed from the undefeated 12th Street YMCA team—Henderson was lucky enough to have watched his dream of organized black athletics come true and mature. Black schools and sports clubs had produced world-class athletes in every major sport and helped to challenge false racial stereotypes.

Henderson also knew that he had to keep pushing for black athletics to stay up-to-date and competitive. "Let us admit that those who worked for school facilities under a passing dispensation did all they could do under the circumstances," wrote Henderson in 1948. "Tomorrow's school will require large gymnasia, space for spectators, swimming pools, rooms for apparatus and games, ample locker space, and many acres for athletics for boys and girls." Yet again, Henderson would be correct about the coming trend in sports.[6]

Henderson also kept pushing hard as a civil-rights activist, either organizing or taking part in numerous protests against segregation. These protests ranged from picketing the local branch of the American Athletic Union to force it to hold mixed-race boxing championships in Washington to demonstrating against Jim Crow policies at the city's best theaters and arenas, all battles that Henderson and colleagues won decisively.

Henderson also sensed greater victories to come on the athletic field. With his uncanny intuition for future trends in sports, he wrote the following in 1948:

Nineteen-forty eight in sports may one day be called the turning point on the road towards complete integration. Among the significant happenings in the world of sports we cite a few:

The Olympics gave us the fastest human, the strongest man, the only American girl champion, the longest jumper, and a star in the basketball firmament.

. . . Some would say on the debit side is the decline of Negro baseball as a business. We say otherwise. The decline and fall of Jim
Crow business is a good sign. We see the beginning of the collapse of
institutionalized exploitation of segregation, and a greater stride towards integration in sports and business.

It is a healthy sign when Negro business in sports, when Negro
schools, when the Negro press and the NAACP, Urban League,
Negro YMCA, and Negro churches begin to go out of business.

It will be a great day for America when by Supreme Court or leg-
islative action there will be no such citizens as Negro citizens, but
just Americans in the United States.

Let us not look apprehensively at the decline of Negro baseball. It
is a hopeful indication. The only great sufferers will be the vested interests and leaders who must now begin to find other fields in which
to operate.

[Larry] Doby, [Marion] Motley, and [Jackie] Robinson had a lot to
learn to compete in the integrated field of sports. So must our business men, educators, our doctors, lawyers, and statesmen.[7]

On February 3, 1977, Ed Henderson passed away at the age of
ninety-three. Having dedicated his life to the advancement of black athletics, Henderson wrote a decade before his death words that could
have served as his epitaph: "It is our opinion that when the final record
is written as to contributing values in the battle of human and civil rights
our Negro athletes should be accorded high esteem."[8]

Almost twenty years earlier, in January 1958, longtime Howard University basketball coach John Burr died after a brief illness at the age
of fifty-nine. After his rocky introduction to Howard basketball in the
early 1920s—when his team severed its ties with the Colored Intercollegiate Athletic Association—Burr had persevered to see better times.

"It is safe to predict that diplomatic relations between the former al-
lies will be restored before the snow begins to melt in the spring," wrote
the *Amsterdam News* at Christmas 1927. "The sudden change in attitude of both belligerents may be attributed to the spirit of good will that
is sweeping over the earth at this time of the year. Maybe, however, it
is also reasonable to assume that the depleted state of the Howard University athletic treasury and the stagnant condition in the C.I.A.A.
household since their big brother 'ran off and joined the navy' has been
the deciding factor."[9]

In December 1928, Howard University officially rejoined the CIAA. Howard president Mordecai Johnson vowed that all brushes with professionalism would cease on the university's campus. "No man who has been around our colleges in the East, white and colored, has failed to see that there has been a considerable amount of professionalism in these schools, a considerable . . . use of money, violating written understandings and creating mistrust between institutions, and destroying morale of the institutions themselves," Johnson told his colleagues. "The one thing that the trustees and president of Howard University set out to do was to develop an absolutely clean, open, and above board amateur situation with men playing the game because they love the sport."[10]

For the most part, during these separate and unequal times, Johnson, Burr, and their CIAA colleagues succeeded. By 1934, Virginia Union professor Arthur Davis could in good conscience comment, "It is indeed a far cry from that small group of six colleges which assembled in 1912 to form the CIAA to the present large and highly-trained group of coaches and faculty members representing thirteen schools of the present organization. This group in itself is concrete evidence of the progress made in those intervening years in training, in equipment, and in appreciation of the place of athletics in our Negro colleges."[11]

Today, though only Virginia Union remains of the original members, the CIAA continues under the name of the Central Intercollegiate Athletic Association. Playing on the NCAA Division II level, the CIAA each year produces many outstanding student athletes at small, traditionally black colleges.

In 1979, Bob Douglas passed away. Several years before he died, the Naismith Basketball Hall of Fame enshrined him for his long career with the Rens. Later joining him in the Hall of Fame were Pop Gates and Tarzan Cooper.

"Bob Douglas was a very direct, very positive person," recalled Gates in words that also summarized Douglas's career in basketball. "He knew the ball game, and he knew the players. There was nothing that he wouldn't do for you, if he could. But he wouldn't take no stuff from anybody. He was a very smart, astute, tough person."[12]

The heart and soul of the Rens, Fat Jenkins, has never been inducted into the Naismith Basketball Hall of Fame, a major oversight and injustice. Also missing is the greatest player that Jenkins said he ever faced, Cum Posey.

NOTES

ONE In the Beginning

1. L. N. Coursey, *The Life of Edwin Bancroft Henderson and His Professional Contributions to Physical Education* (Columbus, 1971), pp. 20–21, 43; *Congressional Record—Senate,* Apr. 5, 1977, S5572–S5573.
2. *Washington Evening Star,* Nov. 26, 1907.
3. Coursey, *Life of Edwin Bancroft Henderson,* p. 54; *Washington Afro-American,* Feb. 28, 1953; Jul. 31, 1954.
4. YMCA Campaign Book of 1908.
5. Jones, *Washington YMCA,* 1909, p. 5.
6. Henderson often said he introduced basketball to the male students in Washington's black public schools in 1904. This is correct in that he introduced the sport during gym class for exercise. He also organized an exhibition game in early 1907 (see *University Journal,* Feb. 15, 1907). But Henderson did not formally organize black basketball until his encounter with Beckett in late 1907.
7. *University Journal,* Jan. 10, 1908.
8. Ibid., Feb. 10, 1908.
9. Ibid.
10. Ibid.
11. Ibid., May 10, 1908.
12. *Howard University Journal,* Feb. 5, 1909.
13. *Washington Evening Star,* Mar. 31, 1954.
14. *Howard University Journal,* Feb. 5, 1909.
15. In William Joiner Collection, Moorland-Spingarn Memorial Library, Howard University.
16. *Annual Handbook of the Inter-Scholastic Association of Middle Atlantic States, 1911,* Spalding's Athletic Library, p. 47; *New York Age,* Apr. 8. 1909.

17. In Edwin Bancroft Henderson Collection, Moorland-Spingarn Memorial Library, Howard University.

18. Anyone who attempts to pin down the identity of the "original" black basketball teams quickly realizes the futility of the undertaking. Most of the few copies of newspapers of the era that remain today covered sports sporadically at best, and virtually all paid no attention to basketball firsts. The players and fans of the era passed away long ago, and based on their few remaining accounts of early basketball, it seems unlikely that any of them considered or knew the correct answer to the question.

19. Coursey, *Life of Edwin Bancroft Henderson,* p. 173.

20. *Amsterdam News,* Apr. 13, 1932.

21. *Washington Evening Star,* Apr. 14, 1905.

22. *Messenger,* Jun. 1927.

23. Quoted in *Cycle Age,* Apr. 18, 1901.

24. G. Astor, *The Baseball Hall of Fame* (New York, 1988), p. 52.

25. *New York Age,* Sept. 27, 1906; *Indianapolis Freeman,* Jan. 12, 1907.

26. *New York Age,* Sept. 20, 1906; *Boston Guardian,* Feb. 15, 1908.

27. *Indianapolis Freeman,* Dec. 28, 1912.

28. *Washington Evening Star,* Jul. 30, 1905; *New York Times,* Jan. 1, 1907.

29. *Annual Handbook of the Inter-Scholastic Association of Middle Atlantic States, 1910,* Spalding's Athletic Library, p. 25.

30. *Year Book of the Young Men's Christian Associations of North America,* May 1, 1905–Apr. 30, 1906, pp. 7, 184.

31. Coursey, *Life of Edwin Bancroft Henderson,* pp. 20–24.

32. *Washington Evening Star,* Dec. 22, 1897.

33. *Annual Handbook, 1910,* foreword.

34. Coursey, *Life of Edwin Bancroft Henderson,* pp. 28–29.

35. Ibid., pp. 22–23.

36. Ibid., p. 40.

37. *Washington Afro-American,* Aug. 7, 1954.

38. *Howard University Journal,* Mar. 11, 1910.

39. Washington Playground Association pamphlet, Playgrounds folder, Washingtoniana Room, Martin Luther King Library, Washington, D.C.

40. *Report of Commissioners of District of Columbia,* 1908, p. 251.

41. Ibid., pp. 251–52.

42. *University Journal,* Nov. 4, 1904.

43. Ibid., Dec. 1, 1903.

44. Ibid., Apr. 15, 1904.

45. *Annual Handbook, 1910,* pp. 15–23.

46. W. Irwin, *Highlights of Manhattan* (New York and London, 1927), p. 20.

47. M. W. Ovington, *Half a Man: The Status of the Negro in New York* (New York, 1911), p. 53.

48. Ovington, *Half a Man,* p. 119.

49. The parish house was located at 25th Street between Sixth and Seventh Avenues. In 1911, St. Philip's Church moved into an elaborate new church and

parish house in Harlem between 133rd and 134th Streets near 7th Avenue. The parish house was a fairly large three-story building in the middle of a residential block. The new gymnasium, while too small to host large crowds, was by far the best facility of its kind among the black clubs in New York. See *New York Age*, Jan. 19, 1911.

50. *Annual Handbook, 1911*, p. 27.

51. *Amsterdam News*, Jan. 20, 1932.

52. K. T. Jackson, ed., *The Encyclopedia of New York City* (New Haven and London, 1995), p. 582; Ovington, *Half a Man*, pp. 48–50.

53. Ovington, *Half a Man*, p. 177.

54. *Indianapolis Freeman*, Mar. 7, 1908.

55. *Howard University Journal*, Feb. 25, 1910.

56. *Annual Handbook, 1910*, p. 21.

57. *New York Age*, Feb. 17, 1910.

58. Newspaper article found in Ed Henderson's personal scrapbook, Moorland-Spingarn Memorial Library, Howard University.

59. *Washington Evening Star*, Apr. 3, 1910.

60. *Howard University Journal*, Apr. 8, 1910.

TWO The Golden Era of Amateurism

1. When the 12th Street YMCA played Smart Set for the 1910 title, nearly two thousand fans attended the championship game. However, the contest was part of a much larger athletic carnival, not a stand-alone attraction, as Alpha promoted its first game against 12th Street. It is noteworthy that prior to intercity competition in 1907, most basketball games drew crowds in the low hundreds in New York. After intercity play began, the crowds remained modest. The Smart Set–Armstrong High School game of 1907, for instance, attracted only about five hundred fans. As this figure suggests, an athletic club had to step forward and market the game to the public, as Ed Henderson had done in Washington. Alpha was that club, turning the game into a social event and dance. Smart Set, which had a better basketball team, might have filled this role had it not committed itself to promoting expensive track meets and athletic carnivals.

2. *Washington Evening Star*, Dec. 29, 1910.

3. *New York Age*, Oct. 13, 1910.

4. Ibid.

5. Ibid., Jan. 5, 1911.

6. Ibid., Feb. 23, 1911.

7. *Howard University Journal*, Dec. 1, 1911.

8. *Amsterdam News*, Mar. 16, 1932.

9. *New York Age*, Mar. 28, 1912.

10. *Amsterdam News*, Jul. 27, 1927.

11. *Washington Bee*, Sept. 9, 1911.

12. *Washington Tribune*, Mar. 4, 1922.

13. *Washington Evening Star*, May 1, 1905.

14. *Washington Bee*, Oct. 28, 1911.

15. Ibid., Oct. 23, 1913.
16. Ibid., Dec. 20, 1913.
17. F. J. Grimke, *The Things of Paramount Importance in the Development of the Negro Race* (Washington, DC, 1903), p. 1.
18. Given that so much information has been lost from this era, I recognize that it is a bit of a leap to label this game as the first. As writer Ocania Chalk noted, students at Fisk College began playing basketball intramurally as early as 1900. (O. Chalk, *Black College Sports* [New York, 1976], p. 71.) It is possible that Fisk scrimmaged a rival black college soon thereafter. Nevertheless, the Howard-Hampton game was significant because it was the first involving major black colleges that had skilled basketball teams. With the success of this game, the two heavyweights began a healthy rivalry that would encourage other local black colleges to pursue the sport. These rivalries would lay the groundwork for the rise of black intercollegiate basketball after World War I.
19. *Pittsburgh Courier*, Dec. 16, 1911; Jan. 13, 1912; Apr. 6, 1929.
20. Ibid., Dec. 19, 1942.
21. Ibid., Mar. 16, 1912.
22. *New York Age*, Mar. 14, 1912.
23. *Pittsburgh Courier*, Mar. 16, 1912.
24. *New York Age*, Mar. 14, 1912.
25. Ibid. The newspaper probably was hesitant to crown Monticello as the champion because Posey and company had yet to play any of the New York teams. However, reading between the lines, the sportswriter implied that any team that could beat Howard must be the best in the game.
26. *Howard University Journal*, Dec. 5, 1913.
27. C. H. Williams, "Twenty Years' Work of the C.I.A.A.," in *Bulletin of the Colored Intercollegiate Athletic Association*, 1932, pp. 1–4.
28. *Annual Handbook of the Inter-Scholastic Association of Middle Atlantic States, 1912*, Spalding's Athletic Library, p. 49.
29. Williams, "Twenty Years," p. 3.
30. *Annual Handbook of the Inter-Scholastic Association of Middle Atlantic States, 1913*, Spalding's Athletic Library, p. 63.
31. *Annual Handbook of the Inter-Scholastic Association of Middle Atlantic States, 1910*, Spalding's Athletic Library, p. 69.
32. Ibid.
33. Undated newspaper article titled "Athletic Notes," written by Ed Henderson. The article is in Henderson's personal scrapbook, Moorland-Spingarn Memorial Library, Howard University; *Southern Workman*, Apr. 1915, p. 251.
34. *Baltimore Afro-American*, Apr. 6, 1929.
35. The exchange of letters between Richardson and Norris was published in the *New York Age*, Jan. 23, Feb. 6, and Feb. 13, 1913.
36. *Howard University Journal*, Mar. 28, 1913.
37. Ibid.
38. Ibid.

39. Ibid., Apr. 12, 1913.
40. Personal interview, 1991.
41. *Pittsburgh Courier,* Jan. 14, 1928.
42. *Washington Bee,* Jun. 27, 1914.
43. *Messenger,* May 1926.
44. *Washington Evening Star,* Nov. 12, Nov. 25, 1912; Jan. 7, 1913.
45. Ibid., Nov. 6, 1912.
46. *Black Sports,* Feb. 1972, p. 65.
47. *Washington Bee,* Mar. 17, 1917.
48. E. B. Henderson, *History of the Fairfax County Branch of the NAACP,* Oct. 1965, p. 4.
49. L. N. Coursey, *The Life of Edwin Bancroft Henderson and His Professional Contributions to Physical Education* (Columbus, 1971), p. 272.
50. Coursey, *Life of Edwin Bancroft Henderson,* p. 250.
51. *Pittsburgh Courier,* Dec. 19, 1942.
52. *Amsterdam News,* Feb. 10, 1932.
53. *New York Age,* Feb. 3, 1916.
54. Ibid., Apr. 9, 1914.
55. Ibid., Mar. 26, 1914.
56. Ibid., Apr. 23, 1914.
57. Ibid., Dec. 10, 1914.
58. Ibid., Oct. 22, 1914.
59. *Amsterdam News,* Jan. 2, 1929.
60. Ibid.; *New York Age,* Dec. 10, 1914.
61. *New York Age,* Nov. 26, 1914.
62. Ibid., Dec. 17, 1914.
63. Ibid.
64. *Washington Sun,* Jan. 1, 1915.
65. *New York Age,* Dec. 31, 1914.
66. *Washington Sun,* Jan. 1, 1915.
67. The white amateur movement weathered numerous small scandals during the decade, most of which involved college and club teams' fielding ineligible players. But the white movement already had succumbed to obsessive rivalries and an emphasis on winning, particularly among the prominent white colleges of the day. As more university presidents viewed football and other games as Saturday afternoon social events staged before tens of thousands of students and alumni, the amateur ideal was becoming more susceptible to the pressures and taint of money.
68. *Washington Sun,* Jan. 1, 1915.
69. *New York Age,* Jan. 7, 1915.
70. Ibid., Nov. 4, 1915.
71. *Pittsburgh Courier,* Feb. 28, 1925.
72. Ibid., Nov. 25, 1915.
73. Ibid., Apr. 20, 1916.

74. Ibid., Mar. 17, 1928.
75. Ibid.
76. *New York Age*, Mar. 23, 1917.
77. Ibid.
78. Ibid., Dec. 21, 1916.
79. Ibid., Apr. 26, 1917.
80. *Competitor*, 1919.
81. *Spirit of Jefferson*, Charles Town, WV, May 29, 1917.
82. *Washington Bee*, Aug. 25, 1917.
83. Ibid., Apr. 28, 1917.

THREE   The Decline of Amateurism

1. *Washington Bee*, Nov. 2, 1918.
2. Ibid., Jan. 18, 1919.
3. A. Locke, "Harlem," in *Survey Graphic*, March 1925, p. 630.
4. *Crusader Monthly*, Feb. 1920.
5. Quoted in D. L. Lewis, *W. E. B. Du Bois: Biography of a Race* (New York, 1993), p. 580.
6. *Amsterdam News*, Apr. 13, 1927.
7. *This Fabulous Century, 1920–1930* (New York, 1988), p. 4.
8. G. Myrdal, *An American Dilemma: The Negro Problem and Modern Democracy* (New York and London, 1944), p. 225.
9. *Washington Evening Times*, Jul. 9, 1921.
10. R. Roberts, *Papa Jack: Jack Johnson and the Era of White Hopes* (New York, 1983), pp. 69–70.
11. *New York Age*, Aug. 21, 1930; *Buffalo Morning Express*, Jan. 16, 1921. It is worth noting that not all whites below the Mason-Dixon line were filled with race hatred. For example, after black middleweight boxing champion Tiger Flowers won the world middleweight title from white boxer Harry Greb, blacks and whites in his hometown of Brunswick, Georgia, celebrated the news. "[A] parade was formed to march through the city," wrote the *Pittsburgh Courier* on Apr. 3, 1926. "Headed by the Chief of Police of Brunswick, those taking part in the parade increased in numbers until there were in line about 100 automobiles of every description from a coughing, rattling truck to a softly purring seven-passenger sedan lined with downy plush. . . . One truck carried an orchestra, including a piano. . . . The tooting of horns, clanging of bells, and shouts of the paraders, which could be heard all over the town, sounded like the inevitable din which accompanies the return of a mob of victorious college students from a football classic."
12. *Washington Herald*, Jul. 6, 1921.
13. C. Samuels, *The Magnificent Rube: The Life and Gaudy Times of Tex Rickard* (New York, Toronto, London, 1957), p. 276.
14. *Pittsburgh Courier*, Dec. 15, 1928.
15. L. Koppett, *24 Seconds to Shoot: An Informal History of the National Basketball Association* (London, 1968), p. 39.

16. *Baltimore Afro-American,* Sept. 5, 1924.

17. *Messenger,* Feb. 1927.

18. S. Frank, ed., *Sports Extra: Classics of Sports Reporting* (New York, 1944), foreword, xiii.

19. T. Hayes, *With the Gloves Off: My Life in the Boxing and Political Arenas* (Houston, 1977), p. 159.

20. R. W. Peterson, *Cages to Jump Shots: Pro Basketball's Early Years* (New York and Oxford, 1990), p. 69.

21. *Washington Evening Times,* Jan. 11, 1923.

22. T. Meany, "The Original Celtics," in E. Fitzgerald, ed., *A Treasury of Sports Stories* (New York, 1955), p. 145.

23. Ibid., pp. 151–52.

24. Ibid., p. 145.

25. Ibid., p. 143.

26. Ibid.

27. J. Lapchick, *50 Years of Basketball* (New York, 1968), p. 14.

28. *Crusader Monthly,* Dec. 1919.

29. *New York Age,* Jan. 31, 1920.

30. Ibid., Feb. 28, 1920.

31. Ibid., Mar. 13, 1920.

32. Ibid.

33. Ibid.

34. Ibid.

35. E. Rust and A. Rust Jr., *Art Rust's Illustrated History of the Black Athlete* (Garden City, NY, 1985), p. 298. Late in his life, as might be expected, Douglas sometimes retold the story of watching his first basketball game with somewhat altered details. In the quote cited here, Douglas places the year as 1903 and the location of the gymnasium as "52nd Street on Tenth Avenue." In Douglas's obituary on July 21, 1979, the *Amsterdam News* cites Douglas as giving the same address for the gymnasium, but lists the year as 1905.

36. Rust and Rust, *Art Rust's Illustrated History,* p. 298.

37. *New York Age,* Aug. 27, 1914.

38. Ibid., Dec. 17, 1914.

39. Ibid., Apr. 20, 1916.

40. *Chicago Defender,* Jan. 16, 1926.

41. *New York Age,* Dec. 14, 1916.

42. Ibid., Dec. 4, 1920.

43. This theme emerged several times in some of my personal interviews. While one could dismiss it as hearsay or sour grapes, the Carlisle-Spartan game offers a vivid taste of the home cooking that visiting teams could face in Harlem.

44. *Baltimore Afro-American,* Dec. 24, 1920.

45. In addition to the revolving names in the box score, several former Washington players from the 1930s and 1940s talked about the difficulty of working full time and rearranging their schedules to play in games. Many said they were em-

ployed as messengers, elevator operators, or custodians. Given the menial nature of these jobs, most were easily replaced if they missed a work shift. All said they couldn't afford to lose a regular paycheck to play a basketball game for free or, in some cases, a few extra dollars.

46. *New York Age,* Jan. 1, 1921.
47. *Washington Bee,* Jan. 8, 1921.
48. *New York Age,* Nov. 13, 1920.
49. Ibid., May 29, Oct. 9, 1920.
50. Ibid., Dec. 4, 1920.
51. Ibid., Apr. 16, 1921.
52. Ibid., Feb. 2, 1920.
53. *Competitor,* 1919.
54. *Crusader Monthly,* Jan. 1921.
55. Ibid.
56. Ibid.
57. *New York Age,* Dec. 11, 1920.
58. Ibid.
59. Ibid., Nov. 27, 1920.
60. Ibid.
61. Ibid.
62. *Chicago Defender,* Apr. 2, 1921.
63. *Baltimore Afro-American,* Feb. 18, 1921.
64. *New York Age,* Jan. 22, 1921.
65. Ibid., Apr. 9, 1921.
66. Ibid., Feb. 12, 1921.
67. *Baltimore Afro-American,* May 27, 1921.
68. *New York Age,* Nov. 19, Dec. 17, 1921.
69. Ibid., Dec. 17, 1921.
70. Ibid., Dec. 3, 1921.
71. Ibid., Jan. 7, 1922.
72. Ibid., Jan. 14, 1922.
73. Ibid., Jan. 28, 1922.
74. Ibid., Feb. 11, 1922.
75. *Washington Tribune,* Mar. 18, 1922.
76. Ibid., Jun. 11, 1921.
77. Ibid., Jan. 28, 1922.
78. Ibid., Feb. 18, 1922.
79. *Washington Bee,* Jan. 21, 1922.
80. *Washington Tribune,* Mar. 18, 1922.
81. Ibid.
82. The Commonwealth Casino was formerly the Palace Casino, where Douglas's Spartan basketball team had tried several years earlier to break into the Harlem basketball scene. See *New York Age,* Oct. 2, 1920.
83. *Amsterdam News,* Dec. 6, 1922.

84. Ibid., Jan. 3, 1923.
85. Ibid.
86. Ibid., Feb. 28, 1923.
87. Ibid., Jan. 3, 1923.
88. *New York Age,* Dec. 16, 1922.
89. *Amsterdam News,* Feb. 28, 1923.
90. *Chicago Defender,* Mar. 10, 1923.
91. *Amsterdam News,* Mar. 7, 1923.
92. Ibid.
93. *Chicago Defender,* Mar. 23, 1923.
94. Ibid.
95. *Amsterdam News,* Mar. 21, 1923.
96. Ibid.
97. *Pittsburgh Courier,* Apr. 14, 1923.

FOUR The Rise of Professionalism

1. *New York Age,* Feb. 19, 1921.
2. Ibid., Jan. 29, 1921.
3. Ibid., Feb. 24, 1923.
4. *Baltimore Afro-American,* Jan. 11, 1924.
5. *Amsterdam News,* Sept. 26, 1923.
6. *Pittsburgh Courier,* Nov. 17, 1923.
7. Ibid., Nov. 3, 1923.
8. E. Rust and A. Rust Jr., *Art Rust's Illustrated History of the Black Athlete* (Garden City, NY, 1985), p. 299.
9. Ibid.
10. *New York Age,* Aug. 4, 1923.
11. *Amsterdam News,* Sept. 19, 1923; *Pittsburgh Courier,* Oct. 27, 1923; *Baltimore Afro-American,* Oct. 12, 1923.
12. *Amsterdam News,* Oct. 17, 1923.
13. Ibid.
14. *Pittsburgh Courier,* Dec. 1, 1923.
15. *Washington Tribune,* Feb. 16, 1924.
16. *Pittsburgh Courier,* Feb. 16, 1924.
17. *Washington Tribune,* Jan. 5, 1924.
18. *Amsterdam News,* Sept. 19, 1923.
19. Ibid.
20. Ibid., Oct. 17, 1923. According to Pop Gates, the Renaissance Casino had holes drilled at each end of the dance floor where long poles could be inserted. The poles had a backboard and basket attached at the top. Ceiling wires that dropped down and attached tightly to the sides of each backboard kept the basket from shaking. Gates said folding chairs were set up near courtside for the more fashionable fans.
21. *Amsterdam News,* Oct. 31, 1923.

22. Ibid., Nov. 7, 1923.

23. *New York Age,* Mar. 1, 1924.

24. Ibid., Mar. 15, 1924.

25. *Chicago Defender,* Apr. 26, 1924.

26. *Washington Herald,* Apr. 22, 1924.

27. Ibid.

28. Personal interview, 1991.

29. *Chicago Defender,* Apr. 26, 1924.

30. Ibid., May 2, 1924.

31. W. E. B. Du Bois, "Of Our Spiritual Strivings," in *The Souls of Black Folk* (New York, 1903), p. 4.

32. *Chicago Defender,* Dec. 27, 1924.

33. *Washington Tribune,* Jan. 24, 1925.

34. Ibid.

35. Ibid., Feb. 7, 1925.

36. Ibid., Mar. 8, 1924.

37. Ibid., Jan. 17, 1925.

38. Ibid.

39. *Philadelphia Tribune,* Jan. 2, 1926.

40. *Baltimore Afro-American,* Jan. 16, 1926.

41. *Washington Tribune,* Jan. 29, 1926.

42. *Baltimore Afro-American,* Jan. 30, 1926.

43. *Philadelphia Tribune,* Jan. 30, 1926.

44. *Pittsburgh Courier,* Apr. 17, 1926; *Amsterdam News,* Apr. 21, 1926.

45. *Baltimore Afro-American,* Mar. 13, 1926.

46. *Washington Tribune,* Feb. 18, 1927.

47. *Chicago Defender,* Feb. 19, 1927; D. Zinkoff, *Go, Man, Go* (New York, 1971), pp. 21–22.

48. *Washington Tribune,* Jan. 14, 1927.

49. Ibid.

50. Ibid., Feb. 25, 1927.

51. Ibid.

52. *Baltimore Afro-American,* Feb. 18, 1927.

53. *Chicago Defender,* Apr. 30, 1927; *Atlantic City Daily Press,* Mar. 16, 1927.

54. C. S. Johnson, "Black Workers in the City," in *Survey Graphic,* March 1925, p. 643.

55. The nickname "Heavenly Twins" was borrowed from white basketball and the moniker for the popular 1920s duo of Barney Sedran and Marty Friedman. Though a newspaper reporter originally used the nickname sarcastically, it soon took on a life of its own. Among white basketball fans, it meant that the tandem could do no wrong. By extension, Harlem fans believed the duo of Jenkins and Fiall could make all the plays.

56. *Amsterdam News,* Mar. 18, 1925.

57. Ibid., Mar. 4, 1925.

58. *Pittsburgh Courier,* Mar. 28, 1925.

59. Ibid.
60. Cum Posey referred occasionally to differences in the black and white games. See a brief mention in the *Pittsburgh Courier,* Nov. 28, 1925. Posey indicates that the black game was built on speed, not size or seamless teamwork. This idea is echoed by Madden in his above critique of the Ren-Celtic matchup and, over the next few years, by Romeo Dougherty of the *Amsterdam News.*
61. N. Holman, *Winning Basketball* (New York, 1934), pp. 43–44.
62. *Washington Herald,* Jan. 11, 1923.
63. *Philadelphia Tribune,* Apr. 4, 1925.
64. *Amsterdam News,* Oct. 7, 1925.
65. Ibid., Oct. 21, 1925.
66. Ibid., Dec. 9, 1925.
67. Ibid., Apr. 1, 1925.
68. *New York Age,* Nov. 7, 1925.
69. *Messenger,* Feb. 1927.
70. *Amsterdam News,* Dec. 23, 1925.
71. *Reach Official Basket Ball Guide, 1926–1927* (Philadelphia), p. 215.
72. *Amsterdam News,* Dec. 23, 1925.
73. *Pittsburgh Courier,* Mar. 28, 1925.
74. *Washington Herald,* Nov. 28, 1925; *Reach Official Basket Ball Guide, 1926–1927,* p. 214.
75. Quoted in *New York Age,* Mar. 26, 1926.
76. Quoted in *Amsterdam News,* Dec. 23, 1925.
77. Ibid.
78. *Pittsburgh Courier,* Dec. 26, 1925.
79. *New York Age,* Oct. 9, 1920.
80. *Baltimore Afro-American,* May 18, 1923.
81. Ibid., Jan. 2, 1926.
82. *Messenger,* Feb. 1926.
83. *Amsterdam News,* Dec. 23, 1925.
84. Ibid., Feb. 24, 1926.
85. Ibid., Dec. 18, 1929.
86. Ibid., Oct. 6, 1926.
87. Ibid., Aug. 4, 1926.
88. Ibid., Mar. 30, 1927.
89. Ibid., Jan. 5, 1927; *Washington Herald,* Nov. 30, 1925.
90. *Amsterdam News,* Dec. 29, 1926.
91. *Pittsburgh Courier,* Mar. 12, 1927.
92. *New York Age,* Nov. 27, 1926.
93. *Philadelphia Tribune,* Apr. 9, 1927.
94. *Pittsburgh Courier,* Mar. 12, 1927.
95. *Philadelphia Tribune,* Apr. 9, 1927; *Chicago Defender,* Mar. 5, 1927.
96. Douglas clearly was on good terms with the management of the Renaissance Casino, which allowed him to use the hall not only for basketball games but for

dances and other social events. In 1933, Douglas was officially named manager of the casino, a title he held for many years.

97. *Washington Tribune*, Mar. 23, 1928.

98. J. W. Johnson, *Black Manhattan* (New York, 1930), pp. 157–58.

99. *Washington Evening Times*, Jan. 11, 1923.

100. Two examples: *Washington Tribune*, Dec. 15, 1923, and Jan. 12, 1924. Many other games could be cited.

101. Personal interview, 1999.

102. *Washington Evening Star*, Oct. 19, 1965.

103. *Washington Herald*, Jan. 2, 1926.

104. Personal interview, 1999.

105. Ibid.

106. R. Lapchick, *Broken Promises: Racism in American Sports* (New York, 1984), p. 155.

107. Personal interview, 1994.

108. Rust and Rust, *Art Rust's Illustrated History*, p. 328.

109. Personal interview, 1999.

110. *Pittsburgh Courier*, Nov. 12, 1927.

111. *Amsterdam News*, Dec. 28, 1927.

112. *Philadelphia Tribune*, Dec. 22, 1927.

113. *Pittsburgh Courier*, Mar. 28, 1925.

114. *Washington Tribune*, Dec. 5, 1925.

115. *Pittsburgh Courier*, Dec. 31, 1927.

116. *Washington Tribune*, Feb. 3, 1927.

117. *Amsterdam News*, Nov. 16, 1927.

118. *Pittsburgh Courier*, Jan. 7, 1928.

119. *Washington Tribune*, Dec. 30, 1927.

120. Ibid., Feb. 3, 1928.

121. Ibid.

122. *Baltimore Afro-American*, Mar. 10, 1928.

123. *New York Age*, Feb. 4, 1928.

124. *Amsterdam News*, Oct. 10, 1928.

125. *Washington Tribune*, Mar. 16, 1928.

126. Ibid., Oct. 26, 1928.

127. Ibid., Jan. 18, 1929.

128. Ibid.

129. See, for example, an advertisement for the Morgan–Renaissance Big Five game in the *Baltimore Afro-American*, Jan. 19, 1929.

130. *Washington Tribune*, Jan. 25, 1929.

131. *Amsterdam News*, Feb. 6, 1929.

132. M. Nelson, *The Originals: The New York Celtics Invent Modern Basketball* (Bowling Green, OH, 1999), p. 165.

133. T. Gould, *Pioneers of the Hardwood. Indiana and the Birth of Professional Basketball* (Bloomington, 1998), p. 25.

134. Personal interview, 1999.

135. Ibid.

136. Z. Hollander, ed., *The NBA's Official Encyclopedia of Pro Basketball, 35th Anniversary Edition*, New American Library, 1981, p. 35.

137. R. Lapchick, *Five Minutes to Midnight: Race and Sport in the 1990s* (New York and Lanham, MD, 1991), p. 164.

138. A. R. Ashe Jr., *A Hard Road to Glory. Basketball: The African-American Athlete in Basketball* (New York, 1993), p. 13.

139. Hollander, ed., *NBA's Official Encyclopedia*, p. 35.

140. Ibid., p. 36.

141. Personal interview, 1999.

142. *Indianapolis Recorder*, Jan. 19, 1935

143. *Anderson Herald*, Jan. 11, 1935; *Anderson Daily Bulletin*, Jan. 12, 1935.

144. Rust and Rust, *Art Rust's Illustrated History*, p. 300.

145. *Evansville Courier*, Jan. 17, 1934.

Epilogue

1. *Pittsburgh Courier*, Mar. 20, 1943.

2. Personal interview, 1999.

3. Personal interview, 1991.

4. Personal interview with Buck Covington, who played for the Bruins, 1994.

5. *Washington Afro-American*, Dec. 20, 1941.

6. Ibid., Mar. 6, 1948.

7. *Norfolk Journal and Guide*, Jan. 8, 1949.

8. Newspaper clipping in the Edwin Henderson papers at Moorland-Spingarn Research Center, Howard University. Henderson's letter to the editor is dated Oct. 22, 1966, and it likely was published in a white Washington newspaper.

9. *Amsterdam News*, Dec. 14, 1927.

10. Ibid., Oct. 23, 1929.

11. *1934 CIAA Bulletin*, p. 2.

12. Personal interview, 1999.

INDEX